The Sweatshop Regime

This book explores the processes producing and reproducing the garment sweatshop in India. Drawing from Marxian and feminist insights, the book theorizes the sweatshop as a complex 'regime' of exploitation and oppression, jointly crafted by global, regional and local actors, and working across productive and reproductive realms. The analysis illustrates the links between the physical and social materiality of production, unveiling the distinct circuits of exploitation corresponding to different clothing items. As these circuits change across India, on the basis of regional patterns of product specialisation, so does the logic of the sweatshop, its composition, the social profile of the labouring poor engaged in garment work, and their working conditions. T' ' the eyes of sourcing actors, the whole country can be re-imagined as a gia garment collections exhibited at different floor different sets of labourers.

Highlighting the great social differentia factories, workshops and homes scattered a narrative also unveils the multiple patterns of to. These exceed narrow definitions of unfreedom mainly base— which are becoming dominant in the debate on global labour standards and 'modern slavery'. By discussing interplays between productive and reproductive realms and processes of commodification and exploitation, on the contrary, the analysis highlights how social difference and unfreedom pre-exist the sweatshop and at the same time are also reproduced by it. It also highlights the role different actors – like global buyers, regional suppliers and retailers, and labour contractors – play in these processes. Indeed, the book depicts the sweatshop as a complex joint enterprise against the labouring poor, shaped and steered by multiple lords, and where production and circulation – of garments, processes and people – intertwine in manifold ways. It also shows how the labouring body is systematically and inexorably depleted and consumed by garment work, until it is finally ejected from the sweatshop. Finally, the book highlights how the study of India's sweatshop regime informs contemporary debates on industrial modernity, comparative advantage and cheap labour, modern slavery, and ethical consumerism.

Alessandra Mezzadri teaches at the School of Oriental and African Studies, University of London. Her research interests focus on globalisation and processes of labour informalisation; materialist approaches to global commodity chain analysis and global industrial systems, labour standards and CSR; gender and feminist theory; and the political economy of India. She has investigated in depth the Indian garment industry over a span of ten years, and illustrated the different ways in which distinct regional sweatshops are formed and reproduced across the subcontinent.

Development Trajectories in Global Value Chains

A feature of the current phase of globalization is the outsourcing of production tasks and services across borders, and increasing organization of production and trade through global value chains (GVCs), global commodity chains (GCCs), and global production networks (GPNs). With a large and growing literature on GVCs, GCCs, and GPNs, this series is distinguished by its focus on the implications of these new production systems for economic, social and regional development.

This series publishes a wide range of theoretical, methodological and empirical works, both research monographs and edited volumes, dealing with crucial issues of transformation in the global economy. How do GVCs change the ways in which lead and supplier firms shape regional and international economies? How do they affect local and regional development trajectories, and what implications do they have for workers and their communities? How is the organization of value chains changing and how are these emerging forms contested as more traditional structures of North-South trade are complemented and transformed by emerging South-South lead firms, investments, and trading links? How does the large-scale entry of women into value chain production impact on gender relations? What opportunities and limits do GVCs create for economic and social upgrading and innovation? In what ways are GVCs changing the nature of work and the role of labour in the global economy? And how might the increasing focus on logistics management, financialization, or social standards and compliance portend important developments in the structure of regional economies?

The series includes contributions from many disciplines and interdisciplinary fields and approaches related to GVC analysis, including GCCs and GPNs, and is particularly focused on theoretically innovative and informed works that are grounded in the empirics of development related to these approaches. through their focus on the changing organizational forms, governance systems, and production relations, volumes in this series contribute to on-going conversations about theories of development and development policy in the contemporary era of globalization.

Series editors

Stephanie Barrientos is Professor of Global Development at the Global Development Institute, University of Manchester.

Gary Gereffi is Professor of Sociology and Director of the Center on Globalization, Governance and Competitiveness, Duke University.

Dev Nathan is Visiting Professor at the Institute for Human Development, New Delhi, and Visiting Research Fellow at the Center on Globalization, Governance and Competitiveness, Duke University.

John Pickles is Earl N. Phillips Distinguished Professor of International Studies at the University of North Carolina, Chapel Hill.

The Sweatshop Regime

Labouring Bodies, Exploitation, and
Garments *Made in India*

Alessandra Mezzadri

CAMBRIDGE
UNIVERSITY PRESS

CAMBRIDGE
UNIVERSITY PRESS

University Printing House, Cambridge CB2 8BS, United Kingdom

One Liberty Plaza, 20th Floor, New York, NY 10006, USA

477 Williamstown Road, Port Melbourne, VIC 3207, Australia

314-321, 3rd Floor, Plot 3, Splendor Forum, Jasola District Centre, New Delhi - 110025, India

79 Anson Road, #06-04/06, Singapore 079906

Cambridge University Press is part of the University of Cambridge.

It furthers the University's mission by disseminating knowledge in the pursuit of education, learning and research at the highest international levels of excellence.

www.cambridge.org
Information on this title: www.cambridge.org/9781108799249

© Alessandra Mezzadri 2017

First published 2017
First paperback edition 2020

A catalogue record for this publication is available from the British Library

Library of Congress Cataloging in Publication data
Names: Mezzadri, Alessandra, author.
Title: The sweatshop regime : labouring bodies, exploitation, and garments made in India / Alessandra Mezzadri.
Description: New York : Cambridge University Press, 2016. | Includes bibliographical references and index.
Identifiers: LCCN 2016030023 | ISBN 9781107116962 (hardback)
Subjects: LCSH: Sweatshops--India. | Clothing trade--India. | Clothing workers--India.
Classification: LCC HD2339.I4 M49 2016 | DDC 338.6/340954--dc23 LC record available at https://lccn.loc.gov/2016030023

ISBN 978-1-107-11696-2 Hardback
ISBN 978-1-108-79924-9 Paperback

To Bianca, who taught me about resistance.
And to Silvia, who taught me about resilience.
They are the roots of it all.

Table of Contents

List of Tables, Figures and Pictures

Acknowledgements

This book is the outcome of years of research in India, across multiple research sites. The personal intellectual trajectory on which the book is based was also developed across many 'sites' - namely, Italy, the United Kingdom and India. For this reason, it is particularly challenging to acknowledge and thank all those who helped, either professionally or personally, along the way. I will try my best here to name at least some of those who were central for the development of the main arguments of the book, and some of those who provided key help during the many field rounds conducted in India.

I am intellectually indebted to Jens Lerche, my former PhD mentor and current SOAS colleague. In its early *avatar*, this project started under his guidance and has benefited from his generous engagement. Some of the arguments that are central to the development of this book are greatly inspired by the work of Jairus Banaji, Henry Bernstein, Barbara Harriss-White and Jan Breman. I wish to thank them all for their support and comments on my work, at various stages and in different academic *fora*. I also wish to thank all the members of the 'SOAS Labour, Social Movements and Development Research Cluster' and the 'regular crowd' at the Agrarian Change seminar series and its wonderful dinners. Special thanks to T.J. Byres, for his comradeship and for sharing his lecture notes. I hope that sooner or later he will consider publishing them. Thanks to Adam Hanieh, Elisabetta Basile, Geert De Neve, Becky Prentice, Peter Lund-Thomsen, Karin Siegmann, Khalid Nadvi, Kanchana Ruwanpura, Florence Palpacuer, Kaustav Banerjee, Leandro Vergara-Camus, Naila Kabeer, Ravi Srivastava, Praveen Jha, Indrani Mazumdar, Supriya RoyChowdhury, Jeemol Unni, Sumangala Damodaran, K. V. Ramaswamy, Patrick Neveling, Alpa Shah, Tamaki Endo, Sarosh Kuruvilla, Jane Tate, Matilde Adduci and Subir Sinha for useful comments and feedback on parts of the manuscript, or on parts of the analysis on which it is based. Cambridge University Press offered me great editorial support. Thanks also to the editors of the CUP global series 'Development Trajectories in Global Value Chains'; Stephanie Barrientos, Gary Gereffi, Dev Nathan and John Pickles.

Some of the empirical evidence analysed here has been collected during fieldwork rounds linked to two research projects. One is the ESRC-DfID project

'Labour conditions and the working poor in China and India' [ES/I033599/1], led by Jens Lerche, where I acted as India co-investigator together with Ravi Srivastava. The other is the British Academy small grant 'The global village? Homeworking in the global economy' [SG100684], which I designed, and managed with the research assistance of Saagar Tewari and Debabrata (Dev) Baral. Thanks to all the ESRC-DfID project team in Delhi and London and to Saagar and Dev for their extraordinary work in Uttar Pradesh. Thanks also to Roger Jeffery, for his generous encouragement. I am very grateful to the ESRC and to the British Academy for their financial support.

Despite its many labour regulations, India remains an extremely difficult arena for the upholding of workers' rights. The current rise of the 'Make in India' agenda is unlikely to change this scenario, as it further reinforces the idea of 'flexible' (read cheap and informal) labour as being one of India's key comparative advantages. In such hard climate, the work of many activists and labour NGO workers has been crucial, and is likely to remain so for many years to come. I engaged with many of them during the years, and learnt a lot from their political commitment and dedication. Special thanks to Pallavi Mansingh, Gopinath Parakuni, Ashim Roy, Aloysius, Rohini Hensman, Sujata Modi and Sanjay Kumar Singh. Thanks to the staff of SEWA Bareilly – Mary, Rochini, Sangeeta and Gulnaz – who greatly facilitated my work in Uttar Pradesh. Most of all, thanks to all respondents, in particular the many garment workers who dedicated precious time to answering my questions and who shared their stories with me, whilst endlessly toiling to cut, stitch, mend, embroider or pack stacks and stacks of clothes.

Finally, I owe immense gratitude to a number of friends and comrades, scattered across Italy, London and New Delhi, who have supported me professionally, personally, or logistically during the years and facilitated this research in different ways. Thanks to Neha Wadhawan, Carlotta Barcaro, Koyal Verma, Keshab Das, Vijayabaskar, Swati Narayan, Jaya Narayan, Peter Ter Weeme, David Kuefler, Orlanda Ruthven, Michela Cerimele, Elisa Van Waeyenberge, Rossella Ferrari, Carmen Gloria Sepulveda Zelaya, Jessica Lerche, Jonathan Pattenden, Thomas Marois, Tim Pringle, Dae-oup Chang, Rafeef Ziadah, Benjamin Selwyn, Satoshi Miyamura, Elena Baglioni, Paulo Dos Santos, Jenn Yablonski and Liam Campling. I also want to thank my family in Italy: my parents Stefania and Carlo, my sister Paola, my grandmother Silvia, aunt Daniela and uncle Luca, and Sonia. Thanks also to uncle Maurizio, my 'American uncle', for his wise academic advice, and to aunt Susan. Finally, thank you Paolo, for putting up with all the ups and down of a greatly inspiring but harshly taxing writing process. I know I owe you, I do.

List of Abbreviations

AEPC	:	Apparel Export Promotion Council
BHG	:	Bareilly Homeworkers Group
CEC	:	Centre for Education and Communication
Cividep	:	Civil Initiatives for Development and Peace India
CMAI	:	Clothing Manufacturers Association of India
COTEX	:	Consortium of Textile Exporters
CSR	:	Corporate Social Responsibility
DCMSME	:	Development Commissioner for Micro, Small, and Medium Enterprises
DISHA	:	Driving Industry Towards Sustainable Human Capital
EOI	:	Export-Oriented Patterns of Industrialization
ETI	:	Ethical Trade Initiatives
GATT	:	General Agreement on Tariffs and Trade
GATWU	:	Garment and Textile Workers Union
GCC	:	Global Commodity Chains
GGCC	:	Global Garment Commodity Chain
GLU	:	Global Labour Union
GPN	:	Global Production Network
GVC	:	Global Value Chain
HF	:	Handwork Foundation
ILO	:	International Labour Organisation
MFA	:	Multi-Fibre Arrangement
NCEUS	:	National Commission for Enterprises in the Unorganised Sector
NCR	:	National Capital Region
NHG	:	National Homeworkers Group
NTUI	:	New Trade Union Initiatives
SAVE	:	Social Awareness and Voluntary Education
SEWA	:	Self-Employed Women Organisation
SIHMA	:	South India Hosiery Association

SMEs   : Small and Medium Enterprises
TEA   : Tiruppur Exporters Association
UNIDO   : United National Industrial Development Organisation
UP   : Uttar Pradesh
WTO   : World Trade Organization

Introduction

The Sweatshop as a Regime

Every day, as we clothe ourselves, we wear the endless circuits of exploitation at work in garment sweatshops. Who is in charge of these circuits; who is subjected to them; and based on which processes are such circuits created and recreated? To what extent do our jeans, jackets, sweaters and T-shirt hide common stories of exploitation, and to what extent instead do their seams and features conceal the struggles of different working lives, exposed to and consumed by distinct production practices? At its broadest, this book unveils the processes leading to the creation and recreation of the garment sweatshop in India, in the context of greatly differentiated garment commodities and markets. This is hardly a trivial exercise, given that, as astutely observed by Karl Marx (1990, p. 280), employers always carefully and jealously guard the mysteries and secrets of the 'abode of production', 'on whose threshold there hangs the notice "No admittance except on business"'. These mysteries and secrets are particularly numerous in the garment sector, where the 'abode of production' is fragmented and organized in composite production circuits connecting different spaces of work and geographical domains. Admittedly, many of such mysteries and secrets – even some of the most repugnant – have been unveiled throughout the last decades by the work of numerous committed scholars, researchers, journalists and activists (recent contributions come from Hoskins, 2014; Seabrook, 2015). Lately, the *World Factory* has even become the object of a political play interactively illustrating our false commitment to ethical capitalism once this threatens profitability (see Paul Mason's review in *The Guardian*, 2015). In many ways, one could say that this book simply aims at joining these critical voices by exploring the workings of the sweatshop in India, one of today's great emerging economies whose success is undoubtedly happening on the shoulders of its millions of working poor.

However, while joining the numerous concerned accounts that attempt to describe the sweatshop and its impact, this book also aspires to *theorize* the sweatshop. In particular, the analysis developed in the following pages will try its best to convince the reader that the sweatshop must be conceptualized as a *regime*. Namely, the sweatshop has to be understood as a complex system of labour subjugation and social oppression establishing a strong interrelation between different clothing 'things' and the people who make them across multiple (factory and non-factory) spaces of work; organized in a joint enterprise set-up and strongly managed by multiple global, regional and local masters; banking on a complex matrix of social differences and patterns of labour unfreedom spanning across both productive and reproductive realms; and implying greatly depleting effects on the labouring body of the workers involved. The analysis will aim to demonstrate that only by paying attention to the solid and capillary organization of the sweatshop as a regime one can fully understand its great resilience, despite the many attempts at intervention and regulation following industrial disasters and scandals in recent years. In fact, many interventions and regulations, particularly those based on corporate approaches – which can be gathered under the umbrella of CSR initiatives – may well have even reinforced the exploitative and oppressive mechanisms of the sweatshop.

The word 'regime' has been already deployed by studies aimed at unveiling the secrets of abodes of production. The most renowned attempt comes from the sociologist Michael Burawoy (1985), who deploys the term 'factory regime', as a dispositive encapsulating not only different relations *in* production – linked to the labour process – but also relations of production more broadly, as defined by the overall balance between capital and labour in a given society. Building on, and perhaps also going beyond his work, authors like Chris Smith and Pun Ngai (2006; see also Pun, 2007) have more recently turned their focus on labour regimes, hence shifting the attention from the factory to labour, while also accounting for realms of daily social reproduction of the workforce. Attention to the workings of labour regimes is also present in Henry Bernstein's (2007) theorization of 'classes of labour' as the outcome of the complex process of proletarianization at work in contemporary capitalism and deepening patterns of labour informalization, and in the work of Jens Lerche (2007; see also Lerche, 2010), who develops this framework in relation to India (see also Pattenden, 2016). Other studies, particularly in the field of geography, have deployed the term, although perhaps in more descriptive ways. Moreover, some labour scholars have placed emphasis on single aspects of labour regimes, for instance on patterns of labour control (see Jonas, 1996, on labour control regimes) and how they relate to different forms of workers' resistance (e.g. Anner, 2015).

While the concept of sweatshop regime I propose here clearly benefits from the work of many of these authors, it also aims at further expanding as well as delineating the social boundaries of the analysis. In particular, I deploy here the term sweatshop regime rather than labour regime as this allows me to place emphasis on three issues, which are crucial for the development of this book.[1]

Firstly, I deploy the term sweatshop regime to centre the analysis on garment production, which this book is concerned with. In reality, this rather simple correlation conceals a more ambitious design, namely that of stressing the strong correspondence between specific commodities – specific garments in this case – and the spaces of work and people composing and inhabiting the sweatshop. This link between the physical and social 'materiality' of production is a key thread running throughout the analysis, and it is presented as one of the first crucial components of the sweatshop regime. The term 'sweatshop' is also better equipped, in my view, to capture the process through which the garment industry has been able, across time and space, to always reconstitute itself as a realm of harsh labour conditions and relations. Briefly, emphasis placed on the word 'sweatshop' helps underlining the continuities in the oppressive and exploitative labouring experience generated by garment work. In stressing the poor historical record of the industry for workers, the analysis will also discuss the role of neoliberalism in 'exporting' the sweatshop across the world, drawing particularly, albeit not only, from the work of Silver and Arrighi (2001).

Secondly, in the characterization proposed here, the sweatshop regime is not only meant to be the expression of capital–labour relations, *in* as well and *of* production (Burawoy, 1985). It is also meant to encapsulate broader networks of oppression that exceed (or pre-exist) the constitution of 'labour' and 'labouring' in the sweatshop and that strongly shape them at the same time. These networks cross realms of social reproduction that are not only confined to the daily survival of the workforce (as in Pun and Smith, 2007) but that also include workers' place of origin. Strongly shaped by social structures, divisions and differences, these networks are mediators of processes of working class formation (Harriss-White and Gooptu, 2001; Harriss-White, 2003) as well as constitutive elements of processes of accumulation (Mies, 1986; Federici, 2004). This emphasis on social reproduction also aims at capturing a glimpse of 'embodied' labour, not only as the outcome of given labour relations but also as their constitutive part. Moreover, it aims at including the signs of labouring hardship worn by the labouring body as yet another key component of the sweatshop regime; namely, as the 'signature' of the sweatshop.

---

[1] I have deployed the term labour regime in the past, and will most likely deploy it again (see Mezzadri, 2012, 2014a).

Finally, the expression sweatshop regime is also meant to allow for a more flexible consideration of the interplays between processes of production and circulation of commodities as well as people. The term sweatshop already evokes the resilience of mercantile, highly decentralized networks of production, of great importance in the development of the garment as well as the far older textile industry. Both processes of production and circulation are crucial for the workings of the sweatshop, particularly in shaping it as a joint enterprise where processes of surplus extraction are made possible and organized by a complex crowd of global, regional and local lords. For the development of this key aspect of the analysis of the sweatshop regime, as well as for the ways in which it articulates with the management of both 'free' and 'unfree' forms of labour, I draw considerably from the work of Jairus Banaji (2003, 2010) and Jan Breman (1996, 2013). However, the analysis of the patterns of unfreedom at work in the sweatshop regime combines debates on the formal subsumption of labour with considerations on the social traits of labouring (neo)bondage.

After arguing the case for analyzing the garment industry through the lens of its sweatshop, this book illustrates the distinct key features composing the sweatshop as a regime, by drawing from empirical evidence coming from distinct garment-producing areas. Each chapter engages with different theoretical debates and deploys different cases to illustrate its points. This means that this book does not differentiate 'theory' and 'evidence' in a top-down fashion, first elaborating an abstract model and then 'testing it' through cases. Rather, it interweaves theory and evidence throughout the narrative to unveil the key mechanisms of the sweatshop regime. Hence, only by the end of the last chapter the argument proposed will emerge in full, in all its complexities and nuances, and the theorization of the sweatshop as a regime will be complete. In my view, this was the only choice that could give justice to the many debates reviewed to capture the inner workings of the sweatshop, and to the great richness of the empirical narrative, collected in India across a significant span of time.

India is hardly only a case study here. Rather, the ways in which the complex political economy of India interplays and interacts but also reshapes how the supposed 'global' reality of the sweatshop is created and reproduced emerges as a key aspect of the analysis. In fact, it is an aspect that indirectly challenges conceptualizations of globalization and capitalism in general as abstract, disembedded realities. Empirical evidence on the workings of the garment industry in India interweaves inextricably with the theorization of each different aspect of the sweatshop regime. It is not a case that many of the authors greatly inspiring this analysis – Banaji, Breman, Harriss-White, Mies – have worked extensively (or exclusively) on India. In fact, also adopting a view mainly centred on India, the garment sweatshop is best theorized as a regime, as one cannot understand the hardship of India's garment proletariat without considering the garments they produce and the entire set of relations of exploitation, commodification and oppression moulding the sweatshop, as they cross India's factories, workshops and homes, industrial colonies, slums and villages.

In order to capture the regional instantiations of the sweatshop regime in India, the analysis deploys the image of a giant, country-wide clothing mall, 'offering' its customers – buyers and all regional and local sourcing agents – multiple garment collections placed at different floors, represented by different regions of the country. The India garment mall epitomizes the correspondence between the 'physical' and the 'social' materiality at work in the sweatshop, and it is the starting point to analyze the corresponding regional variations in the ways the sweatshop manifests on the ground in the subcontinent. These regional manifestations depend upon the processes of informalization of *both* capital and labour at work in India (Harriss-White, 2003; Breman, 2013), whose history is in fact quite old (Banaji, 2003, 2010).

Under this light, the study of the sweatshop regime developed by this book also contributes to the study of the contemporary political economy of India, by providing a window into the ways in which aspects of the constitution of today's 'Global' India – namely, in this case, the country's engagement in modern global industries – are greatly based on a long-term development systematically banking on the subjugation of India's poor labouring masses. This point will be emphasized in the analysis to debunk ideas of the sweatshop that simply ascribe its features and resilience to global (western) actors and processes. The lords of the sweatshop are instead far more numerous.

The theorization of the sweatshop as a regime developed here also contributes to debates on cheap labour. In particular, it aims at deconstructing this weak analytical category, too often seen as a 'natural' comparative advantage of poor regions and emerging economies characterized by staggering social disparities, like India. I contend that this is a crucial exercise for two reasons. The first is analytical. While a lot has been written to debunk the rhetoric of comparative advantage in relation to commodities and shifting patterns of production and trade in the global economy in historical perspective (Shaikh, 2005; Chang, 2003), labour has been largely excluded from similar debates. Few noteworthy exceptions come from the feminist critique of free trade (e.g. Seguino, 2000; Elson *et al.*, 2007; Perrons, 2004), which has primarily focused on how liberalization has happened on women's shoulders. However, more can be said on how the mythology of comparative advantage has reified working poverty. In particular, while rejecting representations of labour as a commodity, we should also be aware that such representations are powerful producers of real effects. Labour is fetishized as a commodity by capital through processes at work in both the realm of material production and of its representation.

This leads me to the second point, which is instead largely political. Only by deconstructing the myth of the existence of a comparative advantage in cheap labour for some countries one can attack modernizing narratives which are still charmed by the idea that the 'cheap labour model' will eventually, 'naturally' give way to forms of more 'inclusive' capitalism that will finally deliver for the working poor. The model itself is flawed, and largely ideological, based, as argued by Jan Breman (1985), on the paradoxical assumption that organizing capital is still the only way of organizing labour (see also Federici, 2012). Instead, an emphasis on the complex processes through which cheap labour is produced and reproduced, which lies at the core of this analysis, enables us to appreciate how capital is already greatly organized in its process of subjugating labour, even in highly informalized, chaotic settings. The book will return insistently on these issues, in relation to different aspects of the sweatshop regime. Moreover, it will further expand on the problematic nature of modernizing narratives in its conclusions, when it will also engage with debates on modern slavery and ethical consumerism.

The sources and categories deployed to theorize the sweatshop regime reveal that this analysis is clearly informed by a Marxist Feminist approach. Admittedly, political economy as well as feminist understandings of capitalism may vary considerably. This work specifically adopts a view on capitalism as a mode of production mainly defined by processes of extraction of labour surplus, which can manifest, as highlighted by Banaji (2003, 2010) in multiple *forms of exploitation*, combinations of 'free' and 'unfree' labour, as well as complex interplays between production and circulation. Undoubtedly, contemporary processes of proletarianization produce distinct 'classes of labour' (Bernstein, 2007). This said capitalist accumulation always banks on social differences and divisions (Silver, 2003; Harriss-White, 2003), and forms of social oppression starting from realms of social reproduction (Mies, 1986; Federici, 2004). Ultimately, the sweatshop regime theorized here epitomizes a vision of capitalism not as a homogenizing force but rather as a harshly dividing one, driven by and always reconstituting multiple forms of inequality. The embodied aspects of this force in 'producing affliction' (O'Laughlin, 2013) and consuming the labouring body as a key capitalist 'machine' (Federici, 2004) clearly problematize benign visions of industrial modernization as an inherently positive process. In the sweatshop, systematic processes of depletion of the labouring body are even too visible. The way in which the narrative systematically combines insights from the political economy and feminist traditions is discussed in far more detail in each chapter, in relation to the different aspects of the sweatshop regime, and in the concluding sections of this introduction, which present the organization of the book.

On the Complex Social Life in Commodity Chains and Commodity Fetishism

In contending that the sweatshop regime is a more useful methodological and analytical tool than others in representing the harsh workings of the garment industry, the analysis cannot shy away from an engagement with commodity studies; namely studies framed around 'global commodity chains', 'value chains' or 'production networks'. In fact, many studies of garment production have deployed this methodology, since its elaboration by Gary Gereffi and Michael Korzeniewicz (1994). Indeed, in this book, the literature on global commodity chains is deployed as a useful background to reconstruct the progressive development of the industry and its processes of geographical location and relocation, and to identify the multiple nodes of production (and power) that characterize it.

However, at the same time, the chain – namely the global garment commodity chain (GGCC) – is simply considered here as an *object of enquiry* rather than the leading analytical framework. It is the ground for the deployment of a Marxist Feminist analysis of the sweatshop. In this sense, this narrative clearly recalls the study of chains into the far broader framework of political economy (Mezzadri, 2014a, b). Moreover, the adoption of the sweatshop regime rather than the garment chain as the main lens of the narrative further shifts the emphasis from capital onto labour. The sweatshop regime is the *avatar* of the garment chain, a reconceptualization of the latter as mainly framed around labour and labouring aspects, as well as issues of social reproduction.

Admittedly, in recent times, a rising number of scholars have tried to overcome the widely discussed limitations of chain analysis in relation to its omission of issues of labour. Perhaps, the most systematic attempts to address this issue come from Marcus Taylor (2007) and Ben Selwyn (2010). Selwyn (2010, 2012), in particular, has proposed a chain framework reintegrating political economy concerns;

labour and class analysis in general (see also Smith *et al.*, 2002).[2] Other scholars have instead opted for moving away from the study of global commodity or value chains and focus instead on 'global production networks' (GPNs), a framework supposedly more equipped to engage with issues of labour (see Coe *et al.*, 2008; Coe and Hesse, 2013; McGrath, 2013; Barrientos, 2013; Carswell and De Neve, 2013).[3] While recognizing the intellectual relevance of this scholarship, whose strengths and limitations ultimately depend – as spelt out by one of the 'founding fathers' of commodity chains Immanuel Wallerstein (2009, p. 89) – on avoiding the trap of 'looking too narrowly', a focus on the sweatshop regime rather than the chain itself allows framing the whole analysis and representation of garment production on the centrality of labouring.[4] By focusing on the sweatshop, the analysis not only emphasizes the role of workers in commodity chains but it also does so by deploying a representational device already focused on labour.

Furthermore, this representational device maintains a strong concern with garment as a commodity. In fact, it is concerned with the many distinct commodities the broad category 'garment' entails, and stresses the links between different physical and social materialities of production. Obviously, I am aware that this choice can be accused of falling into the trap of 'commodity fetishism', a critique already moved to commodity studies (see Bernstein and Campling, 2006). However, I contend that this would be misleading. Focusing the attention on the ways in which the physical properties of commodities relate to the specific set of social relations of production serves the purpose of unveiling the workings of commodity fetishism, showing its relevance in shaping the world of labour. If indeed, as argued by Marx, commodity production fetishizes the world by concealing the relations of exploitation it entails, this process nevertheless does produce real and differential social outcomes, which must be shown and studied. In other words,

---

[2] For other important contributions of Marxian political economy scholars to commodity studies see, for instance, Newman (2009) on the financialization of the coffee chain and its implication for social relations (which also builds on the previous work by Gibbon and Ponte, 2005) and Starosta (2010a, b) on the relevance of the Marxian 'law of value' to understand the constitution and dynamics of chains. A number of institutional contributions to the debate have also greatly participated in unveiling the complex political economy of chains. See, in particular, Milberg (2008) on the interplays between finance and governance, and Palpacuer (2008) on the relation between financialization and the distribution of wealth along chains. A useful reader on different theoretical and analytical takes on chains can be found in Gibbon *et al.* (2008).

[3] There is an on-going debate on differences and continuities of analyses framed on global value chains or global production networks (e.g. compare Bair, 2009; with Barrientos *et al.*, 2011).

[4] The other founding father of commodity chains is Terence Hopkins (see Hopkins and Wallerstein, 1986; Wallerstein and Hopkins, 1977).

a crucial way to fight against commodity fetishism is to take it seriously, in all its distinct, crucial effects in the social world. This analysis is committed to this purpose. Indeed, as it will be amply illustrated, the different global, regional and local masters shaping the structure and functioning mechanisms of the sweatshop regime in India systematically bank on multiple, different forms of fetishism, targeting both commodities as well as people, namely workers. A notable example of processes of fetishization of labour is the way in which female labour is always deployed in certain tasks based on gendered discourses powerfully shaping the global assembly line (Salzinger, 2003; Caraway, 2005).

Despite not adopting chain analysis as its main methodological tool, the ways in which the chain is deployed here as the fruitful research ground for explaining the workings of the sweatshop can still, in my view, contribute to the literature on commodity studies. In particular, the approach proposed here can be seen as providing a glimpse into the chaotic social life within commodity chains, in regions defined by complex patterns of differentiation in relation to both product specialization and social processes of production. Indeed, great regional differentiation is a key aspect of commodity chains (see Smith *et al.*, 2002; Mezzadri, 2014b). Using the sweatshop as a lens, in other words, social life across the garment production chain can be seen as animated by multiple struggles between capital and labour, between 'capitals' and within labour, unfolding across and impinging upon multiple realms of both production and social reproduction, and bearers of depleting effects on the labouring bodies exposed to garment work. Together with the main aims and contributions of this book as delineated in the previous section, the way in which the sweatshop regime 'brings commodity chains to life' is another useful addition to the existing scholarship.

Methods: Seeing Labour through Capital and Capital through Labour and Reproduction

The analysis presented in this book is based on multiple rounds of fieldwork in India, which started in the early autumn of 2004, and continued across a span of almost 10 years. The first round took place between October 2004 and July 2005, and mapped the differences in garments production and labour relations and practices across the main garment-producing areas in India. During this period of intense and at the same time highly mobile fieldwork, 176 interviews were undertaken, and numerous industrial and labour reports were collected. Out of these interviews, 65 were with garment suppliers involved in export

(20 in and around Delhi, seven in Ludhiana, four in Jaipur, six in Kolkata, eight in Chennai, seven in Bangalore, five in Tiruppur and eight in Mumbai), and five with global buyers working across India. Crucially, the sample of garment suppliers in each area included some of the largest exporters. Towering over local production for many years, large exporters have detailed knowledge of the evolution of production systems and export markets over time. Moreover, they generally command complex production systems and can provide useful access to their 'subordinates'. The numerous other interviews conducted during this fieldwork round were with different sets of key informants, like representatives of apparel business associations; government offices linked to garment export or regulating the activities of small and medium enterprises (SMEs); unions, labour organizations, activists' networks and social auditing companies.

Detailed information on subcontracting and labour was also obtained through repeated field trips to industrial areas across India. I spent certainly long days walking around industrial areas like Gurgaon and NOIDA around Delhi or in Peenya in Bangalore, trying to grasp their pace and rhythm, and reconstruct the different logics through which the multiple regional masters of the sweatshop set up all the distinct parts of the product cycle, the same way in which the labourers they command stitch the clothes we wear.

Admittedly, the method described above is consistent with what many commodity studies scholars committed to empirical work have done (see Stephanie Barrientos' 2002 helpful discussion of how to investigate the chain). On the other hand, this method is also in line with what many sociologists have done during the years to unveil the workings of the abode of production in globalized industries. Indeed, the emergence of multi-sited ethnography, its strengths and limitations, has been a key object of discussion for both world-system scholars and scholars concerned with the process of 'manufacturing the global' (see Marcus, 1995; Burawoy et al, 2000, Burawoy, 2001). This is to say that the deployment of a fieldwork method compatible with chain analysis does not necessarily imply the adoption of chain analysis as the main analytical lens. Since this first round of fieldwork, the garment chain has been treated as a multi-sited terrain of investigation to achieve the main objective of reconstructing the nature of capital–labour relations in the sector and their implications for labour and labouring.

The second round of fieldwork, conducted between March and April 2010 and January and May 2012, focused on the complex patterns of local decentralization at work in the industry. It took the complexity of product cycles at work in Northern India as its point of departure, and focused on garment satellite centres

[handwritten annotation: downward social mobility ie employer to employee]

in Uttar Pradesh (UP). Thirty interviews with labour contractors organizing embroidery activities in Bareilly, UP, were undertaken, and 100 with home-based workers. This round of fieldwork was crucial to reach 'the bottom' of the sweatshop regime, which in India is fed by complex processes of proletarianization of artisanal work. If one learns much from a view from the top of the sweatshop, one also learns immensely from looking up from its bottom echelons. In fact, I must say that it is primarily from this vantage point that the sweatshop finally reveals itself in all its multiple facets and layers, as the complex joint enterprise against the working poor that it is. Moreover, it is from this vantage point that I could fully appreciate the ways in which processes of labour surplus extraction are so tightly linked to circulation, and how the many masters shaping the sweatshop anchor these processes to realms of social reproduction.

The third round of fieldwork was quite complex, and took me back to the Delhi metropolitan conglomerate. Between March and May 2013, and in September 2013, I analyzed current processes of transformation at work in the industry, and explored more in depth the world of non-factory labour in and around Delhi. These field trips overlapped with the far longer fieldwork exercise conducted in the context of the joint project 'Labour conditions and the working poor in China and India', led by Jens Lerche. The mapping of current transformations at work in the industry is based on interviews personally held with 17 exporters, 3 Indian retailers and around 10 key informants (2 global buyers, 1 major social auditing company and several representatives of India's key export council).

Also in this case, the information obtained through the interviews was further complemented by other methods of enquiry, in particular by the informal interaction with exporters during one of their annual business meetings and two All-India garment export fairs, gathering companies working across India (see also Mezzadri, 2015a). The exploration of non-factory-based labour entailed the collection of interviews and questionnaires from 70 labourers, and numerous field trips to explore their daily conditions of reproduction (Mezzadri, 2015b). Ravi Srivastava coordinated the main data collection exercise in relation to workers in factories and larger workshops, based on a sample of over 300 workers placed in units of different size and spread across the Delhi metropolitan industrial hub (Srivastava, 2015). This analysis relies on the joint findings of the project in relation to wages, to labour contracting in factory realms, and to the links between health and social reproduction. The ways in which these issues connect and interplay is explored towards the end of the book, which specifically focuses on the hardship of garment work and the impact of the sweatshop regime on the labouring body.

Overall, the inspiring principles and methods at the basis of the different fieldwork rounds represent an attempt to combine a study of labour and labouring through the eyes of capital (Mezzadri 2009a, 2012) with a study of capital through the eyes of labour (see also Mezzadri and Srivastava, 2015) and through the lens of social reproduction.

Finally, it should be noted that interviews and material collected in each location were not only functional to the study of the social processes of production in that particular site, but were also central to the development of a general picture of the sweatshop and its workings in India. In fact, the overall significance of the production and labour relations at work in the industry and their transformations is understood as a result of years of research, by way of triangulating evidence collected *across* all the different areas analyzed and deploying an organic approach to all material gathered, inspired by what Burawoy (1998) calls the 'extended case study method' and with the political economy tradition more in general.

Organization of the Book and of a Long Journey into the World of the Sweatshop

The book is organized as follows. Chapter 1, '*The Chain and the Sweatshop*', reconstructs the trajectory of the garment industry and its progressive evolution into a globalized chain stretching across a rising number of emerging and developing economies. It is here that moving the emphasis from capital to labour, the global chain is reconceptualized as the global sweatshop. The latter is the *avatar* of the former once emphasis is placed on the features of labour and labouring associated with the global garment assembly line. The narrative insists on the role of neoliberalism and the end of the 'labour-friendly regime' (Silver and Arrighi, 2001) in reproducing the sweatshop and exporting it across the world, thanks to the (re)rise of the powerful ideology of comparative advantage and its reification of working poverty as 'good' for development (Breman, 1995). It also critically anchors the emergence and reproduction of the global sweatshop to the rise of processes of labour informalization entailing processes of both formal and real subsumption of labour (Banaji, 2003, 2010) and currently generating multiple classes of labour (Bernstein, 2007) whose subjugation to the capitalist logic banks on and is mediated by multiple social divides (Silver, 2003; Harriss-White and Gooptu, 2001) and is linked to realms of social reproduction (Mies, 1986; Federici, 2004, 2012). In India, the continuous presence of a huge reserve army of informal and informalized workers (NCEUS, 2007; Kannan, 2008; Srivastava, 2012;

Chandrasekhar and Ghosh, 2015), and of accumulation patterns systematically banking on social structures and divides (Harriss-White, 2003) crossing both productive and reproductive realms (Mies, 1986; Harriss White and Gooptu, 2001) provides the sweatshop with endless possibilities of exploitation. These vary greatly based on commercial dynamics and local patterns of product specialization that open the Indian garment industry to multiple 'varieties of global integration' (Tewari, 2008).

If the first chapter sets the general background of the analysis, Chapter 2, *'The Commodity and the Sweatshop'*, starts the theorization of the sweatshop as a regime with a number of specific features. Here, the analysis dwells into the inextricable link between the physical and social materiality of production, beyond analyses only premised on the labour process, or on commodity 'trails' (e.g. Knowles, 2015). Initiating a long, empirical journey across the production structures and labour relations and practices at work in the Indian garment industry, the analysis illustrates the interconnection between the physical and social features of garments, by placing particular emphasis on the decomposition of product cycles into distinct echelons of the local sweatshop. The evidence presented here comes from Northern and Eastern India; namely from the Delhi metropolitan conglomerate, Jaipur, Ludhiana and Kolkata, where product specialization is particularly complex, layered and fragmented as mainly targeting niche markets, and where the sweatshop is a highly composite reality based on combinations of factory and non-factory, 'free' and 'unfree' labour – or indeed, 'classes of labour'. These garment areas form the first floors of the India garment mall, and the regional manifestations of the sweatshop regime corresponding to these specific types of product specializations.

The sweatshop emerges from the analysis developed in Chapter 2 as a 'material' regime where the physical features of commodity production and the complex social processes leading to its realization are strongly interlinked. Chapter 3, *'Difference and the Sweatshop'*, builds on these insights, but it also complements them with further reflections on the multiple social differences and divides at work in the sweatshop. While these are manufactured by the sweatshop, they also pre-exist it. Briefly, 'difference' is both instrumentally deployed as well as reproduced by the sweatshop regime, as it always is by capital (Bair, 2010). The analysis develops this argument with a particular focus on gender, and by highlighting the links between processes of commodification and exploitation inside the sweatshop. By doing so, it engages with feminist insights focused on the interplays between accumulation and realms of social reproduction (Mies, 1986;

Federici, 2004). The narrative draws from empirical evidence coming from Southern India, namely from the garment areas of Chennai, Bangalore and Tiruppur. These represent the lower floors of the India garment mall, which target more standardized garment commodity markets, and where the regional manifestation of the sweatshop regime entails processes of feminization of the factory workforce (e.g. RoyChowdhury, 2005, 2015; Chari, 2010; Carswell and De Neve, 2013). Crucially, through the lens of gender, the analysis returns to and expands on issues of unfreedom, by emphasizing the interrelations and differences between approaches focusing on dispossession and those instead premised on the oppressive nature of given social norms. From the analysis developed in this third chapter, the sweatshop emerges as a regime based on and shaped by multiple social differences and defined by multiple patterns of unfreedom.

While Chapters 2 and 3 illustrate the workings of the sweatshop regime in different regional settings, Chapter 4, '*The Regional Lord and the Sweatshop*' stresses the relevance of underlining its nature as a complex joint enterprise, rather than simply a top-down, globally led endeavour. Drawing from important debates on the relation between production and circulation in shaping processes of labour surplus extraction (Banaji, 2010) and informed by key sources on the global history of India (e.g. Roy, 2007) and of the textile sector (e.g. Beckert, 2015), the analysis highlights the role of different regional lords in reinforcing the sweatshop regime in its distinct, regional manifestations. Empirically, the analysis supports these insights by looking at processes of 'backshoring' (Hardy, 2013) at work in the garment industry, as they are set in motion by a powerful group of Pan-Indian buyer – exporters, who effectively behave as global buyers (Mezzadri, 2014b). For this purpose, the empirical journey into the world of the Indian sweatshop lands in Mumbai, which represents a key centre for the registration of garment export transactions, one of the key 'cash registers' of the India garment mall.

The discussion on the relevance of processes of circulation in shaping the sweatshop regime is further developed in Chapter 5, '*The Broker and the Sweatshop*'. This also expands on the workings of the sweatshop as a complex joint enterprise by dwelling on the relevance of labour brokers in subjugating labourers across different realms of production and social reproduction, and actively engaging in processes of surplus extraction as informalized petty capitalists (see Mezzadri, 2016). Drawing once more from Banaji (2010), but also from debates on interlocked modes of exploitation in the Indian countryside (Bharadwaj, 1974, 1994; Bhaduri, 1983, 1986, 1999; Byres, 1998; Srivastava, 1989; Harriss-White, 2008; Guerin *et al.*, 2012), the analysis develops these argument by taking the reader to Bareilly, a key embroidery satellite centre strongly connected to northern garment-producing areas, a town of contractors.

Chapter 6, 'The Body and the Sweatshop', reflects on the greatly depleting effects of the sweatshop on the health and wellbeing of its multiple subjects, whose labouring body is inexorably consumed by the harsh toil involved in garment work as a result of employers' systematic externalization of all costs related to their social reproduction. If O'Laughlin (2013) and Federici (2004) clearly inspire the theorization of the relation between the sweatshop and the body, the work of Jan Breman (1996, 2013) on labour circulation helps illustrating the mechanisms through which the labouring body is exhausted and eventually ejected from the sweatshop. Empirically, the analysis illustrates this last aspect of the functioning of the sweatshop as a (body) regime by returning to Delhi and Bareilly, and discussing the ways in which workers experience the sweatshop – literally on their skin – in these areas. This chapter also develops a critique to global labour standards, which have systematically failed workers due to their corporate, top-down, depoliticized and technicistic nature, and proposes a reading of industrial 'disasters' as the tragic but unexceptional outcomes of harsh garment toil.

In the Conclusions, the analysis addresses the problematic nature of current debates on the 'modern slaves' of the global economy, while also insisting on the need to abandon modernizing narratives celebrating labour-intensive production as a necessary but temporary evil. Unfortunately, as this analysis will reveal, it is temporary only because it tears and wears the labouring bodies it deploys – the bodies of millions, in India, as elsewhere – but hardly because it necessarily involves a stagist, progressive improvement of conditions of work. Instead, this must be demanded and fought for, as many garment workers are doing worldwide. The chapter ends with some final reflections on the current politics of ethical consumerism, and on its need to be primarily informed by workers' demands and struggles. Let us now begin our analysis.

1 | The Chain and the Sweatshop

.... the apparel industry, as presently constituted, is exploitative at its core.

(Bonacich and Appelbaum, 2000, p. 22)

Global Products, Sweatshop Labour: Introducing the 'Made in India'

We wear and consume globalization on a daily basis. The majority of the products we purchase are global products, created through a complex organization of production stretching across the world economy. Garments are the global product *par excellence*. If we read the labels of the clothes we wear, we immediately realize that, at present, they come from a staggering number of different countries. Today, even the least remarkable among local clothing shops, malls and boutiques in many developed as well as emerging economies is likely to sell 'global' garments: jeans made in Bangladesh, T-shirts made in India, trousers made in China, Cambodia or Vietnam, coats made in Italy, Turkey or Mexico. Being produced in so many different parts of the world, these garments share a number of common traits. First, they are often extremely cheap. In the last four decades, the price of readymade clothing has fallen massively. In Europe and the US, retail stores such as Primark or Wal-Mart sell garments for the price of an ice cream or a slice of pizza. Second, garments come in myriads of different styles that change more rapidly that even fickle consumer taste could ever do. In fact, it is this continuous process of change – the 'fast fashion' model – that is increasingly leading to shifts in consumer taste among middle classes worldwide. Third, while vaguely indicating the country of production, garments hardly provide any other clue regarding their exact origins. This labelling politics contributes to the representation of production regions as undifferentiated lands, effectively hiding the exact location of production, and with it the source of value.

Eventually, we do learn where exactly given garments come from. Sadly, however, this process of discovery is generally linked to the unfolding of terrible industrial disasters or the unveiling of sweatshop scandals. Until April 2013, consumers had perhaps never heard of an industrial area called Savar, in Dhaka, Bangladesh. Now, many do, after the collapse of Rana Plaza, an eight-storey building hosting garment factories producing for global buyers. Probably the greatest industrial tragedy in the history of the garment sector (see Appelbaum and Lichtenstein, 2014), the Rana Plaza collapse claimed the lives of 1,134 garment workers, severely injuring thousands more (ILRF 2015:12). Sweatshop scandals have multiplied, since the first consumer movements and campaigns of the 1990s (see Frank, 2003) launched the first anti-brands wars, and despite (or perhaps also due to) the many attempts at imposing global labour standards. Today, these scandals are greatly represented in traditional and social media, thanks to the joint work of solidarity networks, consumer movements, academics and journalists. Major newspapers like *The Guardian*, host whole sections on the rise of 'modern-day slavery', often featuring the appalling conditions of garment workers. At times, this news targets a specific global clothing manufacturer or brand, whose unfair labour practices in some factory somewhere are uncovered. Naming and shaming strategies against renowned culprits can pay off, as brands are terrified of reputational damage. For instance, in April 2015, *Labour Behind the Label* and *War on Want* organized a march of Oxford Street in London, naming and shaming brands that had not yet contributed to the compensation fund in favour of Rana Plaza's victims and their families. The compensation target was eventually reached, also due to this mounting public pressure.

Despite the proliferation and increasing sensationalism of actions and demonstrations in favour of garment workers worldwide, their vulnerability is quite resilient. After Rana Plaza, and despite the global public uproar, the global garment sector has witnessed many other 'minor' disasters. In Cambodia, in May 2013, 23 workers were injured when a rest area outside a garment factory located near Phnom Penh collapsed and fell into a pond. The incident came just a few days after part of another garment factory collapsed, killing three people and injuring several others (O'Keefe and Narin, 2013). Besides, in many export-producing countries, even in the absence of disasters or scandals, garment workers are exposed to astonishingly high levels of risk. In January 2014, Cambodian garment workers were shot in the street of Phnom Penh during a demonstration for a rise in their low minimum wage. The Cambodian state was 'protecting' its position in the global economy (Mezzadri, 2014c), where garments and the wages of those who produce them must remain cheap, as they represent a crucial source of 'comparative advantage'.

With the rise of neoliberalism, the law of comparative advantage has increasingly become a globally imposed diktat, establishing an international division of labour in which developing regions should focus on labour-intensive manufacturers due to their cheap labour costs. This diktat had profound implications on the spatiality of garment activities. It progressively extended the geographical reach of the so-called global garment commodity chain, which has systematically relocated to areas characterized by cheaper labour costs (Ramaswamy and Gereffi, 2001; Mezzadri, 2008). At the same time, it has also reproduced the vulnerability of the global garment proletariat (Hale and Wills, 2005; Esbenshade, 2004; Seabrook, 2015). Their working poverty was reconceptualized as an asset for global competition. In short, the global garment chain has always been intrinsically structured as a global sweatshop.

The reproduction of garment workers' vulnerability is strongly linked to processes leading to the creation of 'cheap labour' as a key component of the production process. Often, when it comes to developing regions, the category 'cheap labour' is reified and naturalized, as if it was a promptly available input of production in given settings (De Neve, 2005). However, this is hardly the case. In garment production, cheap labour must be manufactured, no less than T-shirts or jeans. Its process of 'making' entails myriads of capital–labour relations, labour practices and outcomes, resulting in different typologies of vulnerability in workspaces and beyond, in realms of social reproduction. Dormitories, for instance, are becoming key sites for workers' control (Smith and Pun, 2006). In countries characterized by great regional disparities, and by huge reserve armies of labour, the making of cheap labour can 'creatively' bank on multiple socio-economic divides and inequalities. This is definitely the case for India, whose sweatshop this book places under the microscope.

Perhaps, less internationally renowned than the Bangladeshi case – ultimately, unlike Bangladesh, luckily India did not experience major garment sweatshop tragedies so far – clothing production in the subcontinent is hardly an outlier in relation to the overall labour conditions of its workers. On the contrary, the 'Made in India' is heavily produced on the shoulders of India's working poor, which represents the largest army of informalized labour in the world (ILO and WTO, 2009; NCEUS, 2007; Kannan, 2008; Srivastava, 2012; Chadrasekhar and Ghosh, 2015). Garment production is greatly fragmented and scattered across the whole country, and characterized by high levels of fragmentation and 'clustering' of production activities (Mezzadri, 2014a). This fragmentation strongly mediates India's integration into the global garment commodity chain, opening the door to multiple patterns of informalization involving both labour and capital (Mezzadri, 2008). In fact, these characterize India's accumulation pattern as a whole (Harriss-White, 2003; Breman, 2013). Overall, India seems to be made for the sweatshop, and the sweatshop for India.

This first chapter places emphasis on the geographical relocation and spread of the global garment commodity chain and its continuous reconstitution as a global sweatshop, as processes shaped by the rise of neoliberalism. Then, it presents a first general sketch of garment production and labour relations in India. By doing so, the analysis engages with debates on labour informalization and class formation in the context of contemporary capitalism and the rise of 'Global' India, drawing primarily from the work of Jairus Banaji (2003, 2010), Henry Bernstein (2007), Silvia Federici (2004, 2012) Maria Mies (1982, 1989), Barbara Harriss-White (2003, 2010) and Jan Breman (1996, 2013). Insights based on the work of these authors, Banaji in particular, guide the analysis throughout. The last section expands on the relevance of shifting the emphasis from the 'chain' to the 'sweatshop', and of theorizing the sweatshop as a regime. Let us now focus on the vicissitudes of the garment industry and the complex spatiality it acquired in the neoliberal era.

Neoliberalism and the Rise of the Global Garment Commodity Chain

The process of globalization of garment production has been progressive and relentless. This process has been marked by different patterns of location and relocation, which the industry has gone through since the 1960s, and which have actually peaked post-1970s, with the rise of neoliberalism and its emphasis on Export-Oriented Patterns of Industrialization (EOI). Today, the industry shows an extremely wide geographical reach, and incorporates a vast number of emerging economies and developing regions as main garment export producers. Asia, in particular, has increasingly emerged as a key region for the development of the global garment industry. In developed regions, the little garment production left is organized into informalized production pockets, often inhabited by migrant communities.[5]

Effectively, already in the 1950s textile production had started moving east, so much that, in the context of the protectionist paradigms of the time, the US had negotiated with Japan the first 'voluntary' export quotas, in order to protect

---

[5] See Hammer *et al.* (2015) on Leicester, UK, and Lan (2014) on Prato, Italy.

its own domestic production (Spinanger and Verma, 2003). However, it is only in the 1960s that a systematic process of migration of the industry towards Asia kicked off. It specifically targeted East Asia, which became the first site of global garment production. This initial shift of the industry was to be the first of many. By the 1970s, garment or apparel (terms used interchangeably in the literature and here), was one of the leading export sectors of the East Asian Newly Industrialized Countries (NICs) (Gereffi, 1994). Export success in light manufacturing, of which apparel was a key component, was a crucial factor (albeit not the only one) in East Asia's impressive economic take off, central to the accumulation strategies of the region.[6]

In the context of the changing development paradigms and policies of the 1970s, the East Asian 'miracle' (as it was labelled by the World Bank, 1993) of export success in labour-intensive production was soon mainstreamed as the way forward for many other developing countries. The rise of neoliberalism, in fact, attacked the basis of protectionist, state-led development, which had dominated the policy scene since post-World War II (see Preston, 1996). By the early 1980s, in the context of the new rising consensus, 'openness' to international trade was set as the '*deus ex machina*' for development. EOI started being mainstreamed as the 'right' industrial policy to follow, replacing cumbersome and costly Import Substituting (IS) strategies, which were considered unsustainable after the two oil shocks and after the onset of the debt crisis (Johnston and Saad-Filho, 2005). Supporters of the neoliberal doctrine highlighted how, in the context of EOI, countries could specialize according to their comparative advantage. In particular, developing regions had to exploit their abundance of a cheap labourforce and focus on labour-intensive productions. Classic models of international trade, such as the Heckscher-Olin model, highlighted how this choice would have unleashed countries' economic potential, eventually leading to a process of convergence of the price of factors of production (i.e. interest rates and wages, in models based on capital and labour). This would have triggered the economic catch up of the so-called 'Global South', in what Smith and Toye (1979) depicted as the 'happy story' of international trade.

---

[6] Wade (1990) highlights the relevance of import substituting policies; Kohli (1999) points at the relevance of 'path dependence', examining the role of Japanese colonisation; and H. J. Chang (2003, 2012) insists on the role of the 'developmental state' in the economic success of East Asia. On a different note, and paying attention to inequalities, Seguino (2000) highlights the relevance of gender discrimination in promoting growth in the region, and D. Chang (2009a) insists on the ruthlessness of East Asia's developmental project.

The neoliberal counterrevolution triggered a profound process of restructuring of the international division of labour, and of the industrial trajectories of developing regions. In the new division of labour, developing regions were not seen as mere providers of raw materials anymore, but rather as suppliers of cheap manufactures. Labour-intensive manufacturing production, in particular, started migrating towards developing countries, abandoning developed regions and their expensive labour. With the rise and fast spread of outsourcing, many developing areas became the new industrial production sites of the neoliberal capitalist architecture. This process favoured the formation of what Gereffi and Korzeniewicz (1994) conceptualized as global commodity chains (GCCs), i.e., production networks organized around specific commodities, spread globally according to specific spatial patterns, and also globally 'governed' by agents and actors who had a privileged position in the complex industrial hierarchy dominating the world economy. Developing regions were now the new manufacturing production 'nodes' of these global industrial formations, although obviously their incorporation in the world-system had a much longer history in international trade and capitalist production, as highlighted by Hopkins and Wallerstein (1977, 1986), who originally developed the concept of commodity chain to study the evolution of patterns of unequal exchange (on the evolution of the literature on chains, see Bair, 2005; 2009). The long history of the integration of developing regions into the world economy is also mapped by studies in global history illustrating the complex division of labour during colonial times (e.g. Roy, 2013; Beckert, 2015), an issue this analysis will return to later on.

Garment production had a particularly prominent place in Gereffi's first conceptualization of GCCs, as the best example of 'buyer-driven' chain, where the global governance of the chain was in the hands of large retailers, brand-named merchandisers and trading companies; actors who do not necessarily own their own manufacturing facilities, but rather make use of networks of suppliers in a variety of exporting countries (Gereffi, 1994, pp. 97–98; see also Gereffi *et al.*, 2002). One of the key features of this type of chains is its labour-intensity and the 'footloose', mercantilist nature of its dominating capital, prone to multiple relocations, and prone to use these relocations (or threats to relocate) as a way of disciplining its subordinate agents, namely the local suppliers based in developing countries. Arguably, this type of chain best represents the paradigmatic shift from IS to EOI policies, and the shift from the 'development project' to the 'globalization project' (Bair, 2005). In fact, this shift encouraged specialization in the kind of labour-intensive, light manufacturing industries generally associated with buyer-driven governance in the context of globalization.

In East Asia, quite rapidly, local manufacturers managed to move from simple garment assembly to 'full packaging' (Gibbon, 2001), further strengthening the new international division of labour between developed and developing nations (Jenkins, Pearson and Seyfang, 2002). By the 1980s, these suppliers were looking for new sources of cheap labour elsewhere, triggering processes of 'triangle manufacturing' (Gereffi, 1994). As US companies were outsourcing production to East Asia, East Asian firms too were relocating production to 'poorer neighbours' and other developing regions, acting as intermediaries in a process of trade triangulation. This process determined a second geographical shift of the global garment commodity chain (GGCC). By the 1980s, production rose also across Southeast Asia and Latin America, South Asia and – obviously – China (Ramaswamy and Gereffi, 2000).

This second set of processes of relocation was due to a combination of different factors. The process of rapid economic growth in the East Asian 'miracle' economies generated a general increase in wages in the region, partially eroding its original comparative advantage in labour-intensive production. However, also the evolution of international regulation in the sector played a crucial role in the further re-spatialization of global garment production (Mezzadri, 2008). Back in 1955, date in which the US negotiated the first voluntary export constraints with Japan, textile exports were regulated through bilateral agreements. However in 1961, importing and exporting countries started new negotiations with the scope of enabling a more systematic, multilateral agreement. This led to the birth of the well-known Multi-Fibre Arrangement (MFA) in 1974 (Singh and Kaur Sapra, 2007).

The MFA established the creation of standardized quotas for exporting countries. Despite protectionist measures were in sharp contrast with the principles of the new open trade consensus contained in the General Agreement on Tariffs and Trade (GATT), the MFA was the expression of developed countries' protectionist aims (Uchikawa, 1998). While in the 1950s and 1960s barriers had mainly focused on fabric exports (mainly cotton), the MFA signalled a shift of focus towards higher-value added products, such as garments and made-ups (Singh and Kaur Sapra, 2007). Therefore, in a sense, the evolution of developed countries' protectionist efforts mirrored in international trade regulations was somehow coherent with the evolution of developing regions' comparative advantage, and with the shift from the old to the new international division of labour (Mezzadri, 2008). The MFA dictated the rules in global textile and garment trade for two decades, until the birth of the World Trade Organization (WTO) in 1994, when it was phased out. The phasing out was carried out over a period of 10 years and in four different stages, and the agreement finally expired in January 2005. After 2005, some export constraints were re-negotiated on the basis of bilateral negotiations. For instance, in 2005, China, today's major global garment producer, agreed to initially place some 'voluntary' limits on its textile and apparel exports to Europe (Barboza and Meller, 2005).

Since the phasing out of the MFA, the global garment commodity chain has further increased its geographical reach. Today, garment export is also present in Africa. Despite gloomy forecasts, suppliers based in countries like Kenya, South Africa, Lesotho, or Madagascar, have not been completely wiped out by the end of the MFA, although they struggle significantly to compete with Asian economies, China in particular (e.g. see Bezuidenhout et al., 2007; McCormick and Kamau, 2013; Kamau, 2013), which in the post-quota world dominates the global market accounting for roughly one-third of all garment exports (Pun et al., 2015). Moreover, 'newcomers' like Ethiopia are becoming increasingly attractive for global buyers. In fact, they are also becoming attractive for Chinese companies, many of which have upgraded their role within the garment chain, becoming 'giant-contractors' (see Appelbaum, 2008), 'total-service-providers', or 'one-stop-shops' (Merk, 2014). Today, Chinese garment capital is already present in numerous developing regions and emerging economies, like Cambodia or Jordan (see Azmeh and Nadvi, 2013, on Jordan). The rise of these regional players has further complicated the governance patterns characterizing the garment chain (Mezzadri, 2014b). In effect, large regional (non-western) players have always played a key role in shaping production systems and trade routes (Banaji, 2010).

This brief sketch of the vicissitudes of readymade garment industry, and of its processes of location and relocation, highlights two specific points. First, while undoubtedly the garment industry has always been characterized by particular traits – like labour-intensity and ability to relocate easily – from the 1970s onwards these traits have been further reinforced and internationalized, providing the industry with its current global, 'footloose' character. Second, the progressive process of globalization of the industry has been considerably accelerated by its neoliberalization. On the one hand, neoliberalism re-instated comparative advantage – perhaps one of the stickiest concepts of economics, courtesy of David Ricardo – as the golden rule to follow.[7] In a neoliberal world, countries can be competitive in light manufacturing production like garment only insofar they are able to reproduce their comparative advantage in cheap products, manufactured by cheap labour. On the other hand, during the onset of the neoliberal era, the sector adopted a specific global institutional framework, ruled by the MFA, which also participated to increase the geographical spread of the global garment commodity chain. In fact, although clearly dictated by the protectionist aims of developed nations (that have never been incompatible with neoliberalism), the establishment of specific production quotas meant that international buyers and clothing brands were unable to source only from a few countries. Rather, they were compelled to diversify sourcing strategies and work with multiple suppliers in multiple regions. This drew into garment-making even countries with no traditional history or competitive edge in either tailoring or fabric production, as they were still able to become 'cut and stitch' centres, i.e., centres for garment assembly. After all, all they needed was an army of cheap workers sitting in front of a stitching machine.

The Rise of the Global Garment Sweatshop

In the imaginary of many people, garment production is by now considered a synonym of 'sweatshop labour'. Its progressive globalization during the neoliberal era has always been tightly linked to finding reservoirs of cheap labour. Since the 1990s, scholars, researchers and journalists have denounced the harsh labour relations and poor working conditions associated with garment work (e.g. Bonacich *et al.*, 1994; Bonacich and Appelbaum, 2000; Rosen, 2002; Esbenshade, 2004; Hoskins, 2014; Seabrook, 2015). Arguably, these have characterized the industry since its early origins. The first tragedy in the history of garment production, took place more than 100 years before Rana Plaza, on March 25th 1911. On that date, the Triangle Shirtwaist factory, based in New York City, burned down killing 146 workers who were locked into the industrial premises. Even the very term 'sweatshop' is far older than what one may think. It was 1901 when the economist John R. Commons (quoted in Howard, 1997, p. 152, see also Esbenshade, 2004), deployed this expression to refer to the small shop-based or home-based clothing units composing the US clothing industry at the beginning of

---

[7] For a powerful political economy critique of comparative advantage, see Shaikh (2005). A recent attempt to undermine the concept from a legal perspective is made by Kishore (2014).

the twentieth century.[8] Today, however, the term sweatshop hardly simply evokes a particular type of pre-industrial production space. In fact, it is considered strongly linked to the development of contemporary processes of late industrialization. It is broadly associated with a particularly intense and despotic work system based on abysmally low standards, a system by now subjugating millions of workers across developing regions – 40 millions, according to some estimates (Hale and Wills, 2005). Briefly, the meanings and use of the word sweatshop have significantly expanded together with the systematic process of multiplication of the number of labouring bodies subject to its harsh rule. Again, this process of multiplication can only be understood in relation to the rise of neoliberalism.

In fact, by promoting the move of labour-intensive manufacturing production like garment to new production sites, the rise of neoliberalism not only led to the constitution and spread of today's globalized industries but also broadly signalled the end of the 'labour-friendly international regime' (Silver and Arrighi, 2000) and the rise of a 'labour-unfriendly' regime (Lerche, 2007; Mezzadri, 2008). In particular, within the 'new' neoliberal conceptualization of development, based on the diktat of comparative advantage, poor working conditions were reconceptualized as a strategic asset to exploit. As observed by Jan Breman (1995), under the logic of comparative advantage, labour in the developing world was asked to surrender to capital since the very start, for the 'greater good' of development. Unsurprisingly, the neoliberal era triggered a deep process of informalization of labour. It promoted the spread of multiple sets of informal labour relations through multiple 'channels of transmission', ranging from structural adjustment programmes (SAPs), to the multiplication of flexible production circuits, and the rise in processes of labour deregulation (Mezzadri, 2008, 2012).[9] It entailed both the 'informalization of the formal' (Chang, 2009b), as well as the expansion of the traditional 'informal sector' (Mezzadri, 2008).[10]

Processes of labour informalization widely characterize the whole global garment commodity chain (Mezzadri, 2008, 2010, 2012), whose very structure

---

[8] Commons (see Howard, 1997, p. 152) defined the sweatshop as 'a system of subcontract, wherein the work is let out to contractors to be done in small shops or homes', to be contrasted with the factory-system, 'wherein the manufacturer employs his own workmen … in his own building'.

[9] Mezzadri (2012) highlights the presence of three channels of transmission of informality into the global era: structural adjustment programmes (Meagher, 1995; Portes and Hoffman, 2003), the formation of global production chains and networks, and the rise in processes of labour deregulation.

[10] For a review of the debate on the informal sector from the 1970s to date, see Moser (1978), Rakowski (1994), Castells and Portes (1989) and Chen (2012). On the channels of transmission of informality into the global era, see Mezzadri (2009, 2012).

and features make it in fact into a global garment sweatshop. Since its origins, the functioning mechanisms of the chain – labour-intensity, proneness to relocate, low capital investment and complex commercial agreements (all key traits of buyer-driven governance) – could only be a disastrous recipe for labour. By the late 1980s and throughout the 1990s, campaigns against sweatshop labour in developing regions gained momentum. In the US, as underlined by Naomi Klein (2000) in her famous *No Logo*, the year 1995–1996 was re-labelled as 'the year of the sweatshop'. Public campaigning in favour of global garment workers peaked as Katie-Lee Gifford – the American TV celebrity who back then collaborated with Wal-Mart on its clothing lines – cried on national television accused of new slavery (Klein, 2000). From this period onwards, all major clothing giants started elaborating their own private 'codes of conduct' for labour, opening the era of Corporate Social Responsibility (CSR), based on the privatization of labour standards.

Originally, codes aimed at providing an answer to public campaigning (see Jenkins, Pearson and Seyfang, 2002), hence representing a sort of defence strategy for global buyers and brands. However, today, after decades of private regulation, CSR is hardly only a defence mechanism for global actors. It is actively and aggressively deployed to discipline suppliers (De Neve, 2009; Taylor, 2011), as well as to promote processes of 'moralization' of market outcomes (O'Laughlin, 2008) that also carry tremendous economic opportunities. Ethical fashion markets have exploded in the last decade. They represent an incredible new source of revenue for many global buyers and brands, which manage to bank on processes of 'commodification of ethics' (Mezzadri, 2012). Despite the fact that ethical fashion is becoming an increasingly lucrative enterprise, sweatshop scandals have continued multiplying, showing how little the CSR model has done for workers in practice. In fact, Rana Plaza tragically epitomizes the sheer inadequacy of this model.

If sweatshop workers across the globe are subject to harsh working rhythms and conditions, and are exposed to multiple types of occupational and livelihood risks, they can also be fairly different. For one, they may sweat across different spaces of work. The particular nature of the garment product cycle, characterized and defined by numerous ancillary activities – let us imagine a garment product, with its multiple seams, button-holes, embroidered patterns and labels – carries a great potential for the set-up of highly decentralized production systems, where the factory is only one among many production sites. More informal production units are still very common in the sector, as also home-based work, often considered the 'weakest link' of the global garment chain (Prugl, 1996;

Carr *et al.*, 2000; Delaney, 2004; Mezzadri, 2008, 2014a; Burchielli *et al.*, 2008, 2010; Unni and Scaria, 2009). Indeed, today's garment sweatshops are hardly standardized production realms, but rather myriads of different factories, informal workshops and homes linked together by the sweat of different sets of labourers. Differences in spaces of work are strongly linked to different relations of proletarianization.

The debate on processes of proletarianization under contemporary capitalism is complex and rather polarized and has interplayed with that on the rise of labour informalization (see Arnold and Bongiovi, 2013, for a selected, useful review). According to some, we are witnessing an age where 'the proletariat' has virtually disappeared and has been replaced by the rise of a 'precariat'; a new potentially 'dangerous' class made of various social segments with a fairly different relation to both work and citizenship (Standing, 2007a, b, 2010, 2014). According to others, instead, the progressive expansion of capitalist relations has led to the creation of a 'social factory': an extension of the law of value to an increasing number of subjects, as well as its domination across all realms of social life. Originally stemming from the work of Mario Tronti (1966), the concept of the social factory has been popularized by Marxist Autonomists. Many increasingly deploy it to picture the expansion of capitalist relations across the world (De Angelis, 2000, 2007; see also Atzeni, 2013), or in specific regions, where 'value subjects' have risen exponentially (Chang, 2009b, on East Asia). While arguably the theorization of the 'precariat', as already that of the 'multitude' developed by Hardt and Negri (2004), seems to primarily speak to processes of pauperization involving western middle classes, the concept of the social factory provides valuable insights on the process of proletarianization at work in the sweatshop, inhabited by poor and lower classes from the developing world. In fact, to an extent, one could argue that the sweatshop does work as a social factory – or better a global factory, as argued by Chang (2009b) – that subjugates an increasing number of fairly diverse people, at work across different spaces of work, to the capitalist–labour relation.

However, these understandings of the social factory only provide the starting point of the debate. How does the process of subjugation to the labour relation manifest within the global factory – or better, in our case, in the global sweatshop? Insights from the work of Jairus Banaji, Henry Bernstein, Silvia Federici and Maria Mies allow us to start pushing the analysis of the sweatshop and its 'class' a little deeper. According to Banaji (2003, 2010), capitalism has always been characterized by combinations of 'free' and 'unfree' labour; that is, by different *forms of exploitation.* In fact, it is the presence of processes of extraction of labour surplus that defines capitalism, and not, as many orthodox Marxist accounts suggest, by the presence of free (read wage) labour (see also Meiksins Wood, 2002).[11] Ultimately, 'freedom' under capitalism is never the happy term suggested in the liberal dictionary. It simply means dispossession from the means of production and subsistence. Along compatible lines, but focusing on the restructuring of class relations characterizing the neoliberal, global era, Bernstein (2007, 2010) suggests that contemporary processes of proletarianization do not produce a proletariat as a coherent, unified class, but rather as different, multiple 'classes of labour'.

Classes of labour are crossed by multiple social divides. These divides can also be relatively autonomous from class, which they often pre-exist. This is to say that if classes of labour have different relations to reproduction (Bernstein, 2007), reproductive realms crucially shape their very difference. In fact, a stronger focus on reproduction is necessary to understand processes of class formation. As stressed by Silvia Federici (2004, 2012) in her theorization of women's work under capitalism, the social factory always *starts* with reproduction. By the same token, as suggested by Maria Mies (1982, 1986), processes of dispossession and surplus extraction always start from the 'home' and the 'body' of workers. At the very least, social structures and structural differences interplay with and mediate the process of class formation (Harriss-White and Gooptu, 2001; Harriss-White, 2003, 2010; see also Basile, 2013), as capital strategically deploys them to engage in an endless boundary-drawing process (Silver, 2003) to segment labour, cheapen its costs, and subjugate it to its control. Recently, Mezzadra and Nielsen (2012) have placed further emphasis on the 'multiplication of labour' triggered by boundary-drawing strategies, conceiving borders as 'technologies of differential inclusion'. Overall, 'classes of labour' are produced by way of already 'classed' bodies as social oppression always exceeds the capitalist relation, although it powerfully structures it.

Indeed, labour inside the many spaces of work composing the global garment sweatshop comes in different guises. Workers sweating in a Mexican *maquila*, for instance, may be fully 'free', that is dispossessed from their means of production and subsistence. Instead, those working from their 'home' in Cambodia, or from a dirty basement in a residential area of Manila, may still be largely 'unfree';

---

[11] Historical work on India confirms the co-existence of 'free' and 'unfree' forms of labour across many industries since colonial times. See, for instance, van Schendel (2012) and Saptari (2012).

they may own some looms or stitching machines, or even land. Still, they are all nevertheless free from survival outside the market. They represent different classes of labour. Inhabiting different echelons of the sweatshop, these classes correspond to different labouring bodies that live the reality of the sweatshop in different ways. The 'sweatshop experience' changes for women, men, migrants, children or different ethnic (or caste) groups.

Notably, if one also accounts for social profile and differences and realms of reproduction, the patterns of 'freedom' or 'unfreedom' at work in the garment sweatshop get further complicated. Workers appear as subject to multiple forms of unfreedom, which exceed definitions only based on dispossession, as they also exceed definition conflating labour unfreedom with labour bondage. For instance, women, even when fully dispossessed and deployed as 'free' wageworkers inside the sweatshop, are always made socially unfree by patriarchal norms. This point will be developed in Chapter 3, which also discusses processes of feminization of labour at work in the industry. Moreover, debates on unfreedom should increasingly account for the entire livelihood of informalized workers. Many workers live in extremely harsh conditions in industrial hamlets and informal colonies, and are often 'free' from a dignified existence (Breman, 2013). Others instead, based in employers-run industrial hostels, experience aggressive processes of commodification of their whole daily reproductive time, their bodies fully subject to the asphyxiating control of a 'dormitory labour regime' (see Smith and Pun, 2006; Pun, 2007). These issues will be analyzed further in Chapter 6.

The particular combinations of 'free' and 'unfree' labour, the different classes of labour and broader social structures of oppression characterizing the global sweatshop in given geographical settings always depend upon regional or local industrial trajectories and accumulation strategies. Briefly, they depend upon the political economy of the sector in a particular region. Moreover, they also depend upon the commercial dynamics and product cycles of the garment 'things' produced. The physical materiality of the garments produced is no secondary complication to the study of the sweatshop, as it crucially shapes its social materiality (Mezzadri, 2014a). Regions producing hundreds of thousands of basic jeans per month are unlikely to have the same type of labourforce than regions focusing instead on small-batch, niche production involving high levels of ancillary and value-addition activities. This issue should be given far more attention in studies focusing on the garment sweatshop; indeed it will be given considerable attention in this analysis. Focusing on India, let us now explore how the commodity chain 'touches down' there, and which type of labour relations the Indian garment sweatshop can bank on in the subcontinent.

India and the Global Garment Commodity Chain

There is no doubt that India's textile industry had been incorporated into the global capitalist system since colonial times. By 1700, cotton cloth was the East Indian Company's major import from India; plain cotton was deployed as a means of payment in Ocean trade; and coloured cottons were already in great demand for fashionable clothing (Riello and Parthasarathi, 2010; Riello and Roy, 2010; Roy, 2013). Indeed, India was a key player in the rise of what Beckert (2015) calls the *Empire of Cotton*, an issue further explored in Chapter 4. However, despite this long history in textile production and trade, data seem to suggest that India was surprisingly a relatively latecomer into the business of modern, global readymade garment export. This started quite late, towards the 1960s, and remained rather negligible for the following two decades, as India still mainly exported textile fabrics (Thorburn, 2009, see also Fukunishi and Yamagata, 2014).[12] Garment production was organized by different communities than those who took charge of capital-intensive textile production following the demise of the British Raj. It was mainly organized by Marwaris, Sindhis and other Punjabi trading castes who did not necessarily have access to large capital (Mezzadri, 2009a).[13] During these first years, Indian export was mainly linked to the stitching of India's traditionally printed fabrics (Singh, Kaur and Kaur Sapra, 2004), which, overall, had already made the fortunes of many regional traders in international markets. Mumbai and Delhi were the two leading export centres, given their status as new Third World metropoles, and their former colonial past (Ambekar Institute of Labour Studies, 1980). The process of consolidation of India's position in the global garment commodity chain started gaining momentum in the 1980s. As export production relocated from East Asia, India's share of world garment export started growing considerably (Mezzadri, 2010). Tables 1.1 and 1.2 show that production continued growing steadily throughout the Nineties and the Two-Thousands, as India's liberalization phase began, relaxing tariff grids and opening up to the Neoliberal world order (see also Appelbaum, 2005; Hashim, 2004). By 2011, the Indian share of global garment production was 3.4 per cent.

---

[12] Fukunishi and Yamagata (2014, p. 6, Table 1.2) show that India became a top garment exporter in the 1980s. Between 1980 and 2008, India moved from 9th to 6th position in the list of top exporters.
[13] For an analysis of the caste-origins of business in India, the reader can refer to Damodaran (2008).

Table 1.1 Share of readymade garments in India's exports from 1960–1961 to 2000–2011

Year	Total exports	Total textile exports	Readymade garment exports	RMG/total export
Value/%	Value (Rs. Crore)	Value (Rs. Crore)	Value (Rs. Crore)	%
1960–61	643	79	1	0.16
1970–71	1,535	145	29	1.89
1980–81	6,711	933	550	8.20
1990–91	88,669	6,926	4,012	12.32
1994–95	88,669	19,945	10,305	11.6
2000–01	203,571	47,980	25,480	12.52
2004–05	375,339	62,370	29,538	7.87
2010–11	1,142,649.0	125,422	51,069	4.47

Source: Adapted from Table 3.1 in Singh and Kaur Sapra (2007, p. 43) and AEPC data (2013).

Table 1.2 India's share of world exports, apparel and clothing, during 1970–2011 (US$ million)

Year	World	India	India's share (%)
1970	109	–	–
1975	308	–	–
1980	32,365	590	1.8
1985	38,718	887	2.3
1990	94,577	2,211	2.3
2000	201,379	7,093	3.5
2007	364,118	9,930	2.7
2008	378,415	10,968	2.9
2009	332,366	12,005	3.6
2010	369,600	11,229	3.0
2011	432,555	14,672	3.4

Source: Adapted from Table 7.5 of Economic Survey 2010–2011 and 2012–2013.

Table 1.2 also shows that the phasing out of the MFA, albeit primarily benefitting China, today towering over all exporting countries, clearly also boosted Indian exports. It further indicates that the 2008–2009 global financial crisis had a harsher impact on world export than on India's share (see data for the years 2008 and 2009 in the table).

Complementing available data, qualitative information reveals that the crisis had an impact on Indian garment export companies, but a highly differentiated one.

It mainly hit small to medium exporters engaging in middle-end garment production, that is items sold at around 5–7 US$ FOB.[14] For some large exporters, the crisis was even a way to consolidate local market power, as buyers preferred focusing on companies with higher manufacturing capacity. For some small and medium exporters engaging in high-end production, the crisis could pass by with virtually no effect. They effectively engage in luxury goods export, whose demand is generally less 'elastic' to market downturns.[15] Finally, for those who are at the bottom of the production pyramid, that is small concerns focusing on low-end production (less than 5$ FOB), the final effect of the crisis largely depended on fate. It depended on the behaviour of the buyers they engaged with, or the broader exporting networks they were part of (since many small units work as subcontractors). Since 2010, according to exporters and unions (see Table 1.1), export growth picked up again, at least in the main industrial areas (Mezzadri and Srivastava, 2015).

Indian garment export production is scattered across multiple production spaces, and organized into specialized industrial 'clusters', that is networks of small and medium enterprises (SMEs).[16] By 2005, the Apparel Export Promotion Council (AEPC), the government body in charge of the allocation of export quotas during the MFA (and which today has only maintained its export promotion functions), pointed at the presence of eight garment export clusters in India; the National Capital Region (NCR; formed by Delhi and its neighbouring industrial areas in Uttar Pradesh and Haryana), Ludhiana, Jaipur, Calcutta, Mumbai, Bangalore, Chennai and Tiruppur. All these places, except from Chennai, were also identified in the UNIDO list of Indian industrial clusters (DCMSME, 2012). 'Special economic zones' (effectively the equivalent of export processing zones) engaging in garment-making for export could be found in Hyderabad and Cochin, although, according to the Council, production from these two poles was rather negligible. By 2009, the Council had re-mapped the spatial perimeters of the industry in India, and identified a total of 18 key clusters; namely, Okhla, Gurgaon, NOIDA (listed now as separate areas), Kolkata, Mumbai, Tiruppur, Ludhiana, Indore, Bellary, Jaipur, Bangalore, Chennai, Kanpur, Ahmedabad, Jabalpur, Salem/Erode/Madurai, Faridabad and Nagpur (AEPC, 2009). However, while the industry is

---

[14] FOB stands for free on board, and includes all costs until a buyer finally imports a good.
[15] This means that economic downturns are followed by a much less than proportional fall in demand.
[16] For an excellent review of Indian industrial clusters, see Das (2005). See also Uchikawa (2014).

indeed finding new areas, the AEPC confirms that direct export still remains concentrated across the usual eight (pooling together clusters in the NCR). These have developed longer term relations with buyers and importers, and a clear product specialization (AEPC, 2009).

Aggregate data suggest that, within garment clusters, production is highly decentralized and fragmented (see Table 1.3). A relatively old Accenture report (Singh *et al.*, 2004) provided an effective summary of India's overall peculiar garment trajectory, when it observed that, by 2001, India was earning US$ 5.5 billion in export revenues through a network of 10,865 exporters, while Sri Lanka was earning US$ 3 billion via 300 exporters. By 2003, four-fifths of the whole Indian garment sector was of small-scale (Spinanger and Verma, 2003). This trend continues to date, as a more recent survey across Mumbai, Tiruppur, Ludhiana, Indore, Bellary, Jaipur, Bangalore, Okhla, Chennai and Kolkata reveals that 78 per cent of units still have less than 40 machines, while only 7 per cent have more than 100 (AEPC, 2009). Unsurprisingly, UNCTAD identified 'industrial size' as the main issue of Indian garment export, limiting the potential for further

Table 1.3 Turnover, unit number and employment, main Indian garment clusters, 2009

Cluster	Turnover (Crores INR)*			Export share in total	Units	Employment (direct and indirect)
	Domestic	Export	Total			
Tiruppur	3,500	9,950	13,450	74	2,500	600,000
Kolkata**	11,200	1,000	12,200	8	12,291	604,700
Ludhiana	5,600	1,400	7,000	20	2,500	350,000
Gurgaon	750	4,250	5,000	85	675	99,500
Bangalore	1,000	4,000	5,000	80	850	450,000
Noida	1,000	3,500	4,500	78	750	NA
Chennai	500	2,000	2,500	80	650	224,000
Mumbai	1,260	840	2,100	40	6,000	667,500
Indore	1,140	60	1,200	5	2,000	100,000
Okhla	120	680	800	85	250	100,000
Jaipur	50	650	700	93	950	100,000
Bellary	250	25	275	9	1,305	30,000
Total	26,370	28,355	54,725	52	30,721	3,341,700

Source: Combined data from Tables 4.1, 4.4, and 4.7 (p. 10, 13, 17) in AEPC (2009).
Note: Unit number and employment excludes units with less than 10 machines.
*1 crore: 10 million INR. **Projected.

economic development (Appelbaum, 2005). Other accounts, instead, highlighted how industrial 'smallness' had actually become a source of strength for India, carving a competitive edge in small batch production. They stressed how the peculiarity of India's industrial fabric favoured the creation of backward linkages; triggered a stronger reliance on local capital, and created positive externalities for multiple local growth poles. Indeed, the vast geographical reach of the global garment commodity chain does not suggest a single 'ideal' type of incorporation in the global economy. On the contrary, it seems to suggest the presence of multiple 'varieties of global integration' (Tewari, 2008; Mezzadri, 2014b).

In India, the footloose nature of the global garment commodity chain acquires extreme traits. For instance, subcontracting, a key feature of all buyer-driven chains, in India entails capillary processes of decentralization and decomposition of production, including myriads of micro enterprises and SMEs. In his brilliant study of Tiruppur, Chari (2004) highlights the features of the highly decentralized patterns of growth characterizing this industrial town, linked to its agrarian past, and managed by a dominant caste and class of 'fraternal capitalists'.[17] Industrial fragmentation and inter-firm division of labour are so marked in Tiruppur that 'the entire town works as a decentralized factory for the global economy' (Chari, 2010: 446). More recently, De Neve (2014a) illustrates how the cluster has developed a Taylorist segment of production (see also Mezzadri, 2009a).

This extreme industrial fragmentation has not been reproduced 'in the shadow' of the state (Centeno and Portes, 2006), an argument which is often put forward to explain the proliferation of informal economic activities. On the contrary, the Indian state has always been a crucial player in reproducing informality (Basile and Harriss-White, 2010; see also Basile, 2013). This is definitely the case in the garment industry (Mezzadri, 2010). On the one hand, for decades, the Indian government 'reserved' the garment industry to SMEs. This policy of reservation was aimed at preserving employment generation in this very labour-intensive industry. However, it also created and recreated highly decentralized industrial systems, where even large companies preferred owning networks of small units rather than consolidating production under a single industrial roof. Besides, the Indian government also originally favoured a politics of quota allocation based on two principles: 'past performance', and 'first come first served'. Throughout the

---

[17] On inter-firm relations in Tiruppur, see also Cawthorne (1992; 1995) and Vijayabaskar (2001; 2005). The case of Tiruppur is discussed in Chapter 3.

1980s and 1990s, both these principles favoured actors who were in business for a long time, and those with already established connections abroad. These actors could access quotas easily without effectively owning manufacturing capacity, so that merchant capital soon started orchestrating a complex black market for the sale and purchase of export quotas (Mezzadri, 2010). The politics of reservation has been relaxed only since 2000, with the elaboration of the New Textile Policy (see Singh and Kaur Sapra, 2007). Only since then larger industrial set-ups started entering the sector, first in woven production, and only successively in knitwear (whose de-reservation started later, in 2005). In the same period, the government introduced a third quota allocation principle; the 'new investment entitlements', thanks to which manufacturing investment was finally relevant for export quota allocation (Mezzadri, 2010). However, by then, past legislation and practices had already crucially shaped the sector for decades. If, at the international level, the MFA increased the spread and dispersal of the global garment commodity chain globally, India's policy of reservation and management of quota allocation under the MFA had a crucial impact on the spread and fragmentation of the industry *locally*, promoting the mushrooming of many decentralized and diverse production networks across the subcontinent (see Mezzadri, 2010). These networks can bank on multiple processes of labour informalization, which feed the Indian sweatshop with armies of cheap labour (already suggested by estimates in Table 1.3).

The General Traits of the Indian Sweatshop

The Indian garment industry is not new to sweatshop scandals, although it did not experience horrific industrial disasters like Rana Plaza. In 2008, the BBC screened the *Panorama* documentary 'Primark on the Rack', which attacked the unfair labour practices of Indian garment suppliers working for the Irish clothing colossus Primark, formerly known as Penny's, a giant seller of cheap clothes which today sells through a huge network of 237 stores, located in Ireland and England, but also increasingly scattered across Europe, in countries such as Spain, Portugal, Belgium, the Netherlands and Germany. The documentary showed images of young girls and boys employed by the industry in Delhi and Bangalore, and of Sri Lankan refugees employed around the Tiruppur area (McDougall, 2008). In 2010, another scandal hit Marks & Spencer, as well as Next and The Gap. An investigation by the British newspaper *The Observer* unveiled a gloomy, Dickensian industrial reality where workers paid as little

Table 1.4 Employment and value-added, organized and unorganized apparel, 1989–2000

Wearing apparel	Value-added		Employment	
Years	1989–90 to 1994–95	1994–95 to 1999–2000	1989–90 to 1994–95	1994–95 to 1999–2000
Organized	27.0	2.3	17.3	3.8
Unorganized	6.2	14.9	0.7	15.2

Source: Adapted from Rani and Unni (2004, p. 4577, Table 7 based on NSSO 1989–2002, CSO 1985–2002).

as 25p were found in workshops in Gurgaon, one of the main industrial areas around Delhi (Chamberlain, 2010).

Over the last decade, many authors have denounced the poor working conditions Indian garment workers are subject to, as well as the processes of informalization that broadly characterize the sector. Undoubtedly, aggregate data on the sector clearly show a process of *de-facto* informalization at work (Srivastava, 2015). This process started in the mid-1990s, when the unorganized, informal sector started accounting for the lion share of both value-added and employment generation (Table 1.4).

In many ways, this is unsurprising, considering the fact the India shows the highest incidence of informal employment in the world (ILO and WTO, 2009). Overall, a staggering 93 per cent of all Indian employment is classified as informal (NCEUS, 2007).[18] This comprises labour in informal sector activities as well as all labour relations that, although taking place in formal settings, are casualized and subject to similar working conditions to those characterizing the informal economy.[19] In fact, informalized employment in formal settings seems on the rise (Kannan, 2008; Chandrasekhar and Ghosh, 2015). This is the case even in sectors that were previously characterized by substantially better working conditions, a phenomenon which Kundu and Sarangi (2007) call 'formal informalization' (see Srivastava, 2012). The progressive deterioration of labour relations and conditions in sectors like automobile, steel or telecommunication, which increasingly deploy contract labour, are cases in point (see Monaco, 2015,

---

[18] NCEUS estimates refer to both the employment in informal sector activities as well as to informal labour relations in formal production activities.

[19] An early definition of informal employment across both 'formal' and 'informal' sectors can be found in Hensman (2000). See also Hensman (2010).

on the Maruti-Suzuki NCR case; Parry, 2013 on the public Bhilai Steel Plant in Chhattisgarh; Damodaran, 2013, on the mobile telephone sector).[20]

India's global primacy in rates of informal employment is also paralleled by the resilience of forms of bonded labour across the subcontinent. According to the ILO, India is the first country in the world also when it comes to rates of bonded labour (Lerche, 2007). In fact, informal labour and bonded labour are hardly separate phenomena, but rather they are strongly interrelated. Indian labour is best understood as a 'continuum' defined by the presence of more or less 'free' or 'coerced' labour relations (Lerche, 2010, 2012). By the same token, dualist understandings sharply opposing 'formal' and 'informal' labour markets are also inaccurate. While authors like Jan Breman have always stressed the limitation of dualist understandings of informality, in India as well as elsewhere (Breman, 1996, 2013), these understandings seem particularly ill-equipped in the present context, as the process of informalization of labour not only gains further momentum in developing regions, but increasingly expands to the West, effectively becoming the mode of regulation of capital on a global scale (Breman and van der Linden, 2014).[21]

The vast world of India's informal labour is strongly informally regulated (Harriss-White, 2003, 2010; Harriss-White and Gooptu, 2001; see also Basile, 2013), and different social institutions, *in primis* caste – but also gender, the family or geographical provenance – shape 'myriads of networks of exploitation'. They segment and fragment the workforce, impeding the formation of a cohesive working class, and condemning the Indian informal proletariat to endless struggles 'over class' (Harriss-White and Gooptu, 2001; Sinha 2013). In fact, if episodes of labour resistance do manifest, they generally mainly remain unorganized, spontaneous and sporadic (Breman, 2013; Bhattarcharya, 2014). This is also due to the fact that the subjugation of the Indian working poor is first and foremost realized across realms of reproduction, hence tightly anchoring labour exploitation to wider forms of social oppression. Indeed, the labour question, in India, is also a reproductive question (Breman, 2013). Given the interplay among informality,

---

[20] Monaco (2015) looks at the rise of contract labour in the automotive sector to understand changes in industrial relations and struggles in the NCR. Parry (2013) argues that the state-owned Bhilai steel plant in Chhattisgarh has become a highly polarized labour arena, where a small labour aristocracy of permanent workers and a vast contingent of manual labourers neither share common interests nor see themselves as belonging to the same 'class'. Damodaran (2013) highlights the links between aggressive outsourcing strategies and the rise in casual contract labour in the mobile phone industry.

[21] Breman (2013) rightly criticises both old and new accounts stressing the formal/informal dichotomy (see for instance, his critique of Sanyal, 2007).

unfreedom and the social regulation (and oppression) of the workforce, labour in the Subcontinent can be defined as characterized by 'classes of labour' (Lerche, 2010, 2014; see also Pattenden, 2016). However, also in this case, it is clear how these classes are structured based on already existing regimes of social oppression.

Notably, the endless reproduction of the vulnerability of India's informal proletariat has been the result of state action, particularly since the rise of liberalization, in the 1990s (Chandrasekhar and Ghosh, 2008). Undoubtedly, India has crafted its own 'labour-unfriendly regime' (Lerche, 2007). Based for decades on a process of 'reformism by stealth' (Jenkins, 2004; Shyam Sunder, 2005, 2011), this regime has progressively become more actively aligned with capitalist interests, against labour.[22] Under the current Modi government, in particular, pro-capital policies, in favour of the elites and the 'Neo-Middle Class' (Jeffery, 2014), have become far more open and aggressive (Bhowmik, 2015).

In many ways, the garment sweatshop appears as a microcosm epitomizing India's labour relations and outcomes. If this sweatshop is largely characterized by informalized employment patterns (see Table 1.4 and also Unni and Rani, 2008) and appalling standards, it is also inhabited by different 'classes of labour', whose social profile varies greatly, based on multiple forms of social oppression crossing reproductive realms. The organization of the industry in complex production networks and clusters connected to the global economy has not attenuated the social regulation of the workforce; rather, it has placed a further premium on it, as a way to boost India's competitive edge in the global economy, and reinforce its comparative advantage in multiple, distinct forms of cheap labour (Mezzadri, 2009b). Accounts describing the features of the industry in different local settings clearly suggest the great differentiation of Indian garment workers. RoyChowdhury (2005, 2015) describes the abysmally low wages paid to the female garment factory workforce in Bangalore. Singh and Kaur Sapra (2007) and Mezzadri (2008) look at the precarious working arrangements at work in the Delhi garment industry, dominated instead by male migrants from the Hindi belt. Vijayabaskar (2001, 2005), Chari (2004) and De Neve (2009, 2014a; see also Carswell and De Neve 2013a, b) analyze the informal and exploitative labour systems characterizing the Tiruppur garment industry, and highlight the relevance of caste, gender and migration in shaping and reproducing them.

---

[22] Reformism by stealth takes place when the state maintains a specific formal institutional framework but allows certain classes to introduce acts and tactics which de-facto change the framework. See also Bardhan (2002).

As in so many other parts of the global sweatshop, attempts at exploiting the great visibility of the industry and imposing global labour standards have miserably failed. Corporate interventions, in particular, have hardly scratched the surface of the Indian sweatshop. For one, they have always shied away from 'politically charged' concerns, like wages, focusing instead on more mainstream and 'technicistic' interventions in areas like occupational hazard (Barrientos *et al.*, 2010). Moreover, these interventions aim at simply ensuring that factories – workshops and home-based realms of production are generally excluded – are 'safe enough' working places. However, they do not challenge the harsh rhythms and conditions of the sweatshop, and the systematic process of externalization of social contributions at work across its factories, workshops and homes, which increasingly dump onto workers their own labour question (see Mezzadri, 2014a). In this sense, corporate standards are the ultimate expression of that regime of 'self-entrepreneurship' mainstreamed by neoliberalism, a model that India seems in fact to have embraced (Gooptu, 2013). CSR interventions have failed to ameliorate working conditions in other parts of South Asia, in garment and in many other export-led labour-intensive industries (e.g. Kabeer, 2000, 2004; Kabeer and Mahmud, 2004; Nadvi, 2008; Lund-Thomsen *et al.*, 2012; Lund-Thomsen and Coe, 2015; Ruwanpura and Wrigley, 2011; Ruwanpura, 2013). The fight against the sweatshop, in India as elsewhere, has been lost also due to the inadequate weapons deployed. These have been part of the problem rather than the solution.

Unfortunately, if the failure of the western CSR model is now increasingly accepted in international policy circles, India has instead started to internalize it, recently proposing its own 'India-centric' code of conduct for labour in garment units. Elaborated by the AEPC with the support of the Ministry of Textile, this code, called 'Driving Industry Towards Sustainable Human Capital', or DISHA, seems to aspire to increase the competitiveness of Indian SMEs rather than mainstreaming pro-labour measures inside the garment sweatshop (AEPC, 2013; Mezzadri, 2014b). This said, the full implications of these recent developments should be analyzed more in depth in the future, particularly in the context of growing domestic markets for readymade clothing, the rise of regional corporate retailers – like, for example, Trent, the clothing retailing branch of the Tata colossus – and their increasing links with global retailing capital (Mezzadri and Srivastava, 2015). These trends are likely to further boost the number of sweatshop workers in the subcontinent, as well as further sharpen the urgency of their social question.

From the Global Garment Commodity Chain to the Sweatshop Regime

The analysis developed in this chapter has illustrated the inextricable relation between the development of the garment industry into a complex global commodity chain stretching worldwide and its reproduction across time and space as a global sweatshop, characterized by poor working conditions and multiple relations of exploitation and proletarianization. In this light, the sweatshop does not simply appear as the undesirable outcome of the multiple processes of relocation the chain has gone through. Rather, these processes of relocation seem to have been triggered by the quest to find new reservoirs of cheap labour; in short, by the attempt to always reconstitute the sweatshop. For this reason, a focus on the sweatshop, rather than the chain, represents a fruitful methodological and analytical choice in order to centre the analysis of the garment industry on labour. This choice has allowed anchoring the analysis of the sweatshop to current debates on labour informalization and class formation.

The study of the process of constitution and reconstitution of the garment sweatshop worldwide powerfully epitomizes the working of contemporary capitalism, as a system promoting multiple, highly differentiated patterns of proletarianization, incorporating different forms or classes of labour (Bernstein, 2007) – 'free' or 'unfree' (Banaji, 2003) – and systematically banking on multiple social divides, structural differences and divisions (Silver, 2003) crossing realms of social reproduction (Mies, 1982, 1986; Federici, 2004). Undoubtedly, the progressive incorporation of India into the global garment commodity chain has greatly benefited from the availability of the multiple social divides and structural differences that have always fragmented and segmented the working poor, condemning them to endless struggles 'over class' (Harriss-White and Gooptu, 2001). It has benefited from multiple processes of labour informalization, at work in both 'formal' and 'informal' production realms (see NCEUS, 2007; Kannan, 2008; Srivastava, 2012), and which make India the largest reservoir of informalized labour in the world (ILO and WTO, 2009; Chandrasekhar and Ghosh, 2015).

However, what are the defining features of India's sweatshops? On which basis do they vary across the subcontinent? Which type of workers inhabit them, and why? How are they controlled and organized, and by whom? How can the sweatshop be *theorized*? These are crucial questions. In fact, in order to fully debunk the mythology of comparative advantage in cheap labour, one has to unveil the complex processes of power and subjugation that reproduce labour as a cheap commodity for the world market. This can only be done in practice, by descending into 'the abode of production', and illustrate in detail its workings. Embracing this agenda and drawing from detailed empirical evidence from India, the remaining chapters of this book theorize the sweatshop by portraying it as a regime – a complex system of labour subjugation and social oppression with distinct features. One of these features is the strong, inextricable link between physical and social 'materialities' of production, and its implication for the spatiality of production and labour relations. The second is the great relevance of 'difference' in shaping and being reproduced by the labouring experience, in ways that generate multiple patterns of unfreedom. The third is the contested and complex nature of the relations of power and subordination shaping the processes of labour surplus extraction at work in the sweatshop. These involve interplays between processes of production and circulation as shaped by multiple actors, who often tie and control the labourforce across realms of production and reproduction. This is a crucial point, and one that complicates simplistic stories reducing the sweatshop to a sort of *zona franca* mainly moulded by global brands and global retailers. The sweatshop is not an industrial 'enclave' with 'no connection to the local economy' (Fröbel *et al.*, 1984, p. 6). The masters of the sweatshop are numerous, and their role in processes of labour subjugation is greatly complex. The last feature of the sweatshop regime is embodied in the very signs of labouring, which indelibly stain the lives of garment workers, depleting their health and consuming their bodies until their ultimate ejection from the chaotic social world where our garments are manufactured. In Chapter 2, we move to the analysis of the first feature of the sweatshop regime, by taking a closer look at the seams on our clothes, and at how their physical characteristics greatly influence the social processes of production. For this purpose, we travel to the garment areas of Northern and Eastern India. Here, some of the general arguments on processes of informalization, proletarianization and dispossession will be further analyzed and illustrated in practice, in light of empirical evidence.

2 | The Commodity and the Sweatshop

'A recognition that a commodity is inseparable from its physical materiality, and that as a unit of wealth it embodies both its natural and its value form, presents a different view of capitalism.'

(Coronil, 2000, p. 356)

Living in a 'Material' World

An enquiry into the world of sweatshops should entail some reflections over the types of commodities produced by sweatshops. These are no secondary issues for any study of capital–labour relations. Marx himself started volume one of *Das Kapital* with a chapter on commodities. Marx's primary aim was to insist on the social relations underpinning production and showing how the extraction of labour power – exploitation – was a crucial constitutive aspect of any type of commodity production. In Marx's words (1967, p. 72, in Coronil, 1997, p. 60), 'the existence of things qua commodities, and the value relation between the product of labour which stamps them as commodities, have absolutely no connection with their physical properties and with the material relations arising therefrom'. Arguably, there are many ways to interpret this. One is that the physical properties of commodities have very little relation to the social process deployed to produce them. Another is, instead, that in the process of becoming commodities, things should not be viewed as simply linked to their physical status but primarily as an expression of the social relations deployed to produce them. These are fundamentally different explanations. The former suggests that physical and social 'materialities' fundamentally differ, while the latter instead highlights the presence of multiple, different types of 'materialities' epitomized by the commodity form. Marx addressed the complexities of commodity production in relation to their value. Indeed, he did insist on the twofold value of commodities in capitalist production, their use value and exchange value. Given his aim of de-fetishizing commodity production and to deconstruct the concept of 'utility' deployed by classical political economists, his focus was primarily on exchange value which is also the main feature of producing 'things' under capitalism. However, this does not necessarily mean that use value is of no relevance. It simply means that, in the sphere of production, commodities are 'bearers of value' (Marx, 1990, p. 143) in multiple ways. Today, we also know that through their marketization, they also acquire further social and cultural values that add to the complex 'social life of things' (Appadurai, 1986), shaping a world where people are heavily defined based on their differentiated consumption of 'stuff' (Miller, 2010).

Effectively, only very few authors have worked on the relevance of physical materiality for the social process of production from a political economy perspective. Neither Harry Braverman nor Michael Burawoy, for instance – who contributed greatly to the study of the abode of production – have paid much attention to this issue. Braverman (1974), in his seminal work on the labour process, mainly focused on top-down forms of labour control leading to deskilling.[23] Burawoy, instead, illustrated how the shop-floor may produce different relations between people, leading to forms of control also based on 'consent', rather than simply on coercion (Saptari, 2012; Anner, 2015). However, none of them explored the ways in which different physical objects are possibly 'containers' of different patterns of deskilling or relations between people. Briefly, none of them paid attention to how the materiality of things may already betray significant information on the social materiality of their production.

Perhaps, one of the most interesting attempts to deal with this issue is proposed by Fernando Coronil in his critique of Occidentalism (1997). In fact, Coronil openly acknowledged the relevance of 'the physical' to understand the 'social'. However, Coronil's primary focus was on rent and processes of commodification of nature in post-colonial social formations, and he mainly discussed the relevance of physical materiality in relation to land and natural resources (on this, see also Castree, 2003). But the relevance of 'the physical' does not exhaust itself with land or the world of natural 'matter'. Also the physical properties of man-made things can provide interesting insights on the very social process deployed for their production. At a very basic level of analysis, anyone would agree that ships, cars, toys or canned peaches are all products very likely to be produced in different ways not only simply because their exchange value is different but also because they *are* different. The production processes and product cycles deployed vary. So do

---

[23] His concept of 'deskilling' was quite homogenizing. However, different workers experience deskilling in different ways. Feminist scholars criticized Braverman on this basis (see Phillips and Taylor, 1980).

the outcomes, both in terms of actual finished products and in terms of the social processes involved in their realization.

With reference to commodities produced 'transnationally' across globalized circuits, many commodity studies (with the differences of the case, as discussed in the Introduction and in Chapter 1) have placed emphasis on the relevance of the composite process of 'assembly'. Nevertheless, they have dedicated less explicit reflection to the different physical properties of the 'things' processes of assembly result in. Moreover, in the case of assembly, it is relevant, as commodity studies do, to differentiate between broad categories of commodity production: again ships, cars, toys or canned peaches. Indeed, value chain analysis has dedicated considerable effort to the study of this differentiation, particularly in relation to the changing patterns of governance it entails. However, it is also relevant to acknowledge the great varieties of products these broad categories 'contain', particularly in the context of the increasingly diversified markets contemporary capitalism generates. Caroline Knowles' (2014) recent book *Flip-Flop*, for instance, shows how different sub-categories of products – cheap flip-flops in her case – draw specific 'trails' across the global economy. This said, hers remains a trail based on the life cycle of the product and the mobile geography it entails, rather than one centred on production's physical properties and the labour they involve.

Focusing on garment production, the need of accounting for the different physical features involved in product differentiation is fundamental. As briefly suggested already in Chapter 1, the word 'garment' in fact, is hardly exhaustive of all possible commodities that can be produced in this broad category. This point has important implications for the social processes of production likely to be involved in differentiated types of garment commodity production. This is to say that if, generally speaking, garment production is historically associated with the formation and reproduction of sweatshops, then different typologies of garment production are also likely to generate multiple, different typologies of sweatshops. Briefly, the 'making' of different garments is directly linked to the 'making' of different sweatshops. Obviously then, this process of 'making' strongly depends upon production and labour possibilities available in the local contexts where production takes place.

Attention towards the relation between physical and social materialities can also help problematizing answers to the key questions: Who owns what? Who does what? Who gets what? What do they do with it? in today's global economy, which Bernstein (2010, p. 22) rightly summarizes as the leading concerns of political economy. In fact, answers to these questions have been often based on overly simplistic ideas on the international division of labour, where the developing world is fetishized as a 'natural' site of 'cheap labour'. In this oversimplified schema, the presence of sweatshop labour in developing regions is considered as part and parcel of developing countries' contribution to the globalization project. As argued earlier in this book, theories of comparative advantage have contributed greatly to this characterization, highlighting how an international division of labour where some areas are (temporarily) condemned to labour intensity is effectively 'good' for development in the long run (see Kitching's and Cawthorne's critique of Krugman's 'praise of cheap labour', 2001; see also Powell, 2014). While the pernicious ideological aspects of this position have been powerfully spelt out by Jan Breman (1995), who insists on the dangers of representing labour defeat to capital as the 'primary condition' for future prosperity, I would argue that even more can be said about the fallacies of the theory of comparative advantage in misrepresenting development processes and, crucially, the role of labour within them.

On the one hand, as well explained by Anwar Shaikh (2005), these theories negate the very presence of uneven development across the world, and suggest that trade will work as an engine of development, while there is no historical evidence suggesting that specialization in the 'naturally abundant factor of production' leads to anything but further specialization (see for instance Wood, 1994, 1995; Wood and Ridao-Cano, 1997; Schumacher, 2013). This is to say that, often, countries focusing on cheap labour can only aspire to further master their ability to cheapen their labourforce *vis-à-vis* the rest of the world, and not, as predicated by comparative advantage theories, to catch up. On the other hand, and more crucially for the analysis developed here, one should also observe that there is hardly anything natural about the development of comparative advantage, as throughout history these advantages have been broadly 'manufactured'. While this argument is convincingly demonstrated by authors like Ha-Joon Chang (2003) in relation to the historical specialization of some countries in given types of commodity production (quite famous are his examples of ship building in South Korea or rubber production in Malaysia), it is still underdeveloped in relation to labour.[24] Too often, having a cheap labourforce is considered as a by-product of late development or underdevelopment. Labour is 'assumed to be there from the start, naturally available for deployment by

---

[24] For a critique of mainstream accounts reifying natural endowments as 'curse', see instead Saad-Filho and Weeks (2013).

whichever corporation needs it' (De Neve, 2005, p. 90). However, first, if a comparative advantage in given commodities is manufactured, so is the social process underpinning that production, as physical and social materialities are, as argued above, intertwined. Second, the making of cheap labour is hardly an easy endeavour. It results from the historical trajectories leading to a specific type of product specialization. It depends upon product cycles and also on the possibility to reproduce a given architecture of production profitable to those in charge of the production process.

Focusing on garment, the reflections proposed above help setting a clear agenda for this second chapter. Firstly, the chapter aims to illustrate empirically the relation between the physical and social materialities of highly diversified garment commodities with reference to the case under scrutiny, India. Secondly, it aims at showing how the architecture of production and labour control shaping different sweatshops is all but 'natural'. Rather, it is strongly dependent upon different historical industrial trajectories and reproduced by different product cycles, both entailing different social relations of production. Thirdly, after the presentation of the empirical cases, the chapter concludes by preliminary introducing the concept of 'sweatshop regime' as a useful device to capture the interrelation between physical and social processes, while also stressing the multiple types of labour relations at work in sweatshops. For this scope, reference will be made again to the work of Jairus Banaji (2003, 2010), Henry Bernstein (2007), Beverly Silver (2003) and Barbara Harriss-White (2003). In fact, their work will also be the starting point guiding the analysis in Chapter 3. However, further considerations on the exploitative use of 'difference' by capitalism will also be made there. For this scope, the analysis will broaden and will review again, however in more detail, the key insights provided by the work of feminist scholars like Silvia Federici (2004, 2012) and Maria Mies (1982, 1986). It will also engage with a number of important studies on the concrete functioning and gendering of the global assembly line (e.g. Salzinger, 2003; Caraway, 2005; Wright, 2006).

Different Garment Commodities and Sweatshops in India

In this chapter, I aim to illustrate empirically how the production process through which given commodities are produced tells a lot about the reason why sweatshops acquire a specific form and typology and not others. At a very basic level, the more numerous and more distinct the commodities on offer, the more numerous and more distinct the sweatshop regimes one is likely to find. As argued in Chapter 1, while 'garment' is too often treated as one, single type of commodity production, it in fact entails the creation of substantially diverse and more or less complex items, produced through a variety of processes and product cycles. In India, garment production reveals a great diversity of regional product specialization, as production is organized across multiple industrial areas scattered across the subcontinent. This is fully acknowledged by global buyers and brands. Through the eyes of sourcing actors, the country can be re-imagined as a giant, multi-storey, department store, with different garment 'collections' available at different 'floors' (Mezzadri, 2014b).

Different patterns of product specialization are the outcome of multiple and highly differentiated regional industrial trajectories. Distinct regional trajectories imply distinct product cycles, in turn leading to the formation and reproduction of distinct labour relations, rhythms and outcomes. Hence, one specific commodity, with all its characteristics and features, is at once the outcome of a specific industrial trajectory, a specific production process and the set of social relations these entail. In short, with reference to the Indian case, it appears clear how the 'materiality' of commodities is both physical as well as social. Neither of these dimensions should be neglected, as they are strongly intertwined. In fact, the physical features of a given commodity can provide crucial insights on the social relations its production entails.

In her book, *India Working*, Barbara Harriss-White (2003, p. 208) lists 'space' as one of India's social structures of accumulation. While reflecting on India's informal industrial trajectory, she insists on what she defines as the 'quiddity' of commodities produced across the subcontinent; quiddity, being an archaic word meaning 'the essence or particularity of a thing'. Quiddity has two, broad dimensions. One relates to the social meaning of given commodities; that is the cultural – even moral – understanding of their quality. The second, instead, relates to the physical features of commodities, and the way these interplay with the economic, social and spatial characteristics and relations characterizing production and trade. Indeed, across India's garment sweatshops, both different physical and social 'materialities' are manufactured. The garments produced across Indian garment areas are incredibly diverse – jeans, jackets, T-shirts, skirts, blouses. Such diversity is the outcomes of past industrial trajectories and of the availability of highly differentiated markets (Mezzadri, 2014a). It translates into different product cycles, involving distinct types of labour, which, as we will see, are then socially controlled and disciplined in multiple, different ways. Indeed, different varieties of social regulation are abundantly available in India (Basile and Harriss-White, 2000; Harriss-White and Gooptu, 2001; Harriss-White, 2003, 2010, 2014).

Besides being greatly regionally specialized, garment production in India is also generally defined by considerable industrial fragmentation. As noted in Chapter 1, garment-producing areas are organized into clusters of SMEs. By 2009, 78 per cent of units were classified as having less than 40 machines, while only around 7 per cent had more than 100 (AEPC, 2009). While industrial 'smallness' may not be an issue in relation to growth or potential incorporation into global markets (Tewari, 2008), it surely does have profound implications in relation to the structuring of layered and complex 'product cycles'. In turn, this bears crucial implications for the type of sweatshop regime emerging as dominant in particular local areas. Quite simply, in the context of great industrial fragmentation, the presence of highly complex and fragmented sweatshops is hardly surprising.

If industrial fragmentation is to a certain extent a common trait across all garment clusters, it emerges as one of their most striking features in the north of India; namely in Delhi, Ludhiana and Jaipur. Moreover, it also emerges as a predominant feature in the east of India, in the only centre listed by the AEPC as a key garment centre – Kolkata. By 2005, the AEPC used to divide India's garment regions in North, South, East and West. The north and the east of India were the two regions where fragmentation was at its highest (AEPC, 2004; Mezzadri, 2009a). Common to these clusters is an engagement in what can be defined as the production of 'niche', or highly differentiated products, or low-end items; heavily embellished ladieswear in Delhi, winter wear, woollen knitwear production in Ludhiana, printed garments in Jaipur, and cheap nightwear and kidswear in Kolkata. Arguably, this high differentiation in products is mirrored by a considerable variability in the type of labour constituting the sweatshop across these areas. Let us first focus on the most important among these centres in terms of both value and quantities produced – namely, Delhi and its National Capital Region (NCR).

Composite Commodity Production Across the NCR

Delhi, where our empirical journey into the world of Indian garment sweatshops begins, is India's most important centre for the production of ladieswear. The dominant garment commodity here is often characterized by composite and embellished designs. In fact, garment production does not only takes place in

Delhi city; rather, as many other industrial activities, it also stretches across the whole NCR; that is, the Delhi metropolitan conglomerate. This is a huge area, set at around 34,144 km², and incorporating a number of districts in Delhi's neighbouring states of Haryana, Uttar Pradesh and now also Rajasthan (NCR Planning Board, 2015). New districts have been systematically incorporated into the NCR in the last decade, a trend that testifies to the great, strategic relevance of this area in the whole Indian economy. Unsurprisingly, multiple processes of land grabbing and land acquisition have accompanied this process of expansion, as brilliantly illustrated by Rana Dasgupta (2014) in his book *Capital*.

The history of the evolution of Delhi into its current garment industrial landscape is quite intriguing. Delhi's entry into garment production traces back to the *Mughal* period. *Shahjahnabad*, today's old Delhi, was a very renowned tailoring centre during the Mughal empire. Since the middle of the seventeenth century, the city hosted the *karkhane* (workshops) of many highly skilled artisans who catered to royal households. Towards the end of the Mughal period, many craftsmen and artisans left the city, while those who remained gathered in *mahallas* (craft neighbourhoods) scattered across the walled city (Blake, 1993). Production started organizing for market-based forms of distribution, a trend that was accelerated by the arrival of the British. In fact, if initially the import of fabrics and clothes from Britain crowded out the domestic cottage industry, by the 1940s handloom production and tailoring flourished again, thanks to the expensive tastes of the British colonizers (Roy, 1999; see also Riello and Roy, 2010; Riello and Parthasarathi, 2010). After independence, it was the boom of the hippy culture that accelerated the shift from tailoring into 'modern' garment-making (Singh *et al.*, 2004). By the 1960s, Okhla, a low-rent commercial area turned into an industrial estate (Lal, 2004), emerged as a centre for readymade garment (Alam, 1992). Export, however, started peaking only by the 1980s (Ramaswamy and Gereffi, 2001). By that period, as both real estate prices and pollution levels soared (Lal, 2004), production started moving to Noida, in Uttar Pradesh (UP), and Gurgaon and Faridabad, in Haryana.

The NCR became the new, wider spatial container of the industry. Garment companies did not necessarily 'choose' between different areas. Many, particularly those with more considerable production capacity, differentiated their activities and acquired industrial units across multiple industrial areas, a trend which continues to date (Mezzadri, 2015a). This complex spatial trajectory favoured fragmentation, which was further reinforced by international and national policies, a point already discussed in Chapter 1. On the one hand, the regime of export quota allocation rewarded past performance, established business connections, mercantile networks and ownership of multiple units. On the other hand, government policies also favoured the reproduction of industrial 'smallness' via the reservation of the sector to SMEs (Mezzadri, 2010). Most of all, fragmentation was really conducive to the type of product specialization dominating the NCR, primarily geared towards highly 'embellished' production of ladieswear (Ambekar Institute of Labour Studies, 2005; Mezzadri, 2008, 2014a). This particular type of product specialization needs more complex, fragmented and volatile product cycles. While today a number of NCR garment companies have consolidated production and expanded manufacturing capacity, ladieswear still remains as their primary market segment (Mezzadri and Srivastava, 2015).

The fragmentation of industrial fabric manifests itself in substantial rates of subcontracting, often mediated by what can be (for the time being) loosely defined as mercantile or semi-mercantile forms of organization.[25] In many ways, garment production in the NCR is an excellent, textbook example of Gereffi's buyer-driven chains, as defined by multiple layers and tiers of suppliers and units; incorporating a vast pool of unorganized, unregistered workshops; and stretching all the way to home-based settings (Mezzadri, 2008). Until 2005, suppliers were still quite open about their high subcontracting rates. However, today, due to the greater awareness of compliance norms, and to what suppliers quite amusingly lament as CSR-based 'survey fatigue', this is less the case. Still, visits to subcontracting areas, which are quite scattered around the NCR, reveal that subcontracting units are still numerous. Indeed, the relatively recent boom of domestic production of readymade garment is a new, very important channel of reproduction for these smaller production concerns. However, overall, the resilience of subcontractors and of what will be defined below as the 'non-factory sector' in general (see Mezzadri, 2008) is due to the actual workings of the very volatile and taste-changing ladieswear production segment. In this market segment, the full integration of production activities is difficult until considerably high levels of manufacturing capacity are reached. In the words of one exporter,

> I do not believe those that pretend they do everything in-house while they do a lot of intricate designs; it is genuinely not economical.
>
> (Deepak D., fieldwork interviews, 2005)

---

[25] In Chapter 4, the analysis will complicate simplistic understandings of mercantile or semi-mercantile organizations of production.

Arguably, some large actors now manage to minimize – rather than avoid – the deployment of subcontractors. However, these are part of a rather exclusive and limited upper production layer. Moreover, even this layer can only manage to minimize what can be defined as 'capacity subcontracting', that is the deployment of a lower tier of actors to expand production capacity. Still, the majority of them would subcontract key processing and ancillary activities. Washing and printing are almost always contracted to subagents. Embroidery, a crucial ancillary activity for the NCR product cycle is outsourced to a highly informalized production segment, composed of combinations of micro-units and home-based production spaces and realms. Overall, the whole NCR cluster is organized into a large composite chain or network (Mezzadri, 2008, 2012).

Focusing on the company size and positioning within this chain or network, one can argue that the cluster is made of four different layers (Mezzadri, 2014a). One is made of large garment companies towering over the cluster. More recent fieldwork (conducted in 2013) highlights that post-MFA many of these actors – primarily engaged in export markets – experienced a substantial growth. As a result, a process of partial industrial consolidation has taken place. Consolidation resulted from complex processes. Post-MFA, several large buyers developed a strong preference for working with fewer companies with greater manufacturing capacity. In a world without quotas, buyers were not compelled to place orders with multiple companies anymore. The channelling of large orders towards fewer companies promoted processes of differentiation within the cluster. These were further exacerbated by the onset of the financial crisis. While the aggregate impact of the crisis does not seem substantial (Table 1.2), fieldwork reveals that it was greatly diversified. At the top, a few large companies even managed to 'bank' on the crisis – as many big fish often do – with one large company reporting opening two new units (Mezzadri, 2015a).

The second layer of the cluster is composed of medium and small companies. This is the largest, most fluid, complex segment of garment production in the NCR. These companies engage in highly diversified export markets and increasingly with domestic markets. In this sense, size is not necessarily a good measure of turnover. Some medium enterprises produce for 'average' (mid-range) markets; however, others do not, and focus instead on high-end markets, which require more heavily embellished products with a higher FOB[26]. Small companies can also produce for high-end production. Many deploy astonishingly high levels of subcontracting,

---

[26] See footnote 14 in Chapter 1.

and, despite owning some manufacturing capacity, organize production according to the logic of the mercantile putting-out system. Some, in this category, may also work as subcontractors for larger companies. Moreover, the exponential growth of the domestic garment sector in the last decade has also further differentiated large companies from medium and/or small ones. In fact, the latter increasingly also turn to the domestic market to minimize the increasingly greater risk of dealing with very volatile export orders, particularly in the aftermath of the financial crisis, which hit the second layer of the NCR cluster substantially. During the crisis, many medium and small companies went bankrupt, particularly those relying only on export, on a few markets, and on a few buyers. For instance, the financial collapse of the German colossus LaQuelle left many NCR companies in a very bad shape; with some still trying to recover from losses incurred.

An intermediate, third layer of the cluster is composed of subcontractors and processing units of different types and engaging in different activities. Subcontractors can either focus on core garmenting activities or on single tasks, although the latter type is now more common in domestic production, and increasingly less so in export. The most common processing activities outsourced by garment companies to specialized operators are washing and printing. As large companies generally own processing plants or units, a substantial part of processors are medium or small units.

A fourth and final layer of the cluster is represented by ancillary activities. The most common ancillary activity required by garment companies in the NCR is embroidery. Visits to garment companies and factories reveal the great complexity of the type of ladieswear produced by the NCR. The sample rooms where suppliers receive guests and buyers reveal a vast array of complex designs and intricate embellishment patterns, organized in relatively small and quickly changing production batches. Embroidery is a key component of the NCR garment success story. It is sold as the quintessential competitive advantage of the NCR *vis-à-vis* other garment centres in India and elsewhere. Indeed, for global buyers, the NCR is the place where to source high fashion lines and embellished clothing collections. After embroidery, the FOB price can even double (Lal, 2004).

There are different types of embroidery in the NCR. One is computerized embroidery, which takes place in specialized units. Larger companies increasingly consolidate this type of embroidery activity in-house, while the majority of medium and small factories rely instead on processors scattered around the NCR. A second type of embroidery, more labour-intensive, is machine-based embroidery. This takes place on single-needle machines in either micro units or home-based units – with the two categories often overlapping. A third type of embroidery is hand-based. It is further diversified into *adda* work and *moti* work. In the NCR, *Adda* work, which takes its name from the simple handloom deployed to make it – the *adda* – is organized in either informal units of variable size or home-based settings. Its organization and origins will be further explored in Chapter 5. *Moti* work, also known as sequin work/beading, is fully organized in home-based settings and performed by individual outworkers.

This subdivision based on company hierarchy and tasks articulates with another, broader distinction between what can be defined as 'factory' and 'non-factory' realms of production (Mezzadri, 2008). One obvious way to distinguish these two is based on formal registration (Singh *et al.*, 2004). A second possibility is based on access (or lack of access) to final markets or on activities-based distinctions, like, for instance, engagement in core garmenting activities or only specific tasks. These two possible categorizing principles partially overlap and articulate in different ways across the different layers of the cluster. Notably, unregistered, informal units have always been predominant in the NCR (Singh *et al.*, 2004; Mezzadri, 2008, 2012). Both recent field findings (Mezzadri, 2015b) and aggregate data (Srivastava, 2015) suggest that the expansion of the 'non-factory' segment of production is continuing to date. The non-factory-realm is where one can locate the vast army of subcontractors at work in the NCR. Their difference with some small companies may be blurred, and primarily based on market access, as many small companies may also only own unregistered units. Non-factory units can be located in industrial areas, but they are more often found in crowded residential or commercial areas. Their size is varied and can also be extremely small – just two to three machines and less than five people at work.

The complexity of this local architecture of production, linking different sets of factories, workshops and home-based settings together, is paralleled by an organization of production inside units that must flexibly adapt to changing designs and incorporate multiple, ancillary processes. Garments often frantically enter and exit production lines, move from unit to unit, and enter homes before going back to the production premise from which they started their complex journey, as finished products with all their final characteristics and features.

Large and medium factories are often committed to organize the shop-floor based on assembly-line production. However, in the NCR, assembly-line production is always rather flexible, as garments must leave the line for the many ancillary processes. This is why many garment companies use the expression 'semi-assembly'. The organization of semi-assembly often borders what is more effectively defined as a 'group system', where a team of tailors, together, work on a garment line. Only very large factories engage in more streamlined, 'pure' types of assembly-line production. And even these have to allow for some flexibility depending upon orders. For instance, even these factories rely on the micro unit or home-based sector for embroidery. Going further down the industrial size spectrum, small factories, and all those working on higher end, heavily intricate garment lines, deploy both group systems and 'make-and-through' techniques, where single tailors stitch the entire garment. Notably, these are also common in low-quality products, where standardization is less relevant for final buyers. In larger industrial units this technique is only deployed for extremely high-end production, generally 'secluded' in dedicated rooms within factories, where highly skilled tailors may be locked in, in order to keep the brand designs secret.

The dominant regional product specialization of the NCR, its composite architecture of production and product cycle are corresponded by very complex labour relations and outcomes. Physical and social materialities are strongly interconnected. Their links are mediated by the cost minimization strategies of garment suppliers and agents, and their struggle to cheapen the cost of labour across the different layers, realms and tasks of production. As it will be illustrated in the section below, it is based on these processes that labour is recruited, deployed, disciplined and controlled and that the NCR sweatshop is created and reproduced.

The NCR as a Composite Sweatshop

The borders across the different layers of the NCR garment cluster are extremely porous and continuously redrawn by representatives and agents of garment companies, vendors and multiple types of agents and intermediaries. These actors establish links across factories, workshops and homes; between different factories; between different workshops and between different homes, crafting multiple vertical and horizontal networks. The mobility of labour across these networks is also considerable; an issue that will be partially explored further later on in this section, and then more in depth in Chapter 6. However, overall, different realms of production also establish demarcated local 'enclaves' for workers. In fact, within the great complexity of the production system at work in the NCR, processes of accumulation entail processes of cost minimization setting clear parameters on which type of workforce engage in which garmenting activities and tasks (Mezzadri, 2008).

The social profile of the garment workforce in the NCR is highly differentiated, and not so much across different layers within the cluster, but primarily across distinct activities and tasks within the production process. In both factory and non-factory realms, where factories or workshops engage in core garmenting activities, the workforce is primarily composed of male migrants coming from the states of Uttar Pradesh (UP) and Bihar (Singh and Kaur Sapra, 2007; Mezzadri, 2008, 2012; Barrientos *et al.*, 2010), although a recent survey of labour in the upper echelons of the industry also indicates a rising marginal presence of migrants from other states, like West Bengal, Orissa and Jharkhand (Srivastava, 2015). Caste or religion-based distinctions were quite relevant during the early developments of the industry. *Darzis*, a traditional tailoring caste, were over-represented among labourers. However, today they do not seem particularly relevant; if something, workers seem to primarily come from the 'castes of poverty' (Mezzadri, 2009a). This said, Muslims are over-represented in both factory and non-factory realms (Unni and Scaria, 2009; Mezzadri and Srivastava, 2015).

The deployment of migrants clearly responds to the need of the industry for a highly flexible labourforce, which can be deployed and retrenched following seasonal patterns. In brief, the deployment of migrants from the poor Hindi Belt allows labour cost minimization in the realm of core garmenting activities. A considerable share of migrants stays in the NCR for less than one year, before going back to their villages, particularly for harvesting and holiday season. This is in June, a period of the year more or less 'fortuitously' coinciding with the lean season of the industry. In the context of fast-changing product cycles, often characterized by numerous but small/average quantities, cost minimization can be realized quite effectively through the deployment of this type of mobile labourforce. In factory settings, women are generally primarily deployed as thread-cutters, a relatively low-skill activity. Overall, numerous studies indicate that around 80 per cent of the labourforce in factory realms is temporary or casual in nature (Singh *et al.*, 2004; Mezzadri, 2008, 2012; Barrientos *et al.*, 2010), and set on a continuum of vulnerability (Srivastava, 2015).

Some large factories, those that consolidated production considerably in the last decade, are now applying a more aggressive policy of hiring women workers as frontline shop-floor workers in tailoring (Mezzadri, 2015a). However, so far, only a very limited top segment of the NCR is experiencing a partial process of feminization. This segment places an increasingly lower premium on extreme flexibility, as their orders have become more considerable and consistent, their products less seasonal, and their international markets more diversified. Trends in women's employment should be increasingly monitored in the future, especially after garment businessmen's successful lobbying to allow women to work during night shifts in Tamil Nadu (Narasimhan and Sethi, 2014). There is so far no evidence clearly indicating that women workers, who are often from nearby areas, enjoy better contractual conditions. Notwithstanding the relevance of these new trends, for the majority of NCR garment companies the dominant labour practice remains largely based on the deployment of a very masculine and mobile workforce. This practice still delivers well to dominant industrial needs, and it is effective in guaranteeing cost minimization across a highly flexible production process. Processors also employ a similar workforce, composed of male migrants, particularly given the higher capital-intensity of some activities, like, for instance, washing (Mezzadri, 2009a).

Ancillary activities, which lay at the very periphery of the NCR industrial formation, albeit crucial to its value generation, are characterized by the deployment of a highly composite labourforce. In each segment or activity, employers minimize costs by employing the type of workforce which is more likely to cheapen the costs of production in relative terms; that is, *vis-à-vis* other possible options available. Machine embroidery is generally carried out by family labour in home-based units. In the NCR, *adda* work, which is a rather labour-intensive task requiring craft-based skills, and some dexterity in the use of handlooms, is primarily organized into units, although home-based production realms are also deployed. Specifically, until 2005, a significant number of migrant children travelling alone to the NCR, primarily – albeit not only – from Bihar (Mezzadri, 2007, 2008), used to crowd the dark basements or over-heated roof terraces where *adda* often took place. Since the end of the MFA and, more crucially, with the increasing spread of what garment companies call compliance 'troubles' – let us remember the previously mentioned 2008 Panorama documentary '*Primark on the Rack*' – this particularly vulnerable and exploitative type of migratory child labour, is less present in the area. A study by Phillips *et al.* (2013) still identifies child labour in the NCR garment export industry. However, the study does not distinguish between child labour and child work – namely children at work with members of their own family in homes.[27] Fieldwork reveals that in export one

---

[27] On the crucial distinction between child work and child labour, the reader can refer to the classic text on the subject by Bequele and Boyden (1988).

can observe a gradual *relative* decline of more hazardous forms of child labour, while child work remains widespread. Arguably, this has to do with increasing migratory flows of male adults or families from traditional *adda*-producing villages, particularly from Western UP (Mezzadri, 2014a), an issue that this analysis will expand on later. While in export markets *adda* was a male preserve in the NCR, the last decade has also seen the increasing deployment of women, given the rising availability of this work with the expansion of export production (Mezzadri, 2015b). Women, however, only work from their own homes.

Finally, *moti* work, considered the least skilled type of embroidery and mainly involving attaching beads to finished products, is fully organized in home-based settings, and it is an entirely female preserve. Women home-workers carry out this task eventually helped by their children; many combine *moti* with other labour-intensive informal activities, which may vary based on their residential location within the NCR. If caste and religion-based distinctions are not particularly relevant in factory settings and across units engaged in core garmenting activities (although Muslims are relatively over-represented), they are more relevant in relation to more 'peripheral' types of labour. A higher percentage of this labour is composed of low-caste Muslims, like *Ansaris*, whose traditional occupation has often been linked to craft-based embroidery or petty tailoring activities (see also Unni and Scaria, 2009; Mezzadri, 2014a).

This complex and highly mobile network of different people at work across the NCR is recruited, managed and disciplined by what Barrientos (2013) would define as a 'cascade of labour intermediaries'; namely labour contractors. In fact, the capillary presence, differentiation and 'stickiness' of contracting networks across the multiple layers of several garment clusters are quite remarkable. In the NCR, their resilience should also be understood in relation to both the physical and social materialities dominating the cluster. On the one hand, Delhi's complex and long industrial trajectory in garment-making and its highly composite garment commodities and layered product cycle shape a complex spatiality where establishing connections across different production 'dots' is a necessary task. On the other hand, the local deployment of multiple types of labour within this complex spatiality creates the need to recruit, manage and supervise workers subject to different rhythms and constraints. Arguably, contracting seems to satisfy both these needs. Quite importantly, in this fluid, composite system, where different labouring bodies are assigned different tasks across multiple production realms, contracting becomes crucial to ensure *ad-hoc* forms of labour discipline and control across the whole spectrum of possible activities (see Mezzadri, 2008).

A considerable portion of migrant workers in factories and workshops, highly casualized, is recruited and organized by labour contractors. The entire non-factory sector is also crossed by multiple contracting networks, often starting from the same villages where migrants come from and will return to, based on those patterns of circular migration so well described and analyzed by Jan Breman (1996, 2013). Indeed, different sets of labour contractors are at work across the entire 'embellishment' network focused on embroidery (Mezzadri, 2015b). An in-depth analysis of these forms of labour contracting, their relation with processes of surplus extraction, and implications for labour and livelihoods will be discussed in depth in Chapter 6. Here, we shall simply observe how contracting powerfully articulates with the architecture of labour disciplining and control forming the structural backbone of the sweatshop. First, it further strengthens the social boundaries between different categories of workers across the multiple realms of production of the NCR. Second, it also further reinforces the strong social regulation of the workforce, which, as illustrated above, is mediated by patterns of mobility, geographical provenance, age and gender. Besides, this type of informal regulatory mechanism, extremely widespread in the Indian informal economy (Harriss-White, 2008, 2010), seems entirely compatible with the flexible circuits of global commodity chains and production networks, as shaped by the logic of neoliberal globalization (Mezzadri, 2008).

Altogether, the composite architecture of production and labour control at work in the NCR cluster shapes the general traits of sweatshops that are as composite and layered. Suppliers and agents industriously deploy multiple strategies of labour cost minimization, reproducing a highly segmented workforce engaged in different activities and tasks and subject to different rhythms and, often, even to different masters. Arguably, if the NCR is perhaps the most emblematic example of this type of sweatshop regime, similar trends are at work across the other clusters of Northern and Eastern India, also engaged in 'niche' production of highly differentiated garments. It is to these 'minor' centres and their physical and social materialities of production that now the analysis turns to.

Composite Garment Production in Jaipur, Ludhiana and Kolkata

Studies of garment production in Northern India primarily focus on Delhi and the NCR, given its dominance in terms of both value and quantities produced (Mezzadri, 2010). However, a sketch of production and labour outcomes in 'minor' centres also provides useful insights. Appealing again to the picture of our 'giant garment mall' – India as imagined by global buyers – also these areas engage in a particular type of niche products. Field findings reveal that the sweatshops dominant in these minor centres are also very fragmented and layered, along lines compatible to those observed for the NCR. Also across these centres, the physical materiality of the commodities produced impact profoundly on the reproduction of given social relations of production.

Both in Jaipur and Ludhiana, the types of garment produced focus on particular market segments; print-based and embellished garments, and woollen winterwear production, respectively. Also in Kolkata, the only centre in Eastern India listed as a key garment centre, production targets a specific subsegment of the market. Here, a relative decline of industrial production has entailed a sort of 'failure-based' type of product specialization targeting cheap products and low-end markets, particularly in kidswear and nightwear. Notwithstanding the differences of these cases, due to different trajectories and ports of entry into 'modern' garment-making the strong relation between physical and social features of production is striking. Also in these cases, the architecture of the local sweatshop is very much dependent upon the type, form and 'appearance' of the items produced. Let us first reflect on the physical features of production, their history and organization.

Also in Jaipur, Rajasthan, craft-based textile and tailoring flourished during the Mughal period. It was based on 'hand-block' printing techniques, involving the decoration of fabrics with designs carved on blocks of wood and then printed on the cloth with natural pigments. The craft was mastered by printing families belonging to the *Chhipa* ('printer' in Hindi) community, who moved to Sanganer and Bagru, close to Jaipur, from Gujarat and *Malwa*, today Madhya Pradesh (Sarkar, 2005). Printing *karkhane* first catered for royal households, and turned to domestic markets with the arrival of the British. By the 1960s, garment activities emerged, organized by traders from Jaipur, Mumbai, Delhi and Ahmedabad (Joshi, 1995 in Sarkar, 2005). However, they became widespread only by the 1980s, thanks to *Anokhi*, the famous print-based Indian brand (DeNicola, 2004). During this period, screen printing, cheaper and less time consuming, also spread. By the mid-2000s, Jaipur was a small but steady export centre, accounting for 1.36 and 1.27 per cent of Indian garment export, in terms of quantity and value respectively (AEPC, 2004). In the 1990s, a cluster development programme by UNIDO revitalized the Calico Printers Cooperative society and formed the Consortium of Textile Exporters (COTEX), gathering print-based textile and garment producers. At the same time, a network of small garment companies producing 'modern', not necessarily print-based ladieswear also emerged. Post-MFA, some NCR companies started looking at Jaipur for business opportunities.

Due to all these different developments, despite a small size, the cluster is a complex social formation where craft, semi-industrial and industrial activities articulate in multiple layers, locations, and across both 'traditional' and 'modern' realms. Many print-based companies can be found across Bagru, Sanganer and nearby areas. Small printing workshops can be found in these areas, as well as in the nearby villages of Jahopta, Jairampura and Kaladera (UNIDO, 1997, 2004b). Production of modern garment is instead primarily based in the Malviya, Sanganer, Sitapar and Vaishwa Karma industrial areas, as well as in Mansarovar. Small units, generally deployed as subcontractors, can be found in the residential areas of Saket Colony and Adarsh Nagar (Mezzadri, 2009a).

The organization of production partially varies across craft-based and modern segments, shaping flexible networks. Print-based garments entail backward integration with craft activities, which are either home-based or workshop-based. In this case, from the homes and workshops where printing takes place, fabrics enter processing units, linked to dying and washing, to finally arrive to factories and workshops in industrial areas. The 'modern' garment, instead, acquires its final physical features through a process of progressive forward integration of activities. In this case, 'embellishment', print-based or also embroidery-based, takes place after core garmenting activities. Briefly, the integration of craft into Jaipur's garment final commodity can follow a two-way pathway.

This high organizational fluidity does not imply a lack of hierarchy. On the contrary, as in many small clusters, one finds a strong polarization between the few companies towering over the cluster and the 'rest'. Interrelations are dependent upon market segments – which garment commodity one focuses on – with print-based garments, even when produced by larger companies like *Anokhi*, defined by a more complex spatiality than 'modern' products. Often, the print-based segment still shows an organizational layout resembling mercantile putting-out systems of production. At the top of the hierarchy, one either finds traders or companies with some manufacturing capacity. Traders may also come from printing families. In fact, the export boom triggered processes of differentiation of printers, with some turning into 'printer-job workers' and others into 'trader-printers' (Sarkar, 2005).

Differences across commodity types also bear implications for the organization of production inside garment units. Print-based companies, even when of a fair size, tend to organize production through group systems and make-and-through techniques, placing a premium over the artisanal look of the final garment.

Assembly lines are a rare breed in this type of production, as product cycles are complex, based on small and fast-changing orders. Companies and workshops working on more modern clothing, instead, may adopt semi-assembly-line production, although group systems are also found. Few large companies engaged in modern production deploy only few subcontractors, lamenting the lack of the flexible pool of manufacturing capacity available in larger garment centres (Mezzadri, 2009a). The remarkable heterogeneity of this cluster, its multiple production realms and complex spatiality imply that also here, as in the NCR, a great number of agents and sub-agents work around the clock pulling all the different strings of the system together.

If Jaipur is the city of print-based garments, evolving across lines largely compatible with the NCR (it is not a case that NCR companies are extending their reach here), Ludhiana is where any buyer – or Indian garment trader, for that matter – would place orders for woollens.[28] Also in this case, the evolution towards a specific pattern of local product specialization – winterwear – should be understood in relation to Ludhiana's distinct industrial trajectory. The city, situated in Punjab, 400 km east of Delhi, has been involved in 'hosiery' for 100 years. Originally, in the nineteenth century, both cotton and wool production could be found. Cotton was linked to local agricultural activities, while woollen production was widespread across Punjab and Kashmir (Sharma, 1989). With time, woollen production took over. The British Raj transformed Ludhiana into a key production centre for uniforms and socks, worn by British soldiers during World War II (Maini, 2004). By the time India gained independence, Ludhiana was a wool town, which soon managed to develop export links with the Soviet Union. When the Soviet collapsed and cheap imports started crowding out the domestic industry during the onset of liberalization, woollen producers focused on domestic markets, which worked as safety nets (Tewari, 1999). Today, the industry still primarily produces for domestic markets. All Indian domestic brands producing woollen products – Oswal, Montecarlo, Oster and Benetton India – are based in town. Export partially redeveloped since the late 1990s, this time targeting both western and 'secondary' markets (formerly 'non-quota' countries). The typical commodity remains a woollen knitted garment. By the early 2000s, winterwear composed 95 per cent of Ludhiana's production (Shukla and Bansal, 2003).

Also this cluster has different layers, with larger units located in industrial areas at the outskirts of Ludhiana, in Focal point, Ludhiana industrial area,

---

[28] Several new garment factories now appear along the Delhi–Jaipur highway.

Chandigarh road and Jalahandar road. Then, a vast world of small informal subcontractors and tiny units without access to final markets are scattered across residential and commercial areas, particularly in Sunder Nagar, Madhopuri, Brahmpuri, Shivpuri, Purana Bazar, Bahadur KeRoad and Mohalla Naughara (Shukla and Bansal, 2003; AEPC, 2009). They represent 60 per cent of all local garment units (Mezzadri, 2009a). Some ancillary activities are present, and are home-based. The most common home-based activity is not embroidery (present but not hugely incorporated into product cycles), but rather 'knotting', which literally means making knots at the end of woollen strings in scarves, jumpers or shawls.

Ludhiana's woollen, knitted garments differ considerably from both Delithian ladieswear products and Jaipurian print-based clothing items, which incorporate a segments of craft-based production. Nevertheless, fragmentation is still at work. First, it is largely compatible also with Ludhiana's products. Woollen products are way more seasonal than other garments, with a peak season lasting only from June to November. Market seasonality reinforces production volatility and fragmentation. Ludhiana's primary specialization in domestic production further strengthens fragmentation. Even key export suppliers engaged in top quality production generally also continue engaging in domestic production, which is generally lower end (Shukla and Bansal, 2003; AEPC, 2009). Second, fragmentation is also due to the particular local relation between fabric and garment-making. Unlike in the NCR and Jaipur where the activities providing local garments with their key features, namely embellishment and printing, take place in separate production realms, in Ludhiana knitting is hardly separated from garmenting. In fact, also export and domestic productions never separated. Knitting is very much at the centre of the product cycle, being the historical port of entry of Ludhiana into garment (Mezzadri, 2014a). Arguably, this strong interrelation between fabric and garment-making is more possible in knitwear than in woven production, where backward integration would involve a massive investment. This may be a reason why generally textile and garment productions 'inhabit' substantially different economic worlds (see Gereffi, 1994, on this point). However, it is hard to say if one can really talk about backward integration with reference to Ludhiana. It is more a tendency of units to do a bit of everything. In fact, this intertwining between knitting and garmenting trickles down to even tiny units, unlike what happens in other knitwear centres, like Tiruppur (Vijayabaskar, 2001; Chari, 2004). Units with three or four knitting machines may also have a couple of stitching machines.

According to an officer of the 'Knitwear Club', the association of knitwear and garment producers locally financed in the context of yet another UNIDO cluster development project, this 'tendency to do all inside' – as he put it during our interview – undermines efforts towards consolidation. This is, according to him, the reason why Ludhiana looks like what he defines as a *'kachhaparcha'* (confused, disorganized, based on informal arrangements) industrial area. Many garment producers may pay a price for this disorganization, and particularly for what is effectively a bizarrely consistent rumour running around the Indian garment business community; namely that Ludhiana is unable to deliver on both quality and timely delivery. This is a story one hears both in the crowded trains going from Delhi to Ludhiana, where numerous Delhi traders happily disclose stories on the intricacy of the circulation of goods across Indian markets and abroad, as well as during formal interviews with famous garment businessmen. Obviously, this disrepute hardly helps Ludhiana strengthening its export 'potential', despite export promotion efforts by UNIDO and AEPC. However, the few key players dominating the cluster seem hardly interested. They continue carrying out both export and domestic production in the same industrial premises, albeit in different 'divisions'. The visual difference between these divisions is quite striking, with the domestic arm of the factory chaotic, technologically obsolete and dusty, and the export section modern, tidier and ready to please the buyer. Even fairly large garment companies still deploy some hand-driven, flat-knitting machines – widely available and common in domestic production – together with modern automated circular or computerized flat-knitting machines. In Ludhiana, one moves across different technological eras (and market segments) simply by walking around the different rooms of one single factory.[29]

Unlike the NCR and Jaipur, Ludhiana is not characterized by high degrees of merchant capital. One of the largest garment suppliers in town, working for the giant Scandinavian retailer IKEA, took tremendous pride in showing off the first hand-driven, flat-knitting machine with which he started his business as a self-employed knitwear producer. Listening to his rhetoric about his personal business trajectory, one could not help but imagining the 'De Sotoan' (1989) mythology of the self-employed informal, entrepreneurial 'hero'. Single histories of personal business success should always be taken with a pinch of salt. However, these stories may betray some insights on business in a given locale. In this case, this story betrays insights on labour to capital mobility, which, albeit not

---

[29] On technology see AEPC (2009) and Uchikawa (2012).

massive anymore, was relevant in the past (see Tewari, 1996). The local relative importance of manufacturing over trading is confirmed by the AEPC. This does not mean that merchants are not relevant at all. They have always been involved in export (Maini, 2004; Tewari, 1996), and still are important players for the circulation of goods. But it does mean that merchants are not a dominant component of local capital. Locally, production and circulation seem less intertwined in Ludhiana than elsewhere.

With reference to the importance of merchant capital, Kolkata represents a different case altogether. The city was another leading tailoring centre during Mughal times, and continued flourishing during the *Raj*. From the nineteenth century (Vijayabaskar, 2001) to the end of the Raj, it was also an important hosiery centre, similar to Ludhiana. Moreover, it was also the site of the famous jute industry, a legacy lost with Partition. Little seems left of this past glory. Although still listed by the AEPC as a key garment area, it takes a while to identify garment production. The DCMSME (2013) identifies different woven and hosiery clusters at work. Only after a careful mapping process one finds them. The majority of units are highly informalized, tiny cottage units. At the top, merchants, who invested in the industry locally and elsewhere, overwhelmingly dominate. According to the AEPC, around 80 per cent of garment is in the hands of merchant capital, and organized in putting-out systems. By 2005, informal estimates referred to 30,000 woven units and 9,000 hosiery units (Mezzadri, 2009a).

Woven takes place in Maeshtala and Metiaburuj, situated between 24 Parganas North and 24 Parganas South. Walking around the dirty and narrow lanes of Metiaburuj, it is hard to imagine a 'second Lucknow', as once this place was known. This glorious past is only evoked by local legends and stories. One of these refers to the *Imam Bara*, a palace whose few ruins are nearby, where supposedly the last *Nawab* or *Shah* of Awadh (his actual title changes with the story-teller), Wajid Ali Shah, was imprisoned by the British with his tailors and servants in a sort of golden captivity. Another tale narrates the almost mythical skills of two local master tailors working for the British – Waser Molla and Kamalaya. Local tailors take pride in narrating how their forefathers knew them. Some show ancient placards inscribed with the eternal gratitude of British masters for the services offered. It is hard to know how much of this is true or untrue, as it often happens when it comes to oral history. Quite intriguingly, in 2011, an article of the Calcutta Telegraph (Sarkar, 2011) mentions Metiaburuj and the *Imam Bara* story as one big 'unsolved mystery'. The complete informality of this area and its link to some criminal activities is instead hardly a mystery. And, as shown by

Catherine Boo (2012), poor slum economies are often ripe with alternative, illegal circuits of accumulation mediated by local mafias. At the same time, the whole neighbourhood is also organized in ways that resemble a decentralized factory.[30] Different streets specialize in the production of different clothing items within the broad realm of kidswear production. A couple of streets specialize in baby frocks, while others in baby shirts or pants. The distinction between cottage, micro/tiny and home-based units is blurred, hard to apply. Nonetheless, a process of separation of different tasks across units and homes is at work. The very few fairly sized woven garment players have little or no connection with the tailoring clusters. They almost exclusively focus on workwear, a very niche market segment that can be organized in-house; does not require many additional tasks; and still has some vague links with jute. These units are based elsewhere, in industrial areas or centres around Salt Lake.

Hosiery, or knitwear, instead, takes place not only in Howrah but also in Dum Dum and Shovabazar. Like woven, this industry is still organized at cottage level, stretching to home-based realms. It also shows some degree of separation between tasks, with knitting almost exclusively carried out on hand-driven, flat-knitting machines; and stitching, thread-cutting and packing taking place in different production spaces. However, contrary to woven production, this knitwear segment, which caters for local markets like *Chetla Haat* and *Mangla Haat,* seems to have also developed linkages with larger units (Mezzadri, 2009a). Located in the same areas, few sizeable companies mainly engage in nightwear, underwear and kidswear. Some – Rupa, Lux, Gopal and Dollar – are fairly famous in India while also exporting abroad. They are largely merchant enterprises, and deploy armies of fabricators recruited across the cottage industry around. They have only a few stitching machines for export. In the words of Ramesh A., the owner of one of these companies,

'Buyers need a showpiece: we need to have job-work done anyway, but we need to have a factory to show.'

(Ramesh A., interview)

Despite the astounding fragmentation and parcellization of production – and with the exception of the very few companies engaged in workwear – the garment

---

[30] One of the very first scholars analyzing the 'neighbourhood as factory' was Benjamin (1996) in his study of electronic production in Gandhi Nagar, Delhi. See also Chari's (2004) description of Tiruppur.

commodities locally manufactured do have common traits in relation to final markets. The typical Kolkata garment is cheap, not very high quality, mainly targeting domestic markets or lower export market segments in nightwear, underwear and kidswear. It is not a case that 'make-and-through' techniques largely dominate. This type of product can be – as it is – produced in highly unorganized manufacturing settings, as no premium is placed on standardization. Overall, it is a product of industrial decline.

'Minor' Sweatshops Across the North and East

The distinct complex materialities of garment commodities across the minor garment centres of north and east of India result in sweatshop typologies that are no less composite than in the NCR. On the one hand, several differences can obviously be found in relation to empirical outcomes. However, on the other hand, the underpinning logic of sweatshop formation seems quite compatible with general observations establishing links among industrial trajectories, product cycles and the social process of production. First, in all three distinct cases, the particularity of the garment commodities in question shapes important aspects of the local architecture of the sweatshop. Second, the great fragmentation of all product cycles, which, albeit due to different historical and market-based reasons emerges as one of the most striking features of garment production across Northern and Eastern India, translates into typologies of sweatshops largely dominated by migrant, footloose labour. In all cases, moreover, different segments of product cycles set clear boundaries between different 'labours', whose process of proletarianization is as much as a common as it is a distinct experience.

In Jaipur, the sweatshop stretches across craft and industrial realms, as in the NCR, although its specificities reflect the ways in which craft and industrial activities have articulated historically. By 2005, the cluster employed altogether around 50,000 people, directly or indirectly. In printing realms, that are embedded in the very early origins of the industry, and which employ around 14,000 people (UNIDO, 2004b), the development of 'modern' garment production has entailed significant processes of class differentiation. If many printers upgraded to 'trader-printers' and 'printer-job workers', the largest pool of the *Chhipa* community has gone through a process of proletarianization and started working for others (Sarkar, 2005). The export boom, starting from the 1970s, also meant that many newcomers joined in, hence diluting the caste composition of the workforce (DeNicola, 2004). The move from a home-based organization of printing production and labour activities has been largely gender 'unfriendly', with women largely excluded from work in non-family units. The few still engaged in printing production are all home-based (Sarkar, 2005; Mezzadri, 2009a). At the same time, the move to garmenting activities created new spaces for labour recruitment. Since the 1990s, that space is filled by inflows of male migrant labour, particularly from UP and Bihar. Informally recruited through labour contractors, or word of mouth, until 2005 workers in stitching units were entirely paid piece rate, with a few exceptions applicable to those working for few larger garment companies focusing on 'modern' garments. Migrant workers stay in Jaipur between 6 and 9 months, then they go back to their place of origin. Printers, instead, are generally locals, or workers who have stably migrated to Jaipur and surroundings with their families. Garmenting activities are largely a male preserve, with (local) women generally only engaged in thread-cutting, checking and packing. In some units practicing high levels of subcontracting one may find higher women workforce participation rates, but simply because there is little tailoring going on in-house. However, overall, according to COTEX women represent less than 20 per cent of the total workforce. Only *Anokhi* employs a larger share of women workers in its garmenting units, following what its owner defines as a strategy of 'affirmative action'. It is worth noting that, like in the case of embellishment in Delhi, the relegation of printers to the realm of traditional work, that is often organized by separate vendors and agents, sets useful boundaries in terms of cost minimization. In fact, despite printing is still an important locus of value for the Jaipurian garment commodity – what may contradistinguish it from other garments – its circumscription to the realm of 'craft' production comes handy for garment companies. These companies, *Anokhi* included despite its active engagement in fair trade practices, manage to bank on the availability of local craft labour, while appropriating the role of 'innovators' who perpetuate the marketability of India's traditional activities (DeNicola, 2003). In Jaipur, exporters' ability to 'mediate between urban desire and rural labour' becomes their key asset. It becomes 'discursive capital' (DeNicola, 2005, pp. 14–15).

In Ludhiana, the highly heterogeneous composition of sweatshop labour relates to the interplays between knitting and garmenting activities, with ancillary activities also partially adding another, distinct layer of labour. In this case, the peculiarity of the Ludhiana's garment commodity has nothing to do with craft, although still a lot to do with local history. By the 1950s, the Ludhiana knitwear industry used to employ around 5,000 workers (Maini, 2004). The steady growth of domestic production and the initial Soviet-led export-boom both led to a multiplication of the workforce. By 2001, according to the Small Industries Service Institute (2001), registered employment – only a fraction of overall employment – was set at 99,284. Today, the industry is thought to employ around 350,000–400,000 workers, considering both direct and indirect activities (Uchikawa, 2012). Locally, the industry appears as a completely male preserve. According to the informal estimates of the local Knitwear Club, women account only for 5 per cent of the workforce across the different segments of the production process. Knitting has always been a male-dominated activity. As knitting is hardly separated from garmenting, even across micro and small units, it is very likely to set a dominant trend also across all production segments. The few women employed are, once more, mainly employed in thread-cutting and checking. Originally, knitting was a 'local' preserve, with workers generally coming from Ludhiana or surrounding districts, while stitching and other garmenting activities were dominated by migrant labour, once more coming from UP and Bihar. However, in the last decades, also knitting segments hosts rising inflows of male migrants. The end of the MFA seems to have hit Ludhiana quite significantly, and local labour may increasingly find better sources of livelihood (Singh, 2010). Ancillary home-based activities often decentralized to nearby villages deploy instead women home-workers (Mezzadri, 2009a). They are the only segment of the production process showing any sign of significant participation of women to the workforce. Across both knitting and garmenting, labour is entirely recruited by labour contractors, who can either be key workers, such as supervisors or master tailors, or external agents (Singh, 2010).

In Kolkata, whose commodity is a product of industrial decline targeting low-quality markets, and is produced across realms of cottage and home-based production, the sweatshop is almost entirely composed of self-employed, family labour and individual home-workers. Only a few more organized units are found, employing a workforce that is however also highly casualized. Unlike in other centres, this workforce is mainly local, or if migratory it generally comes from nearby villages or districts in West Bengal (Mezzadri, 2009a). The industry, which is hardly booming, does not attract a large pool of migrant workers from more distant locations, like in the NCR, Jaipur or even Ludhiana. However, also in Kolkata, local garment labour, self-employed and home-based, is differentiated along social lines. A first social division corresponds to the two broad garment categories 'woven' and 'knitwear'. In woven production, cottage, self-employed and home-based spaces of production and work are the realm of local Muslim communities. Both Maeshtala and Metiaburuj are almost entirely Muslim neighbourhoods, whose organization still resembles that of the old craft-based *mahalla*. The traders they sell to, instead, are generally Hindu *Marwaris*, as also the owners of the few large units in the city, although these are not necessarily connected with the cottage industrial fabric. The knitwear segment is characterized by a rather different social profile. In Kolkata, the communities engaged in this type of work are quite dismissively referred to as 'Bangladeshis'. It does not take long to realize that, by now, this stress on 'outsiderness' is mainly discursive, perhaps further fuelled by the anti-immigrant rhetoric increasingly dominating across the Indian East. Members of the hosiery communities, who are composed of both Muslims and Hindu families, may have migrated to Howrah following the partition between West and East Pakistan – today's Bangladesh. However, settled in Kolkata for at least one generation, today these workers can be hardly considered migrants. Focusing on gender, the industry appears as highly masculine, with very low rates of participation of women to the labourforce. Women are more substantially excluded from the hosiery sector where, as already in Ludhiana, knitting is constructed as an entirely male activity. However, as also in the woven sector, the participation of women to garmenting activities is slightly higher. Women's participation does not extend to the organization of production in cottage units. In Kolkata, one finds women employed in units only across the few and more sizeable workwear companies. Women primarily work as family labour – largely unpaid – or as individual home-workers. They are almost exclusively engaged in handwork in Kolkata, in activities such as thread-cutting, mending or 'button-holing' (which locally, as often in low-end production, is a hand-based activity). Unlike in the NCR, Jaipur or Ludhiana, women are not involved in checking, which is already considered a semi-skilled activity. Often, in contexts of soaring underemployment, considered by the old West Bengal Tailors' Union as the main local problem, activities with higher return become the preserve of the male adult breadwinner. For the same reason, while one finds the presence of child work linked to apprenticeship systems, it is very rare to stumble across more hazardous forms of child labour in the industry.

As Kolkata's garment commodity is mainly low-quality produce, ancillary activities linked to value addition are not greatly present. This implies that communities of embroiderers, who are often also organized in cottage and home-based realms, are not significantly linked to garmenting activities. This is the case despite many West Bengali communities, and women in particular, are famous across India for their embroidery skills. Besides its relation to product specialization, this lack of incorporation of embroidery activities into garment product cycles is also due to the extremely time-consuming nature of some of these local craft activities, like for instance, the beautiful, but hugely complex *Khanta* stitch and *Baluchari*, produced in Shantiniketan and Bankura. Across both woven and knitwear segments, Kolkata's informalized petty producers and workers are mainly paid piece rate. Even those working for larger units are mainly paid per piece. This may be disguised by payment practices. The owner of Rupa, for instance, pays his workers weekly, but against piece rates targets. Every Saturday, he visits his factory, carrying a massive stack of cash, to pay workers as well as contractors who establish links with the cottage and home-based units that are part of the putting-out system.

The Sweatshop as a 'Material' Regime

This first empirical journey across the world of garment commodities crowding the upper floors of the Indian garment mall – Northern and Eastern India – embeds the initial reflections on the relation between the physical materiality of production and the social processes underpinning it into grounded realities. Composite product cycles, characterized by multiple activities and tasks, entail links between different production realms. These realms stretch from factories or larger workshops in industrial areas to pettier forms of commodity production, organized in micro, cottage units and home-based settings in more informal pockets of garment centres. Across these different realms, the typologies of workers one finds are also greatly differentiated. In the four different centres analyzed in this chapter, combinations of these different realms and typologies of labour vary together with changing industrial trajectories and historical ports of entry into garment-making. However, there are some 'regularities' one can abstract from the particularities of the cases analyzed, in order to define some basic functioning principles of the garment sweatshop.

Firstly, the garment sweatshop cannot be encapsulated into a single type of standardized production space or realm. Unlike what argued by the radical theories of the 1970s, epitomized by the work of authors like Fröbel *et al.* (1984), the sweatshop is not an abstract industrial enclave, with hardly any connection to the local economy where it is located. On the contrary, it is greatly embedded into this local economy, its industrial trajectory and product specialization. Its particular architecture of production is highly composite; formed by a myriad of different factories, informal workshops and homes linked together by the sweat of the different labourers who inhabit them. As argued by Chang

(2009b), the 'global factory' is characterized by the extension of the law of value to different, multiple subjects. However, this does not result into a coherent process of proletarianization. In fact, as illustrated in the cases analyzed here, this process 'proletarianizes' different labouring subjects whilst also entailing the reproduction of social boundaries fragmenting them across a multiplicity of divides.

Secondly, and more importantly, within the sweatshop, the wage relation may appear in multiple forms; it may be explicit but also *disguised*. This is to say that the labourers inhabiting the sweatshop may be more or less 'free' from their means of production, but even when they are not dispossessed, they are still subject to the process of surplus extraction, and they can hardly survive outside of market imperatives. In this sense, the analysis of the sweatshop demonstrates what argued by Jairus Banaji (2003) in relation to the defining feature of capitalism – that this is primarily defined by the extraction and accumulation of surplus value, rather than by the mere presence of 'free' wage labour.[31] Deploying a Marxian terminology, the subsumption into the capitalist relation can be 'real', as in the case of wage work, or 'formal', as in the case of self-employment or petty commodity production, which dominates in cottage and home-based activities (Banaji, 2010: 280). This dual process of subsumption is what gives rise to differential processes of proletarianization, which produce what Henry Bernstein (2007) calls 'classes of labour'. As illustrated by the empirical analysis, within the garment sweatshop, the reproduction of multiple classes of labour is mediated by numerous forms of intermediation, and responds to logics of cost minimization across different production realms and garmenting activities.

Third, within the garment sweatshop multiple processes of proletarianization are mediated by pre-existing structural differences and social divides. As argued by Beverly Silver (2003), capital can deploy multiple boundary drawing strategies to divide the workforce. Indeed, the Indian garment sweatshop can bank on multiple boundaries, social structures and structural differences. In India, these in fact powerfully socially regulate the workforce (Harriss-White and Gooptu, 2001). In the context of the garment sweatshop, the combination of social structures and structural differences deployed in each industrial formation is strongly based on the evolution of local industrial trajectories, and mediates processes of differential proletarianization at work.

---

[31] Banaji specifically writes (2010, p. 144) that "it is accumulation or the drive to surplus value which defines capitalism, not the presence or absence of 'free' labour".

Ultimately, the sweatshop appears as a regime, with a distinct physical and social materiality. Its local architecture is shaped by past trajectories whose relevance is reinforced by present market dynamics, leading to the creation of different garment commodities. It is underpinned by social relations of production that must be able to produce those commodities, and that manifest across multiple production realms, where labour can be more or less free from the means of production, but always subject to harsh processes of surplus extraction. The internal boundaries of this regime are created and managed by a multiplicity of actors – suppliers, subcontractors, agents and intermediaries – who deploy multiple strategies in order to minimize costs and painfully construct a comparative advantage exploiting multiple structural differences and social divides, such as gender, mobility, age or geographical provenance. Despite being subject to the universal laws of capital, the sweatshop creates and reproduces a world of difference. After all, the sweatshop also *starts from* a world of difference. While many of these differences have emerged already in the context of the first chapter, they will be further explored – together with some of these final reflections – in the next chapter, which will bring the analysis to Southern India.

3 | Difference and the Sweatshop

> The nature of capitalism is not to create a homogeneous social and economic system, but rather to dominate and to draw profit from the diversity and inequality that remain in permanence.
>
> (Berger, 1980, p. 136)

Difference before and within Labour

The sweatshop appears as a world of stark differences. It is made of multiple spaces of work whose composite social architecture varies with the physical materiality of the commodities produced. It is inhabited by different typologies of workers who may be subject to the wage relation either directly or indirectly, according to different degrees of 'freedom' from means of production and subsistence. These workers are subject to differential processes of proletarianization. In fact, capital fragments and segments the workforce through multiple boundary-drawing strategies (Silver, 2003); it extracts labour surplus in multiple ways (Banaji, 2003) and it also generates multiple labour outcomes (Bernstein, 2007). However, is 'difference' produced by capital or does it pre-exist capital? This is a crucial question, when it comes to analyzing the complex world of the sweatshop. In rather crude terms, in accounts stressing difference as primarily produced by capital, 'exploitation' emerges as the key process subjugating labour inside the sweatshop. In accounts stressing instead difference as pre-existing capital, emphasis is primarily placed on processes of labour 'commodification'. The way in which 'difference' and 'capital' articulate (Tsing, 2009; Bair, 2010) is hardly a theoretical conundrum. Rather, it is also of utmost importance for political reflection, in a time and age when the income share accruing to labourers worldwide (and not only in sweatshops!) has ruinously fallen, and inequality massively risen to benefit what the Occupy movement (and now renowned inequality scholars, like Thomas Piketty) identified as the infamous '1 per cent'.[32]

A debate counterpoising 'exploitation' and 'commodification' is currently reaching momentum (see for instance, Selwyn and Miyamura, 2014), despite being hardly a novel debate. For instance, by the 1970s, this debate (amongst others) impacted significantly the 'unhappy marriage of Marxism and Feminism' (Hartmann, 1979; see also Molyneux, 1979, and Vogel, 1983). In a recent issue of the academic journal *Development and Change*, where leading labour and development scholars debate the 'labour question' in contemporary capitalism, Amrita Chhachhi (2014), the guest editor, rightly summarizes the political aspect of this debate as one between supporters of, respectively, 'Polanyian struggles' and 'Marxist struggles'. Briefly, between those who consider today's resistance as primarily taking place against processes of commodification, and those instead who consider it as still linked to the labour experience within realms of production – hence against exploitation. In fact, again in rather crude terms, one *could* simplify Marx's and Polanyi's concerns as primarily focused around one or the other process (see the debate between Burawoy, 2010 and Webster, 2010; see also Webster, Lambert and Bezuidenhout, 2008). However, arguably, this contraposition between commodification and exploitation emerges as a false dichotomy when looking at the sweatshop. Particularly, trying to establish a hierarchical or 'stagist' order between the two processes in relation to labour may be unfruitful. For instance, differences in typologies of sweatshop labour should be conceived both in terms of their relation to capital and also in terms of their link to other social structures of oppression and subordination. The different degrees of freedom or unfreedom characterizing different typologies of sweatshop labour, and which are at the very core of processes of differential proletarianization, are crucially anchored to pre-existing social structures and structural differences and divisions. Wage labour, petty commodity producers or home-workers in different segments of the sweatshop are generally also characterized by quite distinct social traits and profiles.

The different social profiles of the labouring bodies at work in sweatshops are – again – no secondary complication to the study of sweatshop creation and reproduction. Indeed, labour is differentiated across realms/spaces of work,

---

[32] Piketty (2014) illustrates the astonishing extent of elites' income share capture since the onset of neoliberal globalization. The significance and implication of elites' income share capture for inequality outcomes is also shown by Palma (2011). On the debate on global income distribution, and particularly for a critique of mainstream takes on global convergence, see Saad-Filho (2013). The mythology of the 'Economics of the 1 per cent' is also debunked by Weeks (2014).

based on the wage relation and degrees of (un)freedom. However, it also includes men, women, children, and, in places where unemployment is an unaffordable experience, the elderly. All workers can be further sub-classified according to specific traits within their broad social profile; for instance, as migrant or local, urban or rural workers. The 'price' of these workers to sweatshop owners and agents is greatly dependent upon all these distinct social features. Meanwhile, however, social profile also sets the boundaries of workers' incorporation into the sweatshop in particular tasks, activities and with given working rhythms and conditions. This is to say that the process of commodification of particular social traits of individual workers is crucial for the exploitation process and vice versa. Across sweatshops, employers know how commodification and exploitation work in tandem and reinforce each other all too well. Their objective is always paying less and extracting more labour surplus, at once.

In this sense, the process of sweatshop creation manufactures 'classes of labour' (Bernstein, 2007) by means of already socially 'classed' (read differentially 'commodifiable') labouring bodies. In the making of sweatshop labour, commodification and exploitation are hardly distinctive moments. Besides, as argued by Federici (2004), in order to understand accumulation, we need to engage with 'embodied labour', not simply with labour in an abstract form, as the human body itself was the first ever 'machine' invented by capitalism. And the female body in particular, as argued by Maria Mies long before Harvey's (2004) popularization of 'accumulation by dispossession', have always been subject to 'processes of on-going primitive accumulation' (Mies, 1986, p. 4).[33] These processes have crucially shaped women's labour as secondary, setting the basis for both its differential (lower) 'pricing' as a commodity to be deployed in production and its differential (higher) rate of exploitation. Indeed, Mies' work crucially unveils the complex nature of the 'wage', as the outcome of simultaneous social processes of 'pricing' workers' bodies and extracting labour surplus; effectively, an indicator of both exclusion from more profitable labouring opportunities and discriminatory inclusion into the production process.

What discussed above further informs our discussions on labour as comparative advantage, developed earlier in this book. As discussed, labour – as any other type of comparative advantage – hardly ever comes 'naturally' abundant and cheap, and ready for deployment by capital (De Neve, 2005). It has to be *made* so. On the one hand, as argued in Chapter 2, this point further illustrates the strong interrelationship

---

[33] On the continuous character of primitive accumulation, see also de Angelis (2007).

between physical and social materialities. On the other hand, however, it also speaks to our present discussion on the relation between commodification and exploitation. In fact, both these processes are crucial for the making of labour as cheap and docile, reproducing it as a comparative advantage for international competition. Let us take the example of East Asia, a particularly successful region in imposing labour relations able to capture a significant share of the international market, and also in developing a labour 'mythology' able to capture the imagination of global manufacturers and retailers. Here, during the economic boom, the export-oriented comparative advantage was largely based on the exploitation of patriarchal relations and the construction of the myth of the 'submissive oriental girl' (Elson and Pearson, 1981; Elson, 1983; for a critique, see also Lim, 1990). Discursive practices and gendered wage differentials reinforced each other (e.g. Caraway, 2005 on Indonesia), manufacturing a comparative advantage clearly based on 'women's disadvantage' (Arizpe and Aranda, 1981; Collins, 2003) and on the 'feminization of survival' (Sassen, 2000). Clearly, discourse already set the basis for women's labour differential commodification (Salzinger, 2003). That is to say that difference mattered far before women entered East Asian sweatshops. In fact, they entered the sweatshop *because* of that difference, as a *source* of comparative advantage (Collins, 2003; Elson *et al.*, 2007; Tsing, 2009), a process greatly mediated by the state (see Seguino, 2000). However, patriarchal norms also greatly increased rates of exploitation inside the sweatshop, once women entered production. Gendered discourses (and stereotypes) greatly informed material shop-floor practices, by imposing harsher and stricter rhythms on a female workforce who was managed with paternalistic intransigence by what Kabeer (2000) defined as 'the capitalist patriarch'.

Focusing on women's labour experience in the sweatshop, commodification and exploitation appear as two sides of the same coin. Women's contribution is concealed across all the different echelons of what Federici (2012) defines as a 'social factory' extending both *inside* and *outside* the walls of the space of work, across realms of production and reproduction (see also Mitchell *et al.*, 2003).[34] Ultimately, difference shapes both the initial conditions of entry into the sweatshop and the process of labouring inside the sweatshop. Along the 'global assembly line', the capital relation both shapes and is shaped by this difference (Bair, 2010), a point now acknowledged by many feminist analyses focused on specific labour experiences (e.g. Salzinger, 2003; Wright, 2006). This is a crucial

---

[34] More recently also Nancy Fraser has engaged with the question of reproduction in Marx's 'hidden abode' (in New Left Review, 2014).

point to deconstruct overly simplistic analyses assuming that women's 'liberation' may simply coincide with their entry into the capitalist relation as paid labour (Federici, 2012). However, given the predominantly masculine nature of the labour process in the Indian garment-producing centres analyzed so far, do gender differences only partially capture the reality of the garment sweatshop in India? Does women's work always remain primarily confined to the more peripheral echelons of production, as in the case of home-based settings of Northern and Eastern India? As we shall see in the following sections, in order to fully appreciate the significance of gender in shaping the garment sweatshop in India, we need to analyze the south of the Indian subcontinent.

How Real is the Bogey of Feminization in the Indian Sweatshop?

Gender differences in the garment industry have always shaped labour outcomes in very concrete ways. The study of what Beneria and Roldan (1987) defined as the 'crossroads of class and gender' has crucially informed understandings of industrial dynamics in the sector since its origin. Already by the early twentieth century, garment workers (in the US and elsewhere) were predominantly women, facing great occupational hazard and dreadful working conditions (Boris, 1994). Women – young girls in fact – represented the majority of victims of the Shirtwaist factory fire of 1911 in New York City, which can be considered as a sort of 'American Rana Plaza'.[35] Since then, the garment industry has continued incorporating rising numbers of women workers worldwide. That is, it has constantly reproduced itself as a 'feminized' industry. Indeed, processes of feminization of labour in the sector have entailed both a progressive increase in women workforce participation rates, as well as a systematic rise in 'undesirable' jobs paying a 'feminine' (that is lower) wage (Standing, 1989, 1999). Across different regions, ranging from Asia to Latin America, gender has always acted as a powerful port of entry for workers in this industry, while setting clear conditions of work inside garment factories (e.g. see Seguino, 2000, on East Asia; Arnold and Pickles, 2011, on South East Asia; Kusakabe and Pearson, 2010; Pearson and Kusakabe, 2012, on Thailand and Myanmar; Goto and Endo, 2014, on Thailand; Kabeer, 2000; and Kabeer and

---

[35] The Triangle Shirtwaist tragedy is still remembered in the US as a particularly dark chapter in the history of American industrialization. It is still acknowledged in the official website of the United States Department of Labour (2015). The best reconstruction of the tragedy is by Leon Stein (1962).

Mahmud, 2004, on Bangladesh; Ruwanpura, 2011, 2013, on Sri Lanka; Pun, 2005a, 2005b, 2007, on China; Plankey-Videla, 2012, on Mexico).

However, this imagery of the industry as predominantly characterized by a feminized production space is relatively challenged once one analyzes India. In India, the very analytical relevance of debates on labour feminization has been the object of careful scrutiny. In fact, women's incorporation in productive activities has lagged behind *vis-à-vis* other countries, not only in garment but also across other sectors (see Abraham, 2013). Here, Esther Boserup's (1989) early forecast of an industrial modernity potentially excluding women – which clearly does not hold in relation to the structuring of the global assembly line in many developing regions – is yet to be fully disproven. In India, only agriculture seems to absorb a significant number of women workers. Often, this is because as men find more profitable non-agricultural occupations, women are often 'left behind' in rural areas, especially when access to non-agricultural work entails male migration (Garikipati, 2008). The service industry also absorbs a considerable percentage of women if primarily in those call centres (Basi, 2009; Patel, 2010) that compose the cheapest strata of what Ursula Huws (2001, 2014) calls the 'cybertariat'. Industrial work, however, is still characterized by low levels of women participation (Ghosh, 2009) and gender segregation (Mukhopadhyay, 1997). Paid work for women in India may be as low as 15 per cent (Mazumdar and Neetha, 2011; John, 2013), as the majority is locked into unpaid activities varying with the complexity of what Palriwala and Neetha (2011) have called 'stratified familialism', where caste and gender powerfully interplay (John, 2013). This pushed Nirmala Banerjee (1999) to ask, in a famous essay on women's work in the subcontinent, "*How real is the bogey of feminisation?*". Overall, aggregate data may in fact suggest a process of 'de-feminization' instead (Abraham, 2013).

During our empirical journey across Northern and Eastern India, the analysis revealed that while gender crucially defines labour outcomes, it generally shapes a largely 'masculine' production process, where male migrants (in many cases circulatory migrants) represent the most significant share of the factory-based workforce.[36] It is only in non-factory realms that gender differences are more articulate and complex, and women appear as key components of the workforce, primarily in home-based settings. Ultimately, across the north and east of the

---

[36] Also in Pakistan the textile and garment industries, overall, show relatively low female employment rates. However, these are higher in garment stitching factories, and they may be currently further increasing (see Siegmann, 2005, 2009; Makino, 2014).

subcontinent, social difference in production seems to primarily play out in relation to spaces of work and typologies of wage relations. This said, one is faced with a greatly diverse production and labour landscape when analyzing the south of India. Here, in fact, the industry seems to follow a pathway far more consistent with the experience of other garment-producing regions, where women compose a key share of the labourforce. In terms of export, the three key production centres in south India are Chennai, Bangalore and Tiruppur. Bangalore, in particular, has emerged during the 2000s as a success story entirely based on labour feminization, with all the unavoidable contradictions that this entails.

These markedly different labour outcomes should necessarily be understood in relation to the different types of commodity production dominating southern garment-producing centres. Moving south, in fact, we leave the upper floors of the Indian garment mall, characterized by multiple typologies of niche production for highly diversified markets, and we reach instead the lower floors, largely dominated by mass production of basic items. As more structured assembly lines replace semi-assembly, group systems and make-and-through techniques, and highly embellished or printed blouses and skirts, woollens and cheap nightwear leave the room to outwear, jeans and T-shirts, male tailors and armies of home-based workers are largely substituted by platoons of women tailors. In effect, employers, in the powerful language of deskilling, always revealing 'the sexual hierarchy which permeates capitalism' (Phillips and Taylor, 1980, p. 84), generally do not define them as tailors, but rather refer to them as 'female line operators'. Indeed, upper and lower floors of India's clothing mall are gendered in substantially different ways.

The following sections of this chapter illustrate in detail the structure and features of sweatshops across the 'lower floors' of the Indian garment mall, namely South India, in order to compare and contrast them with their northern and eastern counterparts. Also in this case, as in Chapter 2, the analysis stresses the links between the physical and social materialities of production – between 'the material' and 'the materialist' – particularly in the light of the cost minimization strategies deployed by garment employers and agents to reproduce their comparative advantage in given segments of the international market. However, here, the analysis also insists on the relevance of embodied labour and of interplays between processes of labour commodification and labour exploitation in shaping the complex world of the sweatshop and multiplying its patterns of unfreedom. Our empirical journey in the world of India's Southern garment-producing centres starts in Bangalore, it continues in Chennai and it ends in Tiruppur.

Bangalore and Chennai and the Mass Production of Basic Garment Commodities

Moving from the north to the south of India, one realizes the stark difference between the garment commodities produced for the export market almost immediately, during the early stage of interviews with garment exporters and producers in their factories or offices. Effectively, this is the stage when interviewees proudly present any guest with their garment samples, to give an idea of the work done inside (or, as we have seen, often also outside) the industrial premises. In the NCR, Jaipur or Ludhiana, garments locally produced for export markets epitomize the great diversity of fast fashion and the endless possibilities of niche market production. Moreover, these garments also often have a specific 'Indian content' – that is, a craft-based component of production – that make them somewhat unique, and explain how India may have carved a specific place for itself in the industry despite fierce global competition. The sample rooms of factories or offices in Bangalore and Chennai reveal a completely different world of products. Here, in fact, production primarily targets basic garment collections – jeans, jackets, shirts, trousers and so on (Mezzadri, 2014b). Bangalore is considered as the key export centre for outerwear production (Ambekar Institute of Labour Studies, 2005). As mentioned above, this is only the first amongst a staggering number of differences between the north and south of the subcontinent. However, it is a crucial entry point to develop an understanding of the others. In fact, once one leaves the sample room and enters a factory shop-floor in Bangalore or Chennai, the difference in products acquires a more profound, social meaning. As we shall see, it literally comes to life, in the bodies of a workforce that differs greatly from its northern counterpart, and that also inhabits a space of work organized in significantly different ways. However, let us start from the beginning and, like in the case of Northern and Eastern India, let us first introduce the specific historical ports of entry of Bangalore and Chennai into garment production, the spatial organization of productive activities and the organization of production between and inside units.

In both Bangalore and Chennai, the port of entry into garment production had a lot to do with the physical proximity of these cities to fabric production hubs. Chennai, in Tamil Nadu, known to many with its old colonial name of Madras, owes its entry into the garment industry to its early history of cotton trade. In colonial times, the Madras constituency was famous for a particular type of cotton fabric, called the 'Madras check'. This fabric became famous in the West via the Dutch East India Company trading operations. The sad irony is that it seems this was the fabric worn by the Scottish regiments occupying India in the 1800s (Ramamurthy, 2004). The Madras check was obtained through a special dying process. Similar to the case of the printing industry in Jaipur, this was based on natural pigments, so that the cloth 'bled' colour – in fact, the Madras check was also known as the 'bleeding Madras' (Chatterjee and Mohan, 1993). In the post-colonial period, the international fame of the bleeding Madras could be deployed by the city – now Chennai – to specialize in garment production. This specialization happened quite slowly. Indeed, the proximity of Chennai first to important textile mills and then to key power-loom centres situated on the road connecting Erode to Salem was an important factor in the local development of the industry. Also, the presence of the tanning industry may have further encouraged tailoring activities (Mezzadri, 2009a). However, production did not substantially take off until the 1980s, as Northern (and arguably Western) India had a clear edge in relation to established trading networks (Lessinger, 2000). Later, as mentioned in Chapter 1, until the 1990s, export quotas were assigned based on the past export track record and connections abroad, providing northern traders (as well as many traders-turned manufacturers) with a clear competitive edge (Mezzadri, 2010). Since the 1970s, Delhi was considered as the centre benefitting the most from what were seen as 'political' principles of quota allocation. In fact, this issue was also discussed by trade unions, which always considered the sector crucial for its potential employment generation, while never really managed to organize the workforce, at least not until very recently. The report of a 1979 meeting between trade unions and garment exporters clearly refers to the great geographical bias in quota allocation.

> There is a feeling in some parts of the country that manufacturers who are operating from areas in and around Delhi have an edge over those operating from distant centres in securing quotas.
>
> (Ambekar Institute of Labour Studies, 1980, p. 49)

It was only in the 1990s that the south of India carved its own space in the national and international garment export scenario, as quota allocation started considering manufacturing investment as well. According to AEPC data (2004, 2009), Chennai's garment export turnover rose in this period. In 1971, there were only 13 garment units registered; these increased to 91 in 1980 (Kalpagam, 1994) and to 350 in 2005 (Mezzadri, 2009a). The relatively late entry of Chennai into garment export, together with its historical trajectory as a fabric-producing centre, explains its patterns of product specialization focused on basics, and particularly menswear garment commodities (Ambekar Institute of Labour Studies, 2005). This type of specialization had clear implications for the development of the production space, where garment units are more concentrated and organized around a few key industrial areas and estates. Pushed by the need to obtain quotas, garment exporters invested more in manufacturing activities than in northern areas. In fact, already by the early 1990s, merchant exporters were a 'diminishing breed' (Kalpagam, 1994, p. 189), while what the AEPC classifies as 'manufacturer exporters' were on the rise.

The main industrial areas involved in garment production for export are located in Ambattur and Guindy, while Tambaram hosts the Madras Export Processing Zone (MEPZ), established in 1984 and turned into a Special Economic Zone (SEZ) in 2003. Indeed, these areas represent the main production layer. There are smaller, informal units spread across the neighbourhoods of Kanchipuram, Chengalpattu and Tiruvallur; however, their links with the top production layer are not as strong as in Northern India. In fact, subcontracting rates, which were considerable in the 1980s, and established links between registered factories and a world of unregistered units (whose number was and still remains unknown) have considerably declined since. The decline in subcontracting was linked to a process of formalization of the industry, and to its progressive move towards the production of items whose value addition is primarily based on the deployment of specific fabrics. With time, the Madras check has been largely substituted by man-made fibres, not necessarily produced in the subcontinent, and often fairly more expensive than cotton. Also, this change in product specialization has responded to the need to carve a specific production niche for the centre *vis-à-vis* northern industrial areas (Mezzadri, 2009a).

In a context of declining subcontracting rates, centralization of the production space, and evolving product specialization geared towards the production of basic items whose value addition primarily rests on fabrics, rather than craft-based ancillary activities, the average unit size is fairly larger than that in northern garment clusters. Moreover, the organization of production inside the units is considerably different. While throughout the 1980s and 1990s, garment exporters still deployed group systems and make-and-through techniques together with an early organization of assembly-line production (Kalpagam, 1994), by the mid-2000s assembly-line production came to largely dominate across export-oriented industrial units. This is hardly surprising, given the fact that Chennai's garments are mainly factory-based products. Arguably, they are 'global garments', which, contrary to those of northern clusters, do not reflect anymore the craft-based platform of the industry. Effectively, one could argue that amongst all the garment-producing centres surveyed so far, Chennai is the first global 'cut-and-stitch' centre, primarily focused on assembly, and hence comparable to many other garment areas across Asia and Latin America. The garment commodities produced are a proper 'global product', which could be produced here as elsewhere. Indeed, they are produced in Bangalore, which was in fact fairly more successful than Chennai in building its competitive advantage in this type of production in India.

Bangalore is the youngest amongst India's garment export centres. The historical origin of the garment industry, also in this case, can be partially traced back to its proximity to fabric centres. The handloom industry was present in and around the city already before the British conquest (Holmström, 1976). Moreover, given its geographical position, Bangalore could benefit from fabric centres based in both Tamil Nadu and Kerala (like Kannur, previously known as Kannanore). The production and trade of silk fabric, situated in small artisanal clusters around the city, was perhaps even more relevant in the early development of the industry.[37] In fact, silk commerce is crucial to understand the early social history of accumulation in the garment industry. The 'Gokaldas family', who initiated garment production in Bangalore, and who still towers over local garment export activities to date, owes its fortunes to silk trade from the Sindh (Mezzadri, 2009a). Bangalore's garment export started peaking even later than in Chennai, by the early 2000s. In 1989, the centre only contributed 4.4 per cent of total garment exports from India; by 2003 its share was 9 per cent (Mezzadri, 2008, 2009a). The reasons for the garment export boom are also in this case partially linked to the introduction of investment-based principles in quota allocation. Locally, this principle facilitated the transition of merchant capital into industrial capital. Jagdish Hinduja confirmed that the 'Gokaldas' invested massively into the garment business from this period onwards, undertaking a steady path towards industrial consolidation. Their organization of production moved from putting-out systems to in-house production. Their industrial units remained numerous, but increased in size.

---

[37] Ramanagaram, for instance, a small town of 60,000 people situated outside Bangalore is Asia's largest silk cocoon market. There, by 2005 the silk industry supported 55,000 people directly and indirectly, and included the town and its surroundings. Kanchipuram, in Tamil Nadu, is famous instead for the weaving of silk saris. Around 90 per cent of its inhabitants are involved in the silk industry and trade (Benjamin, 2000).

The rise in unit size was also boosted by the introduction of the New Textile Policy in 2000, which started de-reserving garments from the list of industries reserved to SMEs (Singh and Kaur Sapra, 2007; Kalhan, 2008; Mezzadri, 2010). From the 1980s onwards, this transition to manufacturing capital was further strengthened by the investment of large domestic textile players into the local readymade garment business, and by the rising sourcing activities of both international and national retailers. Indeed, by early 2000s, Arvind Mills, India's largest denim manufacturer, had set-up one 180,000 shirts a-day factory in Bangalore. Raymond, another key textile manufacturer in India, had built a plant able to make more than 1,000 male suits a day (Kalhan, 2008). Arguably, the relocation of numerous garment units from Mumbai played an important role in attracting domestic and international capital (Mezzadri, 2009a). This issue will be addressed in the next chapter.

Increasing manufacturing capacity and the consolidation of production inside factories was a key component of Bangalore's ability to rise as an export centre. This process proceeded hand in hand with what commodity studies' analysts may call 'product upgrading', which manifested with a shift from the use of cotton to man-made fabrics. According to local exporters and the local branches of the AEPC and CMAI, it is this shift, mediated by the relations with buyers like Nike and Rebook that turned Bangalore into the key centre for outerwear production. Aggregate data on quantity and value turnover clearly indicate the move to higher value garment commodities (AEPC, 2004). As these changes took place, production moved from Lalbagh, a 'crowded commercial neighbourhood' (RoyChowdhury, 2005, p. 2250), to industrial areas in the outskirts of the city. From the mid-2000s onwards, production clusters around the Peenya and Yeswantpur industrial areas – the former is one of the largest industrial conglomerates in Asia – and in Boomasandra, Bommanahalli and Mysore Road, although some garment units can also be spotted in Whitefield and Hosur Road (Kalhan, 2008; Mezzadri, 2009a, 2012; Cividep and Somo, 2009). By 2003, there were 788 garment units in Karnataka; 729 were in Bangalore (Sharma, 2005). By 2005, according to the CMAI, the city hosted 300 exporters and 600 units. As in the case of Chennai, these data exclude the non-factory sector. In fact, the development of an industrial trajectory more geared towards consolidation and the factory production of 'global' basic garments implies relatively lower degrees of subcontracting than those needed in small-batch, niche market-based production. All garmenting tasks are carried out inside factories, with the exception of washing and printing, which may be carried out by specialized operators. As in Chennai, embroidery is largely irrelevant in the core segments of the local export industry, and it is mainly computerized.[38]

The rationale behind declining rates of subcontracting can be further understood by looking at the organization of production inside individual factories. Here, assembly lines largely dominate, as the organization of the shop-floor producing basic items allows for a more systematic 'taylorization' of activities and tasks. Indeed, one could argue that Bangalore (like Chennai) epitomizes a Fordist production landscape, as much as the NCR (like the other garment-producing centres in the north and east) epitomizes a Post-fordist one. Assembly-line production takes place in batches composed of a variable number of machines and workers. However, generally, one line is composed of 25–40 machines – the number of workers can vary, although the ratio machine/worker is generally 1.5 (Mezzadri, 2009a). Ultimately, it is the logic of assembly-line production that significantly limits subcontracting rates, in Bangalore as in Chennai. In fact, subcontractors can be incorporated into the local production network only if they can guarantee at least one whole line to exporters. In the NCR, it is not uncommon to find garment factories with 25–40 machines and 40–60 workers with direct access to the export market. In Bangalore, these actors only make it into the second production tier, if they make it at all. Besides, the number and types of seams needed to stitch a pair of jeans or a jacket differ significantly from those needed to stitch a patterned blouse or skirt. The hands at work to make these different garment commodities also belong to different people. As underlined by Jagdish Hinduja, in assembly-line production, women are the 'perfect' operators. The tale of the 'submissive oriental girl' has indeed made it to Bangalore. As always, albeit just a tale, it has nevertheless very real effects, as it is told repeatedly by the masters of the shop-floor.

The Feminization and Re-Feminization of a Global Garment Workforce

Walking around the industrial areas of Chennai and Bangalore, the different gendered system at work in garment production immediately reveals itself to the visitor in the guise of a placard placed outside factories that simply says: 'ladies tailors needed'. Such a sign would be extremely rare across the hyper-masculine,

---

[38] The largest factories have computerized embroidery systems in-house. Others may deploy specialized operators like in the case of washing and printing.

northern industrial areas, but here it is indeed very common. Arguably, as we shall see below, this placard talks about gender, but also about labour provenance and recruitment strategies. In Chennai, women workers seem to have dominated the production landscape since the initial development of the industry. In Bangalore, instead, the shift towards the current type of labourforce has gone hand in hand with transformations in products, product cycles and the organization of production. However, in both cases, the feminization of labour was crucial for the local industry to efficiently minimize costs in the specific garment market segment it operates in.

In the 1970s, when the Chennai garment industry was composed of only a few registered units linked to an informalized production segment, it employed around 32,000 workers (Ambekar Institute of Labour Studies, 1980; Kalpagam, 1981).[39] These workers were women since then. The local office of the Centre of Indian Trade Unions (CITU), the union politically affiliated with the Communist Party of India-Marxist (CPI[M]) has one of its main offices just outside the MEPZ. Labour relations are particularly harsh inside the zone, and the union wants to be close enough to be able to speak to workers. As in many other centres, traditional unions (all politically affiliated) have hardly made a dent into the garment industry, whose flexibility and labour informalization make it as difficult to organize as India's informal 'sector'. According to CITU, as well as local exporters and the local branch of CMAI, garment units inside the MEPZ were set-up as 'feminine' spaces as the organization of the shop-floor was inspired by systems at work in other Asian countries. However, even the bulk of production, which did not take place in the zone, but in and around Chennai, employed mainly female workers since its early origin. In fact, when Uma Kalpagam (1981, p. 1957) first discussed the case of Madras garment production she highlighted the exceptionality of a case where both factory and non-factory production segments were feminized. In the 1970s, debates on the informal sector mainly focused on male workers (e.g. Kalpagam mentions Joshi and Joshi, 1976 and Holmström, 1976; see also Breman, 1977).

In Bangalore also, in the 1970s, garment workers were predominantly male piece rate earners. The industry employed around 11,000 in Karnataka (Ambekar Institute of Labour Studies, 1980). By the early 2000s, after the export boom, there were already 153,000 workers registered in the industry, 95 per cent of whom

---

[39] Out of these 32,000, around 24,000 were employed in the informal sector and the other 8,000 in the formal sector (Ambekar Institute of Labour Studies, 1980).

(i.e., 146,835) in Bangalore. This estimate did not include casual and contract workers (Sharma, 2005). By the mid-2000s, the overall number of workers reached 300,000 (Mezzadri, 2009a) and by the late 2000s, peaked at 750,000 (Kalhan, 2008). The massive increase in employment was paralleled by a shift in workers' social profile. Following a number of strikes in the early 1980s, Gokaldas retrenched male labourers and started employing women workers. Soon also the other local garment units followed the same strategy. By the mid-2000s, the garment sector was the largest employer of women in Karnataka, together with the *beedi* (Indian cigarettes) industry (Sharma, 2005).

Coupled with the progressive, steady shift to assembly-line production in the context of changing product specialization, the local process of labour feminization in Chennai and Bangalore aimed at ensuring both labour cost minimization and labour discipline. Overall, women were far cheaper workers than their male counterparts, because largely perceived as secondary earners. Moreover, the strict division of tasks on the shop-floor deployed by local factories also contributed to the construction of the local workforce as deskilled, and hence only entitled to lower wages (Mezzadri, 2012). In the context of more basic type of garment production, where non-factory-based activities are largely absent, labour cost minimization plays out primarily at the factory level. In this light, feminization was the 'right choice' for local exporters in order to boost competitiveness in this specific market segment. In terms of labour control, the deployment of women fitted well also with local perceptions of docility and of what constitutes a dedicated but 'disposable' workforce that, as argued by Melissa Wright (2006) in her study of Mexico, for local exporters are as crucial as considerations over costs. In the process of construction of the comparative advantage in cheap labour, labour cost minimization strategies and discourse are inextricably intertwined, as the latter often successfully guarantees the reproduction of the former. The advantage of employing women is spelt out by exporters in Chennai and Bangalore on the basis of comparisons between the behaviour of women and men on the shop-floor, and essentialist understanding of 'femininity' and their implications for labour. The locally perceived difference between women and men in relation to costs and discipline is efficiently summarized by a Bangalorean exporter (in Mezzadri, 2009a, p. 275):

> Men are troublemakers; their quality is not consistent, not disciplined. There is a continuous bargaining with men, you say I give you 3 rupees, one says no, 5 rupees, and if you do not accept they all sit down and wait.

Some exporters have a chillingly aware understanding of the reasons behind women's docility. Jagdish Hinduja, when asked about this particular issue, candidly answered that women guarantee lack of unionization 'because of the double-burden they carry'. However, the majority of business actors show a far more essentialist understanding of the advantages of employing a feminized workforce. They appeal in fact to a number of different stereotypes. Some highlight how women 'can sit for a longer time', while men 'cannot sit straight for eight hours'. A few even venture into pseudo-scientific explanations according to which women urinate less than men – in their view, an established biological 'fact'. Others argue that women are indeed 'naturally gifted in this specific job', hence stressing women's innate ability in engaging with given activities and tasks. None of this seems really new. In fact, existing studies focusing on women workers and processes of feminization indicate that employers use similar gendered stereotypes in other types of labour-intensive productions and different regions of the world economy (Salzinger, 2003; Caraway, 2005; Pun, 2005a; Wright, 2006). Notably, this jargon should never be easily dismissed, as it sheds key insights into processes of knowledge production in hugely unequal societies and settings. The point is not that the information contained in these comments is false – obviously it is so. Firstly, what Foucault (1969) called the 'archeology of knowledge' is hardly built only on the basis of true information. Secondly, in contexts characterized by harsh patterns of subjugation of one group to another, issues of representation can hardly be addressed simply in terms of a statistical average between 'true' and 'untrue' (Breman, 1995). The point is, instead, that exporters' comments, albeit based on false premises, have the power to turn into a self-fulfilling prophecy with *real* effects – namely, to produce and reproduce labour feminization, together with given shop-floor practices. As elegantly put by Leslie Salzinger (2003, p. 9), images of women as nimble-fingered workers with innate abilities to engage in given tasks are important 'not because they reflect reality, but because they produce it'. These gendered stereotypes impact upon working conditions and rhythms in quite practical ways. Notably, returning to our initial reflections over commodification and exploitation, it is easy to see how such stereotypes may reinforce differential processes of commodification and exploitation of women's labour at once. Let us consider women's supposed ability to need less toilet breaks than men. This stereotype implies higher rate of surplus extraction, as it shortens breaks on the shop-floor. Moreover, it also further cheapens the cost of female labour as a commodity. Unsurprisingly, these outcomes are obtained through the deployment of paternalistic forms of management of women's labour inside industrial premises. Women are often shouted at, and may endure verbal abuse and sexual harassment by male supervisors (Sisters for Change and Munnade, 2016). Supervisors, in their role of 'factory fathers' to 'disposable daughters' (see Wright, 2006), may also engage in naming and shaming practices or other forms of public humiliation when workers do not meet targets (Cividep and Somo, 2009; Jenkins, 2013). Ultimately, factories reproduce familial relations of subordination. Notably, patriarchy sets, at once, the possibilities and boundaries of both commodification and exploitation. In fact, overtime, albeit present, is not as chronically systemic as in the NCR. Indeed, women often punch their cards by 5:30 pm while may continue working until 7:00 pm. However, they do not stay for night shifts, as legislation only allows this (a relatively recent change) if employers provide transport, which involves rising costs (Jenkins, 2013).

The process of feminization of labour in Chennai and Bangalore has also gone through different qualitative phases. In this respect, the women workers employed by the industry can hardly be understood as a homogenous category. The gendering of production processes always articulates with intra-gender differences, particularly as capital responds to changes in competitiveness as well as potential shifts in the balance of industrial relations. While initially the industry mainly employed married women (Kalpagam, 1994), from the late 1990s onwards garment companies started employing unmarried women, particularly after a series of strikes organized by CITU in Bangalore, which challenged ideas of women as never engaged in union activities (Mezzadri, 2009a). Besides clearly responding to employers' need to re-establish labour discipline, this further shift in the social profile of the workforce also responded to considerations over labour costs. The hiring of young, unmarried girls who generally still live with their family of origin allows employers to pay an even lower wages. In fact, these young new recruits are considered subsidiary workers, even by some older women workers. Many work to gather a dowry at the end of a relatively short employment period (Kalpagam, 1994; Mezzadri, 2009a, 2012; Cividep and Somo, 2009).

Effectively, the actual 'timing' and typology of the labour relation should also be understood in relation to women's contractual position in the industry. Contrary to northern garment-producing centres, where workers are mainly in casualized and temporary contractual positions, as either casualized factory labour or non-factory 'unorganized' labour, in Chennai and Bangalore the industry is characterized by what appear as permanent labour relations. A significant percentage of women workers are generally on companies' rolls, and are paid Provident Fund (PF) and Employee State Insurance (ESI). In fact, it should be noted that in the context of the more standardized product cycles locally dominant employers place a premium on the relative greater continuity of labour relations. It is not a case that, contrary to northern garment export areas, for a long time women garment workers were not migrants from distant villages, but rather from areas surrounding Chennai and Bangalore. They were not recruited by contractors – often perceived as less needed in a context where patriarchy is the main mechanism at labour discipline (see Mezzadri, 2012) – but rather through advertisement on those boards and placards that, as mentioned earlier in this section, commonly appear outside industrial premises. Today, these trends have changed significantly, with rising number of migrants landing in Bangalore, even from Northern India.

One should however not be fooled by the relative continuity of labour relations in Southern India. This can be guaranteed only insofar it satisfies industrial needs without ever threatening profitability. In fact, in this case, permanent labour relations seem to be subject to a given 'deadline'. The attrition rate – or labour turnover – is very high, so that women workers can be at best defined as 'permanently temporary' (Kalhan, 2008). Some studies indicate that women may be employed within the same industrial unit for a period ranging between 1 and 3 years (again, see Kalhan, 2008). In any case, as bitterly put by a local activist in Chennai, women workers are permanently employed for 'no more than 4 years and 11 months'. After 5 years, they would mature bonuses and key social contributions set by Indian labour laws, like, for instance, gratuity (Mezzadri, 2012).[40] Indeed, the entry of younger workers and migrants in the industry has further facilitated 'break in service'. Women are compelled to leave in order to access their PF funds, which they may use as dowry. By 2005, this 'politics of PF retention' (Mezzadri, 2012) was extremely widespread, and it still seems to be largely deployed (Jenkins, 2013). Sadly, by the same period, young girls were often seen as those responsible for the acceleration of labour turnover and the negative implications this entailed, as older workers were instead more prone to fight with employers over contributions and wages (Mezzadri, 2009a). However, recently, new forms of workers' solidarity are emerging (Jenkins, 2013; Kumar and Mahoney, 2014; Kumar, 2014). The pre-union work carried out in the area across the 1990s and 2000s (mainly by Civic Initiatives for Development and Peace, Cividep), which focused on education around labour rights and entitlements, played an important role in crafting these solidarities (Jenkins, 2013). Women workers subsequently

---

[40] Gratuity involves the payment by the employer of 15 days of work for every year spent in the same firm.

founded the women's movement *Munnade* (literally 'Front') as well as the unions GLU (Garment Labour Union) and GATWU (Garment and Textile Workers Union). The latter is affiliated to the New Trade Union Initiatives (NTUI) (Jenkins, 2013; Kumar and Mahoney, 2014; Kumar, 2014). In 2012, the unions obtained a tremendous victory, when they successfully mobilized their members for a substantial increase in wages and the payment of Dearness Allowance (DA).[41] Even so, wages remain low, and they also vary massively across factories, depending upon suppliers and/or retailers. A report by Framtiden I Vare Hender (FIVH) and Cividep (Parakuni *et al.*, 2015) indicates a further upsurge in female migration from the rural hinterland and from the north, as well as the opening of new factories in rural areas, where often ESI is not paid, health provisions for the workforce are effectively privatized, and where many young women workers increasingly live in employers-run hostels and dormitories significantly limiting their freedom also outside labouring time.

The women workers of Chennai and Bangalore represent yet another of the multiple 'classes of labour' (Bernstein, 2007) inhabiting the Indian clothing mall and shaping its local sweatshops. The social profile, contractual relations and patterns of labour subjugation of these classes vary based on the changing industrial trajectories and product specialization, confirming the interplays between the physical and social materialities of production. In the south of India, the 'bogey' of feminization seems pretty real, as it fits well with the logics of cost minimization and labour discipline needed by the local industry. Indeed, based on industrial needs, the sweatshop takes different forms and sizes, and it is characterized by distinct patterns of labour commodification and exploitation. Notably, so far, different sweatshop realities seem to correspond to a somewhat clear geographical distinction between north and south of India. This would also make sense in relation to gendered patterns of employment at a more general level. In fact, the south has always been characterized by higher workforce participation rates for women. However, it would be inaccurate to interpret these labour outcomes purely in terms of path dependency. As we have seen so far, markets and commercial dynamics count enormously. In fact, this last point is further confirmed by the analysis of the last key garment export cluster found in the south of India – Tiruppur. Here, in the 'T-shirt town' of India (Chari, 2004), producing a garment commodity easy to be decomposed, the industry can again bank on

---

[41] See NTUI (2014). The recent attempt by the Government to change rules in relation to workers' access to PF contributions has triggered a new wave of labour militancy (Yadav, 2016).

multiple, differential patterns of commodification and exploitation, forging a highly composite local sweatshop that sits somewhere in between northern and southern industrial and labour trajectories.

The Complex T-shirts of Tiruppur

As argued by Sharad Chari (2004) in his engaging account of the rise of Tiruppur to international fame as a key garment centre in India, by the early 2000 the whole town already appeared as a 'decentralized factory' for the production of knitwear – T-shirts in particular. In fact, already in the 1990s, Pamela Cawthorne (1992, 1995) had theorized Tiruppur's knitwear production as a case of 'amoebic capitalism', characterized by a dense proliferation of micro and small units that intertwined based on a complex division of labour and tasks. Appearing as a very complex, 'democratic' socio-industrial formation (Vijayabaskar, 2001; Vijayabaskar and Kalaiyarasan, 2014), where caste has supposedly acted as social, 'fraternal' capital (Chari, 2004) rather than social liability (Meagher, 2006), Tiruppur is often celebrated as a case of 'clustering success', emulating the glory of the old 'industrial districts' as described by Alfred Marshall (1961) and developed across a number of regions like, for instance, the Third Italy (see Brusco, 1982; Becattini, 1990). This ever-growing manufacturing hub drew from a 'rural past', as *Gounders* (a local rural caste) mobilized agricultural surplus to be reinvested in small-scale, manufacturing units (Chari, 2004). By the late 2000s, numerous studies have focused on different aspects of the 'Tiruppur effect' on the local – rural and urban – economy (e.g. Carswell and De Neve, 2013a; De Neve, 2014a; Heyer, 2013). Given the purpose of this analysis, the extremely rich literature available on this case is mainly interrogated in relation to the task of understanding Tiruppur's place in the context of the overall development of the garment industry in India, and the relation between specific garment commodities and typologies of sweatshops. As the analysis below will show, the Tiruppur's case further reinforces the argument developed so far in relation to the intimate link between physical and social materialities of garment production, and its implications for processes of commodification and exploitation at work in the local sweatshop. Arguably, after reviewing this case, the analysis will also be better equipped to focus on issues of unfreedom, and how they may interplay with debates on commodification and exploitation.

Similar to Bangalore and Chennai, Tiruppur emerged as a key garment export centre by the 1990s, as the overwhelming dominance of trading networks for export success was toned down by the introduction of principles of quota allocations finally involving manufacturing investment (Mezzadri, 2010). However, its successful entry into export was paved by a much longer history of hosiery production. In the nineteenth century, when agrarian commercialization intensified cotton farming in the Madras presidency, Tiruppur became a storehouse for cotton trade (Harriss-White, 1996), attracting traders from Bombay and Calcutta. As Coimbatore developed its own textile production (Harriss-White, 1986), *Chettiars* (a south Indian trading caste) and Muslim communities initiated hosiery, previously mainly located in Calcutta. The first small *banian* (Indian under-shirt or vest) units appeared in Tiruppur around the 1920s (Chari, 2004). By the 1940s, there were around 34 units producing knitwear locally. They increased to 230 by the 1960s (Neetha, 2002). The industry triggered great demographic growth, as units continued multiplying exponentially throughout the 1970s (Vijayabaskar, 2001). In the 1980s, Tiruppur's production started carving its own export niche, gaining direct export orders rather than relying on traders from Northern or Eastern India. Studies agree that this process was triggered by the 'discovery' of the town by an Italian 'buyer', Antonio Verona (Vijayabaskar, 2001; Chari, 2004), whose name was still on everyone's lips by the time fieldwork was carried out (Mezzadri, 2009a). The export boom arrived in the late 1980s and early 1990s, as indicated by AEPC data (2004). By then, Tiruppur had entirely replaced Kolkata as the key centre for Indian cotton hosiery (Vijayabaskar, 2001). Specifically, it had become the 'T-shirt town' of India.

The evolution of product specialization enabled Tiruppur to carve a specific competitive niche in relation to other garment-producing centres, both in the north and in the south. In fact, as northern centres specialized in niche productions of various types, and the southern centres of Chennai and Bangalore were turning into 'cut-and-stitch' global centres for woven garment assembly, Tiruppur could bank on its own history, transforming itself from India's *banian* town into a global T-shirt and knitwear hub. By 2005, it had surpassed Delhi in terms of quantity of garments exported, while remaining second to Delhi in terms of value produced (AEPC, 2009). In fact, although different processes of product upgrading have taken place in the last decade, overall Tiruppur is hardly a centre that bases its fortunes on value addition. T-shirts and light cotton knitwear garments are products with quite distinctive features. They are easily decomposable into multiple activities and tasks. For one, knitwear, in particular, unlike woven, involves backward integration more often, as investment in fabric production might be far less costly. In woven, backward integration means investing in textile mills, or owning a significant amount of power-looms.[42] A few circular knitting machines, instead, can also be owned by small operators, and require far less direct labour involvement (Mezzadri, 2009a). Moreover, the production of simple, basic products for low-end markets does not necessarily require standardized quality and can easily take place in highly decentralized production systems. When it entails more standardized production targets (typically when buyers place large orders), it may instead benefit from an organization in larger industrial establishments.

Overall, given its historical port of entry into garment-making, historical trajectory and product specialization, the spatial organization of production in Tiruppur has also always been highly complex, overlapping in fact with the entire urban space and surroundings. The high levels of possible decomposition of the product cycle manifest in the entire town appearing as a huge, informal and decomposed industrial unit. In this sense, unlike in other garment-producing centres, until the mid-2000s it was hard to identify the 'layers' of the clusters as specifically organized around different activities. Rather, different activities and tasks are spread across neighbourhoods, commercial and industrial areas, and also across surrounding villages (Vijayabaskar, 2001; Chari, 2004; Mezzadri, 2009a; Carswell and De Neve 2013a; Heyer, 2013). Knitting, cutting, stitching, embroidery can all take place in different micro and small units or in homes. Decomposition, in fact, gave even poorer homes the possibility to 'specialize', in areas such as 'packing', for instance (Vijayabaskar, 2001). As argued by Chari (2004, p. 77), this great spatial spread helped the Tiruppur Exporters Association (TEA) (formed in the 1980s to substitute the older South India Hosiery Association, SIHMA) 'to project a fetishism of integrated manufacture despite the appearance of decentralized fragmented production'. In fact, by 2005, Shaktivel, the president of TEA – and now also President of the AEPC – organized estimates on production (industrial and cottage) units in Tiruppur based on specific economic activities and tasks, as if it was presenting to the outside world the image of a massive, town-wide industrial plant (Mezzadri, 2009a).

However, as it often happens, the discourse of fetishism may shape its own reality. In fact, by the same period, the cluster itself already showed clear patterns of polarization, with stitching segments of production going through an effective process of consolidation. The cluster appears increasingly crossed by what Meagher (2006) defines as multiple networks of accumulation and survival,

---

[42] Power-loom production increasingly substitutes textile mills production in India (see Haynes, 2001).

and its trajectory is becoming quite exclusionary when it comes to capturing the most significant business opportunities (Vijayabaskar and Kalaiyarasan, 2014). The opening of the Netaji Industrial Park in 2005 was a considerable boost for processes of consolidation (Mezzadri, 2009a, 2010). Today, as argued by De Neve (2014), Tiruppur is characterized by both Fordist and Post-fordist industrial landscapes. One represents the continuity with Tiruppur's past historical legacy, while the other represents a clear rupture with such a past, and the move towards a production segment targeting basic garment products produced *en mass*. Quite tellingly, across the two landscapes of production, the sweatshop organizes in quite different ways, shaped by and drawing from multiple social differences, on the basis of their relevance in gaining competitiveness and constructing distinct comparative advantages in global markets.

Tiruppur's 'Selective' Feminization Process

The first encounters with Tiruppur's garment workers happen as one slowly drives into Tiruppur by car, when the rural landscape slowly turns into the peri-urban echelons surrounding the town. Already in these areas, placed at the intersection between the rural and urban economy, many households engage in different activities linked to the garment product cycle (see Heyer, 2013). Women are spotted in their homes, packing, often helped by children. Men carry huge bundles of cloth, which leave their homes or the micro units they work in, to be moved where other production tasks take place. These can be in other homes, other micro units or in the more sizeable industrial premises located in Tiruppur's town as well as, by now, in surrounding areas organized in proper industrial estates or industrial parks. Indeed, the chaotic buzz of industrial activities and their spread across the entire town and surroundings seems to be everyone's business. Even so, a systematic read into Tiruppur's many noteworthy studies provides a useful indication of the potential internal 'borders' of the local sweatshop, and which type of labourforce dominates across its different segments.

During the early development of the cluster, the labour regimes at work in Tiruppur were largely based on what Chari (2004) refers to as a 'fraternal hegemony', where caste solidarities were deployed to intensify work. During this period, well into the 1980s in fact, a significant portion of the industry was organized in petty commodity production, hence clear estimates separating the number of 'units' and 'workers' as distinct categories of analysis seem missing (see Neetha, 2002). This said, as argued by Vijayabaskar (2001), by the 1980s many petty commodity producers were in a clear relation of subordination first *vis-à-vis* traders and then *vis-à-vis* upper class *Gounders*. Neighbourhood and family ties also crucially mediated patterns of work. If caste solidarities concealed processes of proletarianization amongst *Gounders*, exclusion from caste networks determined workers' placement at the bottom of the employment ladder. For instance, bleaching and ironing tasks were mainly carried out by *Dalits* (Vijayabaskar, 2001; Chari, 2004). Indeed, the 'grammar of caste' (Deshpande, 2000) powerfully shaped Tiruppur's labour trajectory. The knitting segments of the industry were primarily a male preserve (Neetha, 2002), although women, as it is often the case in petty commodity production, contributed as family aids. In small units, women also engaged in activities such as packing, threadcutting or checking (Cawthorne, 1992). Arguably, while this division of labour may still be partially at work across home-based and micro industrial realities, today women tend to be far more directly included into the labourforce (Carswell and De Neve, 2013a; Heyer, 2013). As we shall illustrate below, this is particularly the case in relation to given segments of the industry and of its local sweatshop.

By the mid-2000s, according to TEA's records, the Tiruppur's garment industry had expanded so significantly to employ 300,000 workers (Mezzadri, 2009a). By 2013, the number of workers had risen further, to 400,000 (Heyer, 2013). This astonishing process of industrial and labour expansion was achieved by accessing new significant reservoirs of labour, particularly through migration. Today, migration patterns are greatly differentiated. They include migrant workers who are more or less settled in Tiruppur; long-distant migrants still committed to return to their place of origin, and daily commuters (Carswell and De Neve, 2013a). Indeed, after decades of export boom, the caste–labour nexus has substantially loosened (Vijayabaskar, 2001), in the same way in which local capital is also increasingly complemented by the many newcomers who have arrived in town to exploit its business opportunities (Mezzadri, 2009a). The rising relevance of migration has gone hand in hand with the restructuring of gender relations in the industry (Neetha, 2002), which effectively moved from a 'fraternal' to a 'gendered hegemony' (Chari, 2004). While, to a certain extent, the knitwear segment has remained a sort of male preserve (as it is, in fact, also in other centres), the garmenting segments of production have gone through systematic processes of feminization of the labourforce (Neetha, 2002; Mezzadri, 2009a; Chari, 2010).

Undoubtedly, these processes of feminization are predominantly, albeit not only, linked to the multiplication of large units in and around Tiruppur. These units generally focus solely on stitching (Mezzadri, 2009a). Knitting, as well as other garmenting tasks, remains instead organized more informally within the cluster. Notably, it also remains primarily anchored to local business, as newcomers generally focus on garment assembly, hence not necessarily challenging the local roots of the cluster in terms of fabric production. In this sense, one could argue that the process of feminization has not necessarily substituted alternative forms of labour regulation; rather, it has become the most successful form of labour regulation within a specific segment of Tiruppur's local sweatshop. By embracing this particular labour trajectory in terms of stitching activities, Tiruppur has followed the other garment-producing centres of Chennai and Bangalore, where feminization already emerged as the leading strategy at cost minimization. However, the non-stitching segments of the cluster continue following a far more complex trajectory, where gender and mobility continue to interplay with caste and 'older' forms of labour management and control. Ultimately, also in terms of labour outcomes, Tiruppur seems to be placed at the intersection of Fordism and post-Fordism (De Neve, 2014a). Also here, changes in labour composition across given segments of the local sweatshop responded to the new industrial needs imposed by the progressive rise in the mass production of basic items. Many of the large factories predominantly employing women target mass markets; their cost minimization strategies primarily rely on volumes and on the deployment of cheap factory labour. Here as elsewhere, women serve this purpose quite well. At the same time, as the rest of the cluster continues engaging in more differentiated markets, which may be characterized by lower quality, smaller orders and/or more flexible arrangements, it can still draw from the multiple typologies of labour anchored to Tiruppur's past.

Also in Tiruppur, like in Bangalore, the move towards labour feminization as a successful strategy at cost minimization in (large) factory settings manifested as a way out from a labour 'impasse' that risked threatening the possibility to consolidate manufacturing activities in larger units. In the 1980s, as Tiruppur was already set on its extraordinary success story, and leading export producers started obtaining significant direct orders from buyers overseas, the local industry was affected by a number of strikes led by the local branch of CITU. Until the 1980s, in fact, local unions in Tiruppur seemed far more active and successful than unions elsewhere (De Neve, 2008), perhaps also partially due to caste solidarities.[43] This wave of strikes was particularly successful, as it gained DA for all workers. However,

---

[43] Moreover, several NGOs are also active in town. Many focus on garment workers' livelihoods, given the fact that knitwear is by far the most prominent economic activity.

it also pushed local capital to trigger systemic shifts in terms of labour recruitment and control. It is in this period, in fact, that the industry started substituting local male workers with women, as well as migrants (Chari, 2004; De Neve, 2008). The change in the labour composition of the industry only partially challenged recruitment methods. In the old, 'fraternal' system, contracting, mediated by neighbourhood and kinship ties, was extremely widespread (Vijayabaskar, 2001; Chari, 2004). In the context of the new, increasingly segmented labour regime, contracting arrangements seem to co-exist with more direct forms of recruitment, particularly when it comes to women workers, who, as in Bangalore and Chennai, are considered more docile to supervise and manage on the shop-floor. This said, also many women workers are organized and managed by family contractors (see Carswell and De Neve, 2013a).[44] Moreover, as a rising number of these women are migrants, the industry has invested in a number of dormitories and female hostels. During the opening of Netaji Park in 2005, Shaktivel proudly announced the inauguration of these new living spaces available to Tiruppur's ever expanding new labourforce (Mezzadri, 2009a). Sadly, rather than ameliorating workers' lives, these new spaces seem to aim at expanding the logic of labour control from the shop-floor well into workers' reproductive time, a trend which is already taking place in China in the context of what Smith and Pun (2006) call the 'dormitory labour regime' (see also Pun, 2007; Pun and Smith, 2007). Moreover, employers seem to also deploy these arrangements, and social reproduction more broadly, in order to tie the workforce to the industry for a number of years, without risking any threat to profitability and maintaining full control over the length of service they consider 'ideal'. In fact, since the early 2000s, evidence suggests that the local garment industry was deploying the *Sumangali* scheme. Arguably, in many ways, the premises and implications of this scheme epitomize the strong relation between commodification and exploitation at work in the sweatshop, and the ways in which capital strategically both exploits and reproduces pre-existing differences.

Originally, in Coimbatore and Tiruppur, the *Sumangali* scheme was primarily linked to cotton spinning. The scheme involves the recruitment of girls from different rural areas of Tamil Nadu and Karnataka by local contractors, and their placement in work across different spinning mills. The scheme involves housing arrangements, generally in crowded hostels where groups of young girls share a single room (SOMO and ICN, 2014). However, since the 2000s, an NGO active in Tiruppur, Social Awareness and Voluntary Education (SAVE), started denouncing

---

[44] Contractors who are members of their family and can therefore negotiate better deals for them.

the spread of this scheme to knitting and garment activities (Mezzadri, 2009a, 2012). In fact, a 2010 report by Vérité suggests that by then the scheme had spread to garment factories, while also worryingly linked to highly exploitative sex trafficking networks. This link between garment work and processes of commodification of the (female) body is also raised by other studies.[45] The 'Sumangali girls' are recruited and placed at work under the promise of the payment of a lump-sum at the end of a 3-year employment period. During this employment period, girls may only be provided with subsistence expenses or given extremely low monthly salaries; harsh conditions which are endured in order to access the final payment. In many cases, families allow their daughters to be part of the scheme to be able to pay for their marriage-related expenses in the future (Vérité, 2010). While the report specifically targets 'domestic' units in Tiruppur, the strong local interrelation between domestic and export production raises some doubts on the possible deployment of the scheme also in export units. Besides, the Tiruppur knitwear industry is not new to problems of bonded labour. In 2008, the Panorama documentary *Primark on the Rack* unveiled even the deployment by the local garment industry of Sri Lankan children from refugee camps as home-based workers. In fact, by 2013, dealing immediately with the '*Sumangali* scandal' was seen as an absolute priority by both TEA and the AEPC. The AEPC itself, by then, had developed its own compliance department. Today, as explained in Chapter 1, the council is implementing its own India-centric code of conduct for labour, DISHA (Mezzadri, 2014b). In the context of DISHA, as explained by the new AEPC Compliance manager Chandrima C., one of the key objectives of supplier training in the south of India is the eradication of the *Sumangali* once and for all.[46]

Arguably, the difficulties in the eradication of the *Sumangali* lie in the interplays between forms of oppression shaped by the social institution of gender and highly discriminatory and exploitative patterns of work. Indeed, in this case 'difference', manifesting in harsh forms of inequality, pre-exists the entry of *Sumangali* girls into the sweatshops. In fact, it sets the basis for the differential, highly discriminatory processes of commodification of their labour. At the same time, it allows for the maximization of exploitation inside the sweatshops. As the report shows, girls may be paid as little as 1,500 INR per month, as they expect with great hopes the end of their placement and the payment of the lump-sum promised, which, according to

---

[45] In Bangalore, for instance, one of the key global centres for 'surrogate motherhood' (see Pande, 2010), studies indicate that fertility clinics often recruit former garment workers (see Rudrappa, 2015).
[46] Chandrima C. was interviewed in Delhi in 2013.

SAVE activists, often does not even materialise, as employers are able to terminate the scheme before time claiming different types of contractual breach (Mezzadri, 2009a). Moreover, the case of *Sumangali* also clearly unveils the complex interplays between processes of commodification and exploitation and patterns of unfreedom in the industry. Specifically, it shows that by introducing a focus on social institutions like gender, the debate on unfreedom acquires a further layer of complexity. In fact, so far, issues of unfreedom in the industry have been addressed primarily in relation to patterns of dispossession from the means of production, and to the presence in the industry of multiple relations of wage labour, in either a direct or in a disguised form (Banaji, 2003; Bernstein, 2007). However, arguably, unfreedom is also powerfully shaped by social institutions and structures of oppression spanning across realms of social reproduction (Mezzadri, 2015c). For women workers (or indeed low-caste workers, albeit these seem relatively under-represented in garment export), unfreedom is not only a contractual experience, or one solely linked to their incorporation into the industry as either factory workers or petty commodity producers. Quite ironically, one could argue that, contractually, women are often the workers who are more likely to enjoy full 'freedom' from their means of production and from subsistence. This is only the case because their subjugation to 'patriarchal unfreedom' already guarantees and reproduces harsh processes of commodification and exploitation of their labour. While in the case of Tiruppur this unfreedom may manifest in what is essentially forced labour, these considerations can also be extended to revisit women's work in other segments of the Indian clothing mall and its sweatshop. Ultimately, these considerations indicate that the sweatshop is as much as a 'material' regime as it is a regime crossed by multiple differences and varied and often contradictory patterns of unfreedom.

The Sweatshop as a Regime of Multiple Differences and 'Unfreedoms'

This second empirical journey across the world of garment commodities produced in the lower floors of the Indian garment mall – namely Southern India – further confirms the strong interrelation between social and physical materialities of production. The garment commodities produced and exchanged in export markets in Bangalore, Chennai and Tiruppur are significantly different from those produced in and exported from the NCR, Jaipur, Ludhiana and Kolkata. By the same token, the social relations underpinning production are also considerably different, and they shape a different geography of work, which is not heavily masculine and predominantly characterized by circular mobility. In Bangalore and Chennai, centres for global garment assembly, the production and export of basic garment commodities predominantly produced in assembly-line production are carried out through the deployment of a heavily feminized workforce, whose cheap cost is reproduced thanks to the same gendered discourses of work which already powerfully shape the garment shop-floor across different geographical settings. In Tiruppur, instead, the production and export of knitwear, which has shaped the very identity of the whole town in the last decades, draw again from more complex circuits of production and work. Nevertheless, Tiruppur's evolution from a *banian* town to the top T-shirt town in India has involved aggressive processes of feminization of work, which, as we have seen, also imply pernicious patterns of forced labour, particularly in the segments of the supply chain linked to spinning and knitting. In all centres, in line with findings for Northern and Eastern India, the historical, local ports of entry into the garment industry have powerfully shaped the evolution of patterns of competition into specific market segments. This interplay between historical industrial trajectories and current commercial dynamics has also in this case been mediated by different state policies, particularly in relation to the evolution of export incentives.

As discussed in the initial sections of this chapter, while confirming the relevance of different commodities in shaping the social reality of the sweatshop, the illustration of the different labouring bodies at work in Southern India also provides scope for reflections on the nature of the 'differences' shaping this sweatshop. In fact, these both pre-exist and are reproduced by the sweatshop. Focusing here particularly on gender, the analysis has insisted on how such differences indicate the strong interrelation between processes of commodification and exploitation deployed by employers to strengthen competitiveness, and manufacture a comparative advantage in cheap labour in line with the specific industrial needs set by local industrial development trajectories. In this light, the sweatshop not only appears as a regime shaped by the type of commodities produced – as argued in the concluding section of Chapter 2 – but also as a regime shaped by and composed of multiple differences. The 'boundary-drawing strategies' deployed by capital to segment and fragment the workforce, as theorized by Silver (2003), impinge upon deeply rooted social boundaries shaped by social institutions and social structures of oppression that already set a highly differential pricing for different 'classes of labour' (Bernstein, 2007) well before they are 'welcomed' into local sweatshops.

Arguably, a focus on these social institutions and structures of oppression also complicates further debates on unfreedom. Surveying the industrial and labour landscapes of Northern and Eastern India, unfreedom powerfully appears as predominantly linked to ownership (or lack of ownership) of means of production, and to contractual, wage and debt relations. In those areas, where the combination of many factory and non-factory production realms emerges as a crucial feature of product cycles that are composite and made of multiple activities and tasks often still anchored to craft production, unfreedom is set on a 'continuum' (Lerche, 2010) of different, more or less informalized forms of labour. Processes of labour surplus extraction and the wage relation may be more or less explicit or concealed (Banaji, 2003; Bernstein, 2007). However, in Southern India, reflections over the highly feminized nature of work also allow for an analysis of unfreedom stretching towards realms of social reproduction. In particular, through the lens of gender, unfreedom appears as not only shaped by material dispossession, contractual relations, or the ways in which labour surplus extraction manifests. It also appears as characterized by a social, patriarchal character which, while deployed by capital for the purpose of accumulation, also pre-exists capital, and has a life of its own. Arguably, while the narrative has so far made reference to a particularly harsh case of what is effectively forced labour – the case of *Sumangali* in Tiruppur – insights on the relevance of patriarchal unfreedom can be generalized far beyond it. In fact, this defines the reality of the sweatshop in profound ways, even when it does not manifest as forced labour. It shapes the shop-floor experiences of women factory workers in Bangalore or Chennai, as they endure verbal and physical violence and sexual harassment that they often cannot challenge or counter.[47] It shapes their exit from the shop-floor, after their marriage, or based on family needs. Actually, it also shapes the experiences of women home-workers in highly masculine production spaces, like the NCR. In fact, across the home-based segments of the NCR, where women are more likely to be found, patriarchal unfreedom makes its great contribution in placing women in specific segments of the employment ladder, and in locking them into chains of intermediation they are rarely able to escape, given their scarce mobility. Besides, even when women are granted this mobility, as in Tiruppur, patriarchal unfreedom accompanies them across contracting corridors running from rural to urban areas. That is, under harsh forms of patriarchy, women are always socially unfree; both when they are the

---

[47] On the violent nature of capitalist 'dream zones' for women, see also Cross (2014). On sexual harassment, see Lyimo (2010) and Sisters of Change and Munnade (2016).

ultimately 'free' (read dispossessed) factory workers, or when they are locked into relations of petty commodity production. Some of these issues will be discussed again in Chapter 5, when the analysis will focus more specifically on the home-based contracting networks that increasingly spatialize India's sweatshop beyond urban conglomerates, and their implications for workers' livelihoods across labour and credit markets.

In theorizing the sweatshop as a regime shaped by the physical and social materialities of production and structured around multiple differences and unfreedoms, the narrative is also clearly suggesting yet another feature that greatly characterizes it. The sweatshop is a complex reality, shaped and moulded by multiple actors. In fact, the multiplicity of relations of power shaping the sweatshop escapes any oversimplified representations. In particular, the social responsibility for the harsh working and living conditions of garment workers, not only in India, but arguably everywhere, does not lie with a few culprits. As the debate on 'modern slavery' continues pointing the finger primarily towards global retailers and brands, at times directly or indirectly assuming a sort of diminished responsibility of 'local' capital due to its supposed subordinate position in the world economy, this narrative insists instead that only a systemic take on the reality of sweatshop creation can fully unveil all the complex processes that impede its eradication. A focus on the current behaviour of key regional actors involved in garment production in India reveals the problematic nature of analyses overemphasizing the distinction between 'global' and 'local' business. It reveals the profound compatibility and coherence in the business agendas of key garment players – global and regional – worldwide. Notably, the strong interrelation between global and Indian capital in the garment industry plays out at the levels of both production and circulation, given the relevance of retailing practices in both global and national contexts. Hence, the harsh processes of surplus extraction at the basis of the formation of India's sweatshops increasingly appear as a sort of 'joint enterprise'; orchestrated by multiple actors, and played out across spheres of production and circulation. There is no better place to analyze these trends at work than in Mumbai. This case will be discussed in Chapter 4.

4 | The Regional Lord and the Sweatshop

> In short, the contrast between capitalism as a commercial system and
> capitalism as a mode of production is schematic and overstated (…). In the
> more developed forms of commercial capitalism, circulation dominates
> production in the sense that production is controlled by a class of capitalists
> who remain merchants and cannot be properly classified as 'industrialists'.
>
> (Banaji, 2010, p. 273)

Surplus Extraction as a 'Joint Enterprise'

In the 1990s, as the first wave of international sweatshop scandals shook the liberal conscience of many western customers, *Wal-Mart* and its then famous line created by Kathie Lee Gifford – the American TV host and actress – were turned into the main capitalist monsters to fight (see Klein, 2000). Today, despite Kathie Lee's role has been usurped by other global figures – in particular by Amancio Ortega Gaona, the billionaire owner of the Spanish clothing giant *Zara* (see Hoskins, 2014) – global brands are still considered the primary avatars of the horrors of capitalist development. In fact, the history of textile production as a whole is linked to some of the darkest chapters in the violent history of world capitalism. Indeed, it is linked to rise of Britain's 'satanic mills' and to the evolution of colonialism. It is also linked to black slavery, as powerfully illustrated by Beckert (2015) in *Empire of Cotton*, where we learn how cotton, which became common currency in Indian Ocean trade (Riello and Parthasarathi, 2010; Riello and Roy, 2010), was deployed as means of exchange to pay for slaves from Africa. Clearly, these chapters in our history were hardly the outcome of the behaviour of a few. Could we demonize the East India Company without making reference to the British Crown, or to the powerful western, and also non-western merchants who benefitted enormously from the colonial enterprise? We could not. Historically, transnational trade networks always relied on imperialist designs, but these were also drawn with the help of the astute enterprising spirit of powerful regional merchants, coming from many corners of the world (Hobson, 2004). As also vividly illustrated by historical novels like Amitav Ghosh' (2011) *River of Smoke*, Indian merchants were hardly only 'middlemen' subordinated to colonial capital (Roy, 2014). This is why Roy (2013), in his analysis of *India in the World Economy*, warns against Western-centric readings of history only stressing the role of European actors in crafting and imposing circuits of exchange. On the contrary, he highlights that

> there was so much two-way traffic that it would be hard to characterize the effects in terms of a model of European influence on India or an Indian 'incorporation' into a European world economy.

> (Roy, 2013, p. 78)

Hence, also when it comes to garment, the younger and more 'modern' rib of textile production, without playing down brands' power responsibilities we should be wary of reducing the functioning (and outcomes) of contemporary capitalism to an oversimplified schema, where a handful of (mainly) western giants orchestrate miserable social outcomes for million workers across the world from their comfortable global chairs. Many commodity studies fall into this trap, as they reify the top of the global chain as the primary locus where surplus is realized, at the expenses of 'the rest'. However, this understanding may suffer from 'cake-division fallacy' (see Gilbert, 2008). It assumes the chain to be a closed system, and that the surplus accrued to some fractions of capital within one chain is necessarily realized at the expense of the others within the same chain. In fact, this picture is inaccurate for at least two reasons. First, it is inaccurate because of the great interpenetration between so-called global and so-called regional or local capital. Global and local actors may quite happily jointly benefit from processes of surplus extraction. Second, it is inaccurate because of the actual functioning principles of contemporary capitalism, where *both production and circulation* inextricably intertwine at multiple levels and scales, hence further complicating the ways in which surplus is *de-facto* extracted from the labouring classes. The analysis contained in Chapters 2 and 3 is a useful starting point to reflect on both these processes and on their relevance in shaping the world of the sweatshop.

The strong interrelation between global and regional actors in shaping sweatshop outcomes clearly emerges from our analysis of India's garment-producing areas, and their architectures of production and work. The features and conditions of the classes of labour-crowding India's sweatshop, from the north and east to the south of the subcontinent, are the outcome of processes of capitalist development which clearly transcend a simple 'North–South' divide. More concretely, the analysis has shown that if global buyers and clothing brands can impose stringent price diktats on local suppliers, it is up to the supplier to orchestrate production in ways which are conducive to the reproduction of their incorporation into global garment circuits. Moreover, these circuits, as we have seen, are made to function and reproduce thanks to the actions and laboriousness of multiple sub-agents as well – not only (direct) suppliers, but also subcontractors, vendors, labour contractors and so on. This is to say that the sweatshop is effectively created at multiple levels and scales by pressures simultaneously shaped by the behaviour and strategies of a complex and highly differentiated group of actors. As one interviews the top layer of regional players in India, with interviews often taking place in their luxurious offices or homes, the rigid hierarchical order assumed by many top-down chain analyses is considerably toned down. Indeed, some of the interviewees epitomize Rana Dasgupta's *Capital* and the astute and rapacious capitalist class it depicts. Notably, many of these suppliers appeal to globalization as the abstract, economic bogeyman to blame for the strengthening of competition and the undesirable social outcomes it implies. However, it is clear that this bogeyman may also be quite generous in providing them with significant possibilities for accumulation. Crucially, as argued earlier in this analysis, these possibilities vary greatly depending upon industrial trajectories, the physical materiality of production and the exploitation of multiple patterns of difference and unfreedom, which shape distinct sweatshop regimes on the ground. This is to say that regional actors are not passive receivers of the capitalist global design, but, rather, they actively participate in its drawing. The process of sweatshop creation is a complex 'joint enterprise', where both global and regional capital set the basis for the complex processes of surplus extraction. Ultimately, the sweatshop is not imposed by the 'global' onto the 'local' but by capital onto labour (Mezzadri, 2014b).

The strong relation between global and local actors can be further appreciated also by looking at the interplays between global and regional processes of production and circulation in the industry. Arguably, the relevance of circulation is indirectly acknowledged by studies focusing on the increasing power of global players in the age of globalization. These studies, in fact, refer to the global, neoliberal period as the one characterized by the '*The Retail Revolution*' (e.g., Lichtenstein, 2009), where giant retailers and 'manufacturers without factories' (Gibbon, 2001) have come to dominate the global production landscape. The early conceptualization of commodity chains elaborated by world system theorists insisted on the relevance of exchange in crafting capitalist circuits (Hopkins and Wallerstein, 1986). In fact, it is exactly this focus on exchange that earned the world system framework the accusation of having a distinct 'neo-Smithian', rather than neo-Marxian, character (see Brenner, 1977). Notwithstanding the relevance of this critique in relation to the risk of representing developing regions as an undifferentiated land plundered primarily via (global) trade channels, one could argue that several Marxist analyses propose too sharp a separation between production and circulation. As argued by Jairus Banaji (2010, p. 255), these analyses see the merchant as 'simply a "circulation agent" of industrial capital ... lacking any independent existence'.

Instead, Banaji convincingly shows that by analyzing the actions and behaviour of merchants operating in the Mediterranean Sea from the twelfth century onwards one is compelled to appreciate their key role in setting the very basis for processes of surplus extraction, an issue which will be explored again, and in more depth, also in the next chapter, which focuses on labour contracting networks in non-factory settings. Commercial capitalism, or what Banaji also calls merchant-led 'company-capitalism', crucially sets the basis for the subsequent development of corporate capitalism. It was a system heavily based on advances, in either money or in commodity form, through which the merchants not only ensured their domination over circuits of trade, but also over production. Their fortune was not based on the simple act of 'buying cheap and selling dear'. Rather, it aimed at setting the basis for accumulation, and as such it entailed engagement in processes of surplus extraction. It is not a case that, in some instances, merchants themselves pushed for the concentration of labour into early prototypes of what will then become the 'factory system'.[48] Besides, also where merchants maintained decentralized (putting-out) production systems, they could effectively transform 'simple' (or petty) commodity producers into (disguised) forms of wage labour (Banaji, 2010). Surely, they never left possibilities of accumulation to market chances or in the hands of direct producers; rather, they tried to control both. Indeed, throughout centuries of trade in textiles, from the Ottoman Empire to China, merchants sought control over 'every stage of production, foreshadowing their central role in the

---

[48] In Northern Italy silk production, already by the seventeen century merchants attempted to concentrate labour to benefit from the productivity of new spinning technology (Banaji, 2010). On putting out systems in Europe, see also Braudel (1981), and Noordegraaf (1997).

nineteenth century construction of a globe-spanning empire of cotton' (Beckert, 2015, p. 20). In fact, control over production was often crucial to guarantee primacy in the sphere of exchange.

In the context of contemporary capitalism, shaped by the neoliberal fantasy of a 'borderless world' for capital (Mitchell, 2004), we witness the strong interrelation between processes of production and circulation in myriad of novel ways, as retailing increasingly dominates our patterns of consumption, particularly in the West, but increasingly also in many emerging economies, where global and regional supermarkets and clothing chains target the 'needs' of the rising middle classes. To an extent, also contemporary commercial capitalism may work on advances. For instance, several garment exporters interviewed in India report that global buyers, at times, may advance a particular type of cloth to be deployed to complete a specific order of garments. However, this is not the dominant practice. Advances are used in contexts of competitive production, to 'lock' subordinates into specific business circuits. This is not necessary when instead dominant parties have a considerable 'monopsonistic' power, control demand and, ultimately, the market. Looking at the British commercial enterprise in West Africa, Fieldhouse (1994) illustrates how, unlike in colonial India, advances were not deployed as a systematic strategy to obtain production from local producers. Control could be guaranteed via the dominance over final markets, and hence did not need any *ex-ante* financial commitment by the company. Notably, in many instances, merchant capital may interplay with production in multiple, distinct ways, which cannot be reduced to a few, abstract typologies (Banaji, 2010). This is true both across old and new global trade and production circuits. For instance, looking at the rise of contract farming in the context of the new 'food regime' (see Friedmann, 2005; or McMichael, 2009) shaped by globalized agriculture, Watts (1994) highlights the multiple socio-economic forms that 'living under contract' may entail. Some contracting agreements imply the subsumption of small, direct producers into wider circuits of capital, and their *de-facto* proletarianization. Others, instead, imply the subsumption of entire sectors of production that may be locally commanded by large, capitalist farmers into the orbit of global corporate capital.

Indeed, in contemporary garment production, buyers and brands are in a position of solid, monopsonistic power. Their global reach is based on exactly the opposite functioning principle than that inspiring the old advance system. It is based on the footloose nature of their operations and on the lack of attachment to local suppliers. In fact, long-term, business relations with suppliers are an endangered species in the industry. In this scenario, advances are neither needed nor are they deployed. This said, one could also argue that in the context of contemporary global retailing, the order itself, which the buyer places with the supplier, may represent a form of 'immaterial' advance. Particularly, when the order comes from a renowned brand, it is an advance on a future commercial relationship that, although rarely implying a stable, long-term commitment, still represents the port of entry into highly profitable networks of production and exchange. For the supplier, the export order (or a multiplicity of export orders) speaks of production volumes that would hardly be possible in contexts where domestic markets are still relatively underdeveloped. As such, the order enlarges the boundaries of production, expanding the possibilities of surplus extraction. Arguably, the price negotiated with the buyer, or better imposed by the buyer when placing the order, sets the initial socio-economic perimeters within which surplus extraction will take place. Furthermore, the supplier will also move across the other socio-economic perimeters locally shaped by the differential price of labour available in the region.

The disciplining role of the export order should also be appreciated in relation to the lack of alternative market channels for the supplier. In fact, in the case of any failed transaction, the supplier can hardly easily re-sell the products to other parties. In the NCR, rejected orders mainly land in local markets like *Sarojini Nagar*; who would buy a batch of 2,000 T-shirts with a Nike logo, 'disavowed' by their own brand? When it comes to branded products, the difference between the 'real' and the 'fake' primarily lies with recognition by the brand itself. Due to patenting rights, no other retailer could legally sell the product. It may as well land – fake only because rejected – in the wardrobe of the lower classes of garment-producing countries. The progressive development of domestic markets for western clothing may partially loosen brand-based forms of control, providing suppliers with alternative (if still often illegal) market channels. Undoubtedly, 'alternative' garment markets of all types proliferate in the world economy, like the one for second-hand clothing whose impact on Africa is vividly illustrated by Brooks (2015).[49]

This strong relation between production and circulation in contemporary global industries is not only relevant at the top. For instance, subcontracting

---

[49] Brooks (2015, pp. 86–87) indicates how, in 2008, the UK 'secondary' textile industry moved around 523,000 tonnes of used clothing items. This is equivalent to 23 per cent of the 2,266,000 tonnes of new textiles consumed in the same year.

practices set the basis for highly composite production processes exactly by introducing internal mechanisms of circulation – of commodities and labour – as an integrant part of such processes. Moreover, and more crucially for the aim of this chapter, the current evolution of the global commodity chains in a number of key labour-intensive industries is one whereby the increasing stretch of production worldwide is increasingly commanded regionally by powerful groups of local capitalists. Focusing on East Asia, Appelbaum (2008) illustrates the rise of giant contractors as key gatekeepers of regional patterns of production and exchange. These large suppliers have turned into 'total-service-providers', or 'one-stop-shops' (Merk, 2014). In China, manufacturing giants like *Foxconn* commands around 200 subsidiaries around the world (Chan, Pun and Selden, 2013; see also Lee and Gereffi, 2013; Andrijasevic and Sacchetto, 2014). Looking at the global garment commodity chain, Azmeh and Nadvi (2013) analyze the penetration of Chinese capital into Jordan, highlighting the ways in which the 'Workshop of the World' is gaining a role of its own in mediating further processes of geographical relocation of the industry aimed at conquering new reservoirs of cheap labour. By the same token, India has witnessed the rise of its own key regional players. Arguably, an analysis of the behaviour and strategies of these players shows that they behave exactly like global buyers and retailers. In fact, their tactics are also largely similar to India's own domestic retailers, many of whom have a very long history in towering over putting-out systems of production across the subcontinent. However, in many instances these regional players do own manufacturing capacity. As such, they epitomize particularly well what Harriss-White (2008) has defined as the 'mutual embeddedness' between industrial and commercial capital in India. Altogether, these actors participate in producing and reproducing India as the giant shopping mall sketched by our empirical analysis of garment-producing areas. They participate in producing and reproducing the differentiation of the garment collections available across its different floors, and in reinforcing its multiple, distinct sweatshop regimes.

The Giant Clothing Mall Called India

The greatly regionally different physical materiality of India's garment production is a huge resource for sourcing actors. Crucially, these actors not only *see* India as a giant clothing mall. They also contribute to *make it into* a giant clothing mall, through their offshoring practices. Interviews with buyers and retailers reveal that they live in a world where geography is understood in terms of accumulation possibilities, and these in turn are given by the availability of specific commodities. The buyer fully operates on the basis of a fetishization of space, seen in terms of its production outcomes. He is a master in 'commodity fetishism'. Marx rightly warned us about the perils of commodity fetishism, as this conceals and naturalizes relations of exploitation. However, as argued in Chapter 2, there is indeed a strong relation between physical and social materialities of production. Moreover, commodity fetishism may create its own reality, an issue that was subsequently discussed in Chapter 3, in relation to the use of (gender) discourse to reproduce differential processes of commodification and exploitation. Buyers' fetishism, the one discussed here, ensures instead that given areas will continue receiving orders for specific garment commodities – ladies' shirts or blouses; men's trousers or jackets; children's frocks; woollens or cotton T-shirts. Local suppliers, who already developed a particular type of product specialization based on the local industrial trajectory and past commercial opportunities, will continue producing these commodities to sustain their incorporation into a given production circuit and so on. This is to say that this fetishism may continue turning its own 'perceived' geography into a very real one. Indeed, it has done so in practice by banking on the patterns of 'offshoring' that crucially crafted the new spatiality – or as argued by Harvey (2001), the new 'spatial fix' – of the current, neoliberal globalization project.[50]

Commodity studies have placed considerable emphasis on the relevance of 'offshoring' for the reproduction of specific global geographies of production. That is, they have placed considerable emphasis on the processes through which different types of manufacturing production have moved from now developed regions to developing areas. However, today, the rise of powerful regional players also calls for the need to look at patterns of 'backshoring' (Hardy, 2013); that is, offshoring practices taking place in producing countries' 'own backyard'. These could also be defined, in a more politically charged way, as a sort of industrial 'self-colonization'. Notably, backshoring exceeds subcontracting, that is generally the term mostly used to indicate processes of fragmentation of production inside the production nodes of global production networks. It exceeds subcontracting, as it is not the outcome of subordination in the production process, either in terms of market access and manufacturing

---

[50] It should be noted that Harvey deploys the word 'fix' not merely in 'spatial' terms but also to stress how processes of geographical restructuring are meant to resolve – or 'fix' – capital's crisis tendencies (see Harvey, 2001).

capacity, or in terms of ability to produce finished goods. Backshoring is the practice whereby suppliers may re-organize the production process in ways that loosen the nexus between an economic activity and a specific production site where they originally operated. It is a way to dis-embed production from a given industrial fabric, to re-constitute industrial space elsewhere, based on the production needs. In the process of backshoring, circulation may in fact acquire a certain primacy over production.

As already the rise and establishment of commercial capitalism in the textile sector, the rise of backshoring in the garment industry should be understood in the context of the political economy of its regional development. In particular, three factors greatly influenced the rise of backshoring: the nature of capital in the industry; a number of state practices that greatly impacted upon the evolution of the sector and the presence of multiple, regional patterns of product specialization. For a start, the garment industry in India has always been characterized by an overwhelming presence of merchant capital. Trading communities, like *Marwaris* and *Sindhis*, played a key role in the early development of the industry. By 2005, merchants still represented the majority of garment exporters across all garment-producing areas (Mezzadri, 2010), notwithstanding important differences in the relevance of manufacturing capital and its consolidation, based on the different industrial trajectories analyzed in this study. It is not a case that also many of today's big industrialists started off as textile traders, like, for instance, 'the Gokaldas' of Bangalore. The key role of merchant capital was indeed reinforced by state practices; namely, through different forms of industrial and trade regulations. In fact, the long-term reservation of the sector to SMEs (see Singh and Kaur Sapra, 2007), which ended in 2000 for woven products, and in 2008 for knitwear, combined with a quota-allocation system largely benefitting established trading networks until the mid-1990s, incentivized the reproduction of decentralized, putting-out systems. Finally, the uneven development of the industry, based on the multiple and complex industrial trajectories illustrated here, further boosted its retail-led nature. After all, if uneven development is intimately linked to inequality, it also perpetuates it. And it is hardly surprising that the same product unevenness and diversity that attracts global players to India may also represent a great asset for regional capital (Mezzadri, 2014a).

Across the India garment mall, virtually all top regional garment players could, in theory, engage in backshoring practices. In fact, as we have observed in the early chapters of this book, putting-out systems of different types dominate across many garment-producing centres, particularly, albeit not only, in Northern India. However, in many of these garment-producing areas, the social embeddedness of production provides crucial competitive edge to suppliers. In the NCR, a few large players do own industrial facilities elsewhere. *Orient Craft*, for instance, possibly the largest local exporter, now operates a unit in Bhiwadi, Rajasthan. A few top players are investing in units along the Delhi–Jaipur highway, to benefit from lower labour costs; a process that may lead to a sort of merge between the NCR and Jaipur garment clusters in the future. *Shahi*, another garment colossus, shares its manufacturing activities between the NCR and Bangalore, obviously organizing production based on the product ranges; namely manufacturing smaller batch ladieswear orders in Delhi and simpler, mass produced items in Bangalore. However, these players remain nevertheless 'attached' to the territory where production takes place. The local space thrives with possibilities for accumulation, particularly for these regional 'masters', who can benefit from a long-term knowledge of production and trade, and of which labouring classes can be deployed across all the complex layers of the local sweatshop.

Arguably, it is in areas where local profitable industrial opportunities may have dried up, but which may still remain crucial trading and/or logistical nodes, that backshoring manifests as a more distinct form to re-organize the production circuit, in ways that significantly reconfigure the local landscapes of industrial production. In some of these cases, backshoring may in fact be a necessary strategy to remain in business. In the Indian garment industry, there is no better place to analyze backshoring than in Mumbai. Here, as the analysis below illustrates, a number of regional actors increasingly behave like global buyers, exploiting their strategic trading position in relation to global garment markets, while relocating production facilities elsewhere across the subcontinent. After all, Mumbai, the 'gateway of India', has been a key trade centre in the world economy since colonial times. Indeed, it has always been a great logistical node for global buyers. It hosts thousands of 'globalized' urbanites and is renowned as the fashion capital of India. Paraphrasing an amusing line by a garment exporter, 'fashion is born in Mumbai, matures in Delhi, ages in Chennai and dies in Calcutta'. So, let us focus our attention on the supposed native land of Indian fashion, which today, however, seems to mainly cover the role of the 'cash register' of our country-wide clothing mall (see Figures 4.1 and 4.2).

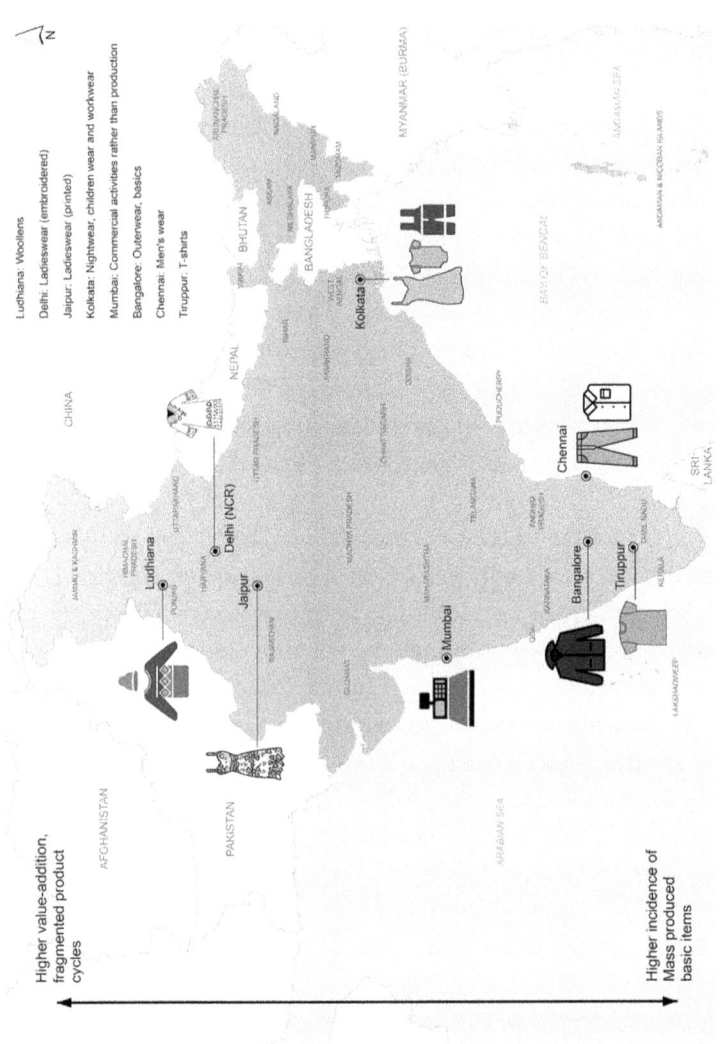

Figure 4.1 The India garment mall and its clothing collections

Source: Author's own design based on field findings (executed by Eseld Imms).

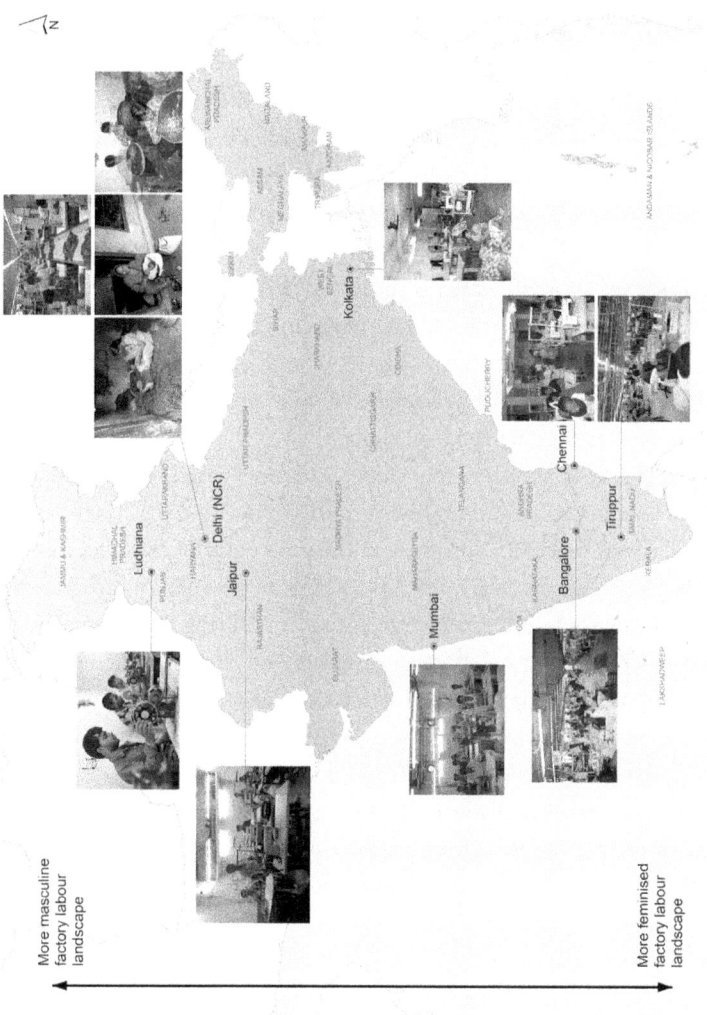

Figure 4.2 Changing sweatshop regime across the Indian garment mall

Source: Author's own design based on field findings (executed by Eseld Imms). Grace Carswell kindly provided the Tiruppur factory picture.

Mumbai: A Tale of Two Production 'Layers'

While Mumbai is still listed by the AEPC (2009) as a key garment export centre, it does not take long to realize that the city today hardly appears as a key industrial hub. Indeed, when compared to the other Indian garment-producing areas, Mumbai appears as a sort of outlier. Today, one cannot distinguish clear patterns of product specialization at work *locally*. Production seems as predominantly small scale and scattered across multiple areas in and around the city. However, unlike the other area hit by industrial decline – namely, Kolkata – export transactions are still rather significant (AEPC, 2009). Obviously, these factors, altogether, do suggest the possible strong presence of merchant capital. However, as it turns out, the story of Mumbai is fairly more complicated, and indeed speaks about the multiple processes through which commercial and industrial dynamics may interplay in today's global industries and certainly in India. As in the case of the other garment areas surveyed in this book, let us first focus on Mumbai's local industrial trajectory, and its peculiar re-organization in the context of the multiple pressures and processes experienced by the city.

If today Mumbai does not seem to produce garments based on clear patterns of local product specialization, it does not mean that the city did not have a very distinct past industrial trajectory. On the contrary, the entry of Mumbai into the garment-making business was clearly linked to its distinctive history and influence as a key centre for the trade and production of textiles. During the colonial years, Mumbai – Bombay – was a key hub hosting groups of powerful regional merchants, who mediated the production and trade of cottons between the East India Company and armies of Indian weavers for stellar profits. In 1800, the Company commissioned the purchase of piece goods from two Bombay merchants – Pestonjee Jemsatjee and Sorabjie Jevangee – for more than one million rupees (Beckert, 2015, p. 34). During and after the British Raj, the city experienced considerable industrial development and also saw the rise of its famous textile mills (Chandavarkar, 1992).

The development of fabric production represented a clear, early port of entry into modern garment-making. According to different sources of information, ranging from the local branch of the AEPC and local business associations, to local exporters and union representatives, garmenting activities were already present in Mumbai by the 1950s, when, as argued by D'Monte (2002) and Chandavarkar (1992), the mill sector was already well established and represented the largest source of employment. In the 1960s and 1970s, the boom of the hippy culture further sustained industrial expansion. Mumbai was the most crucial trade route through which Indian garments reached the 'developed world'. By then, Mumbai's national image as a 'fashion setter' was already established; an image further reinforced by the rapid rise of the Bollywood cinematographic industry. During these initial decades of industrial development, garment production in Mumbai was varied, and it comprised both intricately embroidered items – generally sourced from northern areas – as well as garments made of typically south Indian fabrics, such as the famous 'bleeding Madras' (Mezzadri, 2009a). By the 1970s, Mumbai turned into a large market for low-value products, like children's clothing and undergarments (Ambekar Institute of Labour Studies, 1980, 2005; AEPC, 2009). With time, the centre developed a strong reputation for woven menswear production, whereas Delhi grew its own competitive advantage in ladieswear production (Ambekar Institute of Labour Studies, 2005; AEPC, 2009). According to AEPC data (Mezzadri 2009a), for nearly three decades, until the late 1980s, Mumbai was the second largest garment export centre in India, after Delhi.

As one surveys the local reality of garment production, today little seems to be left of Mumbai's past garment glory. Locally, the industry appears as extremely fragmented and scattered across multiple locations, in residential, commercial, industrial and even slum areas (AEPC, 2009). According to the Clothing Manufacturers Association of India (CMAI), units cluster with particular density in the areas of Navi Mumbai, Parel, Lower Parel, Santa Cruz, Dadar, Andheri and Malad. Krishnamoorthy (2004) also reports the presence of garment production in Mahape, Rabra, Turbhe, Nerul and Vashi, Ghatkopar, Andheri-Kurla road, Bhandup, Byculla and Thane. Officially, the local garment industry is composed of around 6,000 units, and 90 per cent of them operate on less than 50 machines (AEPC, 2009). Unofficial estimates provided by CMAI refer to a much higher number of units; around 16,000, if one does not only account for SMEs, but also for micro and tiny units. Many of these, for instance, are spread across Dharavi, the largest Indian slum. AEPC comparative regional data show that export production declined consistently from the late 1980s onwards, both in terms of quantity and value. In 1989, Mumbai's share of Indian garment export was 39.49 per cent in quantity and 37.31 per cent in value. By 2003, it had plummeted to, respectively, 18.60 and 18.32 per cent (AEPC, 2004). Arguably, however, the seeds of industrial decline were already present in the 1970s, if one pays attention to the number of garment factory closures (see Table 4.1).

The reasons behind this industrial decline are somehow contested. Some explanations focus on land markets and on the transformation of Mumbai into a proper 'global city'. Undoubtedly, Mumbai – landlocked, extremely crowded,

Table 4.1 Number of registered garment factories and closures in Mumbai, 1974–1981

Year	Number of factories	Number working	Number closed
1974	152	139	13
1975	207	188	19
1976	231	214	17
1977	274	234	40
1978	343	289	59
1979	414	346	68
1980	443	336	107
1981	487	388	99

Source: Krishnaraj (1987, p. 8); based on Survey of the Industry, Government of Maharashtra, various issues.

and the main site of the growing Indian financial sector – is far from an ideal industrial location. Real estate prices started soaring in the 1980s and 1990s. By the mid-2000s, new urban land was sought at all costs. From 2005 onwards, the search for 'newly' available precious urban space was obtained through different strategies of land grabbing and sale. On the one hand, it was obtained through the systematic demolition of a considerable number of slum areas; a process of 'accumulation by differentiated displacement' (see Doshi, 2012, building on Harvey's take on processes of accumulation by dispossession), denounced as violent and corrupt by the many grassroots organizations fighting to protect the housing rights of slum-dwellers. According to Sheila Patel, founder of the Society for the Promotion of Area Resource Centers, SPARC, one of the most renowned of these organizations, the 2005 demolitions produced 300,000 homeless in a few months (Mezzadri, 2005a). During the same period, urban land was also obtained by selling the old cotton textile mills, close to the Old Port. Jupiter mill was sold first, at the astronomical price of 268 crore rupees (*The Economic Times*, 2005; *The Times of India*, 2005).[51]

Other explanations, instead, emphasize the role of organized labour in turning Mumbai into an undesirable industrial location. Indeed, many garment exporters like to expressly underline how Mumbai has a particularly compelling 'labour problem'. They refer to the long strike that, in 1982, hit the textile mills. The longest in Indian industrial history, this strike – led by the legendary trade

---

[51] Arguably, also this process of sale was highly controversial and opposed by numerous protests. For instance, in February 2005, the Bombay Environmental Action Group filed a Public Interest Litigation (PIL) against the sale in the Bombay High Court (Datta and Abraham, 2005).

unionist Datta Samant, who will be eventually killed in mysterious circumstances – lasted 15 months, and was never officially called off (D'Monte, 2002). It involved the loss of 64 million man-days and, ultimately, of 225,000 jobs (Gupte, 2004). As powerfully spelt by Chandavarkar (1992, p. 396), it signalled the 'epitaph of the Bombay cotton textile industry', soon replaced by a growing small-scale, power-loom sector (see Srinivasulu, 1996; Haynes, 2001; AEPC, 2009). Bhiwandi, a small town located 50 km away from Mumbai, is one of the sites of this power-loom sector. By 2005, as the first textile mill was sold in Mumbai amidst public uproar, it had turned into a 'village factory' (Mezzadri, 2005b), employing 300,000 workers. Indeed, the fact that garment exporters explain industrial decline by referring to the 1982 strike confirms the strong interconnections between the textile and garment industries in Mumbai. It also further confirms how the local availability of a (cheap and) docile labourforce is perceived and fetishized as the most crucial ingredient for the successful development of a local garment sector. Local 'labour trouble' was hardly the only reason behind industrial decline. However, it was the *primary* reason for local capital.

The decline of Mumbai as a key garment production centre triggered the beginning of a process of dual development in the industry. On the one hand, Mumbai still hosts what can be called 'resident' garment production, which is geared towards low-value items and mainly caters for the growing domestic market (see AEPC, 2009). Faced with multiple spatial constraints, this resident production generally takes place in *galas*, i.e., rooms located in different floors inside a multi-storey, building complex (ASK, 2001; Krishnamoorthy, 2004; Mezzadri, 2009a). The same spatial constraints also explain the reproduction of the great spatial spread of resident garment-making across different areas of the city. On the other hand, larger manufacturing units focusing on export started to systematically abandon the city. The headquarters of these companies are still located in town, and one can visit some of them in the industrial areas of Lower Parel, Andheri or Santa Cruz. They are still registered as Mumbai based, and so are their export transactions. However, their manufacturing capacity is now located elsewhere in India, in areas where they 'backshore' production in order to seize new profitable business opportunities. Notably, the relocation of larger exporters further boosted the industrial fragmentation of Mumbai resident production, while also allowing local merchant capital to survive. In fact, merchants re-established market access for the vast local universe of small, micro and tiny units, which were left orphaned of the upper industrial strata which guarantee them 'job work' during the export boom (Mezzadri, 2009a, 2010).

The backshoring practices undertaken by larger garment companies are highly selective, product-based processes of decentralization of manufacturing production, which are strongly connected with the patterns of regional specialization of the Indian garment mall. In fact, if some argue that relocation of larger garment factories from Mumbai has mainly benefitted Bangalore (e.g., Krishnamoorthy, 2004), field findings reveal a far more complex design.

Backshoring has targeted Bangalore in the case of garment companies specializing in woven menswear and outwear; i.e., more basic items which can be efficiently mass produced in larger industrial units. Indeed, as we have amply discussed in Chapter 3, Bangalore has developed its regional comparative advantage in this type of production (Ambekar Institute of Labour Studies, 2005). Moreover, interviews with exporters reveal that many companies consider the Karnatakan city a prime destination due to its cheaper and 'less militant' labour, its weather and also its lifestyle, compatible with Mumbai. However, relocation is first and foremost dependent upon product range, and this is the basis on which new production centres are carefully chosen. A company named here as Key Export, for instance, slowly started specializing in knits, due to their specific contacts with foreign buyers who mainly branded T-shirts. Due to this product specialization, the company relocated all its production capacity to Tiruppur, where they employ between 1,400 and 2,000 workers.

Companies practicing high product diversification have adopted a complex and fascinating backshoring strategy. They have chosen and moved their manufacturing facilities to different new geographical locations based on the products needed. For instance, a company producing both ladieswear and menswear, and both knitted and woven garments, may have units spread across Delhi, Bangalore and Tiruppur, while retaining its administrative headquarters in Mumbai. The owners of one of the relocating garment companies interviewed highlighted how their relocation choice depended upon the availability of different architectures of production and work suited for different product ranges. The company, which I will call Clothing Creations, has a capacity of around 5,300 machines, employs 7,000 workers, and engages in ladieswear, menswear and basic production. Only its sampling unit is based in Mumbai, so that buyers can actually check compliance with their design specifications *in loco*. However, their capacity is mainly spread across Delhi and Bangalore. In Delhi, they own 4 units, each with 200 machines and 200 workers. In Bangalore, instead, they own 3 units of around 2,800 machines and employ 4,200 workers. Their processing and dying units are based in Vapi, in the State of Daman and Diu.

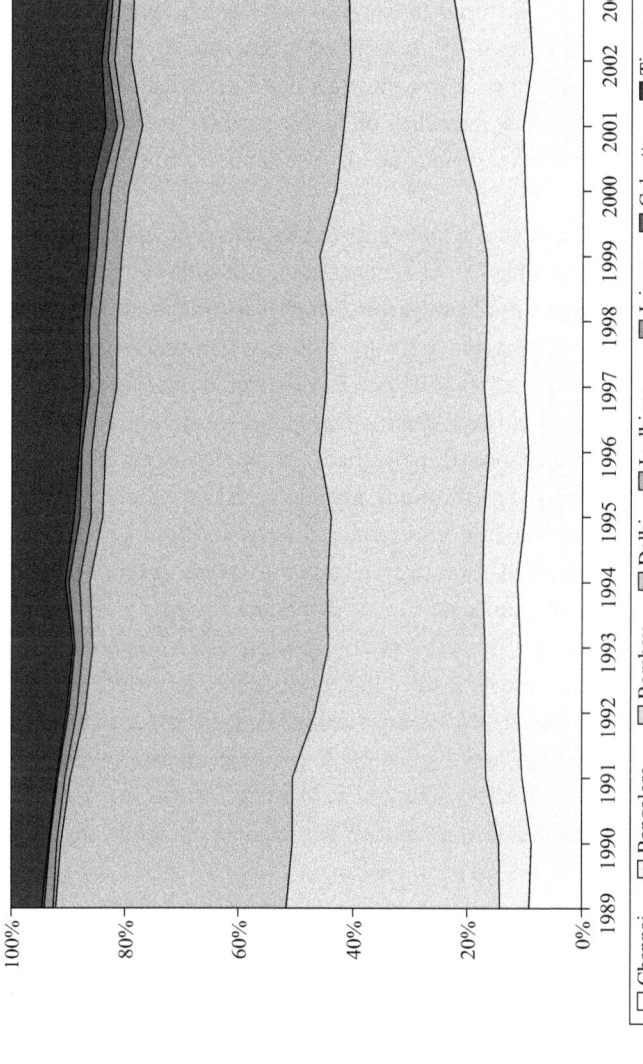

Figure 4.3 Regional value export shares across main garment-producing centres from 1989 to 2003

Source: Mezzadri (2008, p. 618; 2009a). Based on data on regional quantity and value export shares, AEPC (2004). Data tables can be found in Mezzadri (2008, p. 618).

Vijay A., one of the owners, confirms that they produce ladieswear in Delhi, and basics and menswear in Bangalore. He is convinced that Delhi is the only centre which has the 'necessary skills' to engage in embellished products, given the great availability of handwork skills. He also stresses that Bangalore, due to its 'loving population' (ready cheap female workers), is the only centre where they feel they can afford to set-up larger factories to work on mass orders. Bangalore's recent union-led strikes and the rise in minimum wages obtained by women garment workers is a powerful warning against these gender essentialist ideas. However, as analyzed in Chapter 3, new reservoirs of 'loving workers' (read new, cheaper, migrant female workers) are now pouring into Karnataka from different areas of north and south India.

Through these multiple, locally differentiated backshoring practices, Mumbai exporters effectively craft what can be defined as an All-India commodity chain. Contrary to other garment-producing areas, which show higher degrees of what Harriss-White (2003) defines as the 'viscosity' of local capital and where industrial space has a clear local articulation, in Mumbai also a significant share of domestic capital is made footloose. Industrial space is 'destructed' locally and reconstructed as a network of multiple locations. The governance of this network is fully exercised from Mumbai, where design specifications, marketing and other core activities are retained, while its production nodes are scattered across India, in a skilful process of local outsourcing. Indeed, exporters engaged in these practices 'upgrade' to a role that is strikingly similar to that of global buyers, effectively becoming *Pan-Indian buyer–exporters*. This process of upgrading can be defined as purely functional, as it does necessarily involve improvements in terms of processes or products; it is primarily based on a strong local knowledge of different production structures across India, and how best to bank on them. Indian large domestic retailers already behave similarly, although, unlike buyer–exporters, they do not necessarily own any manufacturing capacity. For instance, *Westside*, the clothing retail branch of the Tata retail network *Trent*, a very large Mumbai-based garment player in the Indian domestic market, source its vast range of clothing products from different parts of India, utilizing a wide and diversified network of different factories, workshops and cottage units. Their sourcing manager likes to stress how they indeed 'learnt' a great deal from global retailers. In fact, the liberalization of retail is gaining great momentum in India, a process that, according to some (see Kalhan and Franz, 2009, for example), may threaten the very survival of many small local retail outlets. At the top of the garment chain, however, large global and regional businesses are not only benefitting from liberalization, but they are increasingly converging in their plans to exploit India's large domestic retail opportunities. In fact, *Westside* has established different partnerships and tie-ups with global buyers. It has developed one with *Inditex*, aimed at marketing *Zara* products across its many stores in India. The same regional giant retailer has also a franchising agreement with the Italian clothing giant *Benetton* (Business Standard, 2013). Tie-ups, commercial agreements and even share acquisitions are increasingly common even among national 'ethical' retailers. *Fabindia*, India's famous ethical brand, which started off as a small export company in the 1960s before conquering the domestic market (Singh, 2011), sold 8 per cent of its shares to the Louis Vuitton Moet Hennessy group in 2012 (Burke, 2012, in *The Hindu*).

What analyzed so far indicates that in the Mumbai garment industry one can find different organizational forms, where production and circulation combine in different ways, adding to the already multiple and complex ways in which the garment commodity chain articulates on the ground in India. In Mumbai's resident garment production, local putting-out networks of production are still the primary way in which small units manage to access final markets. These networks have survived since the 1960s.[52] Local traders sit on top of these networks, especially after the departure of larger export units, which used to offer small units alternative channels of distribution via patterns of subcontracting. Indeed, today, the 'jobwork', subcontracting model locally dominant (see AEPC, 2009) is primarily merchant-led. Unsurprisingly, inside the units, the organization of production is mainly based on group systems and 'make-and-through' techniques, with only very few units making use of assembly lines (Krishnamoorthy, 2004; Ambekar Institute of Labour Studies, 2005; Mezzadri, 2009a).

Large garment companies, those that left the 'resident' production layer in the hands of local traders, engage instead in backshoring practices. Arguably, by relocating their manufacturing facilities across different garment-producing areas, and effectively following strategies proper of global and domestic buyers, retailers and brands, these actors craft yet a novel organizational form, where both production and circulation, commercial and industrial capital combine to offer new profitable opportunities. On the one hand, one may characterize this form as

---

[52] A 1980 report on the industry clearly describes the organizational form of the industry since the 1960s, as one where 'the entrepreneur assembles necessary capital (mainly working people) for the purchase of fabric ... mostly what manufacturers call "rags", "fents" and other small pieces... A contractor then comes in; his job will be to collect these pieces on a mutually agreed basis and to promise delivery of finished garments within stipulated time' (Ambekar Institute of Labour Studies' report, 1980, pp. 16–17).

a putting-out system of production stretching across the whole subcontinent and crafting an All-India commodity chain. It clearly shows strong mercantile features. On the other hand, however, the considerable relevance of productive investment within this organizational solution indicates that the accumulation strategy of Pan-Indian buyer–exporters exceeds one mainly based on trading networks.

Notably, backshoring practices promote networked systems defined by a different geographical reach based on the product specialization. In this sense, the link between the physical and social materiality of production is not necessarily lost in the Mumbai garment industry. However, this link is now projected within a more complex and networked industrial reality; that of the 'All-India commodity chain'. It extends to the multiple areas falling into the orbit of the backshoring network practiced by different relocating garment companies. In each of these areas, backshoring further reinforces the distinctiveness of local patterns of product specialization. Hence, the organization of production between and inside the garment units varies across different locations, following the industrial trajectories already analyzed in the previous chapters. After all, the very rationale of backshoring is to bank on the multiple product-based divides and on the unevenness of the Indian garment mall. It does not aim at challenging such divides and unevenness, insofar as they remain profitable. For the same reasons, backshoring practices also do not challenge, but rather further reinforce, the logics of local sweatshop regimes at work across the different floors of the mall.

The Mumbai Sweatshop as both a Resident and 'Backshored' Reality

The dual development of Mumbai's garment industry is paralleled by a dual development of what can be defined as its sweatshop. In the case of Mumbai resident production, the sweatshop presents itself as based on highly casualized labour relations, where workers are often paid piece rate, are not registered, and cannot claim any social security. Workers are scattered around the city in the multiple areas, *galas*, home-based or home-based like workshops where production takes place. Given the great fragmentation of the industrial fabric, in Mumbai, like in Kolkata, factory and non-factory realms exist and overlap in a sort of extremely tight continuum. According to informal estimates provided by CMAI-Mumbai, by 2005 there were 700,000 workers in Mumbai. However, only around 140,000 of them were connected to export markets, while the majority of them sweated in units producing garments for the domestic market (Mezzadri, 2009a). The majority of this workforce is recruited informally and managed via labour contractors, a trend that seems to have reproduced unchallenged since the 1960s (see Ambekar Institute of Labour Studies, 1980; ASK, 2001; Krishnamoorthy, 2004). According to the local offices of India's trade unions, and CITU in particular, contractors are also often garment workers, rather than external agents. Local traders and proprietors of small garment units praise the practice, as particularly functional to the industrial needs of a product cycle that is considerably decentralized and flexible. Being both a worker as well as a supervisor, here the contractor is the employers' 'inside man'; their connecting 'gear' with workers, with a dual role of boosting productivity and also minimizing labour unrest. Both are in the contractor's own interest, in order to reproduce his privileged position. As in the case of northern garment-producing areas, and Kolkata, the majority of workers are male migrants. Many come from rural Maharashtra, but many others circulate from more distant areas, like UP and Bihar. Indeed, the two states of the Hindi belt work as a huge reservoir of labour for the industry across a significant number of areas.[53] Once again, caste distinctions do not seem to actively shape the sweatshop (see also Krishnamoorthy, 2004), whose reproduction is instead crucially guaranteed by mobility, and geographical provenance from India's poverty enclaves. The ways in which Mumbai's sweatshops have consistently reproduced – since the 1980s (see Krishnaraj, 1987) – as rather masculine spaces may be considered somewhat surprising, given the high women workforce participation rates that characterize the state of Maharashtra.[54] However, as we have amply illustrated earlier in this analysis, the Indian sweatshop is hardly simply based on 'path dependence'. It is mainly based on how commercial dynamics and product specialization interplay with local social relations in ways that guarantee the making and re-making of a cheap, disposable and relatively docile labourforce. In the context of fragmented and decentralized product cycles, like the ones at work in Mumbai's resident production, women may not necessarily represent an ideal workforce. Indeed, by 2005, they represented only a third of the whole workforce, and they were

---

[53] Few may also come from Karnataka, Kerala or Tamil Nadu. Within Maharashtra, many migrants come from Ahmednagar, Ratnagiri, Satara, Pune and Raigad (Krishnamoorthy, 2004).

[54] In 1981, more than 85 per cent of units did not employ women at all. Only a few larger factories employed women and generally not in core activities (Krishnaraj, 1987).

primarily employed in the usual activities reified as 'feminine'; thread-cutting, packing and checking.[55]

Mumbai's 'resident sweatshop' appears as a local reality, with distinctively local social features and contours, crafted by given relations of production. However, also the sweatshop 'exported' and de-localized through the backshoring practices of Mumbai's Pan-Indian buyer–exporters remains embedded in specific local socio-economic fabrics; the difference is that its composition varies depending upon the garment centre chosen for industrial relocation. Briefly, by backshoring production buyers–exporters also backshore the process of sweatshop creation. In fact, they engage in the same employment practices found in their new, satellite-manufacturing centres. Some buyers–exporters explain this in terms of their respect for local 'traditions' and (labour) practices. However, his explanations clearly betray considerations over productivity, specialization, labour control and competition across different markets. Rahul M., who owns units both in Bangalore and Delhi, employs male migrants in Delhi and women in Bangalore. His partner openly admits 'whenever we need volumes we go for women, whenever we need tailoring skills, for men' (Mezzadri, 2014b, p. 338).[56] This statement obviously speaks about the social construction of gendered discourses of work. However, it also and more fundamentally speaks about the social construction of local sweatshop regimes as crucial devices to compete in globalized circuits targeting different garment commodities. Buyers–exporters actively participate in reproducing such regimes, as part and parcel of their competitive game, based on a complex combination of production and circulation. They bank on them, cash in the rewards, and by doing so, they further strengthen the architecture of production and work of the Indian garment mall (see Figures 4.1 and 4.2).

Production, Circulation and the Many Scales and Layers of the Sweatshop Regime

The analysis developed in this chapter adds a further, third level of complexity to the characterization of our sweatshop regime. The interpenetration of 'global' and 'regional' or local capital and the interplays between production and circulation

---

[55] Some of these activities have always been home-based in Mumbai, even thread-cutting (Rairikar, 1999; Mezzadri, 2009a).

[56] They are also perfectly aware that both strategies are also conducive to the minimization of labour 'troubles' across different markets. Rahul's partner, Vijay, continues: 'keeping the workforce migratory is the key for avoiding unionisation. The other way is employing women' (see Mezzadri, 2009a).

create and expand platforms for surplus extraction and, ultimately, the sweatshop, which therefore appears as the outcome of a sort of 'joint enterprise'. Indeed, the sweatshop, which, as argued in the previous chapters, is a regime characterized by a physical and social 'materiality' and is crossed by multiple differences and patterns of unfreedom, is also crafted and reproduced at multiple levels and scales. First, it is clearly not imposed by the 'global' onto the 'local'. On the one hand, regional actors of different types actively participate in its reproduction. In fact, they are those who need to manufacture labour as a cheap commodity, no less than they need to manufacture cheap skirts, blouses and T-shirts, in order to reproduce their incorporation into the complex regional circuits of the global garment commodity chain. On the other hand, today, many regional actors also increasingly behave like their global counterparts. Similar to global buyers, they manage to strengthen their power within the chain by expanding and re-organizing their geographical reach, and combining production and circulation in ways that allow them to bank on the multiple differences of the Indian garment mall. By backshoring production across the whole subcontinent and forming what can be defined as an All-India commodity chain, these actors further reinforce the complex and differentiated architecture of production and work of the Indian garment mall. They reinforce the distinctiveness of its local patterns of product specialization. And by doing this, they also reinforce the logics of the distinct sweatshop regimes at work across its different floors. Briefly, the materiality of the sweatshop regime – both physical and social – finds in backshoring practices yet another channel of reproduction.

Second, the conditions that determine the reproduction of sweatshops seem to be dictated by processes of interplay between production and circulation. In fact, both processes, as directly discussed here and, arguably, also as indirectly illustrated by the empirical analyses contained in other chapters, crucially contribute to surplus extraction. Briefly, the process of sweatshop creation is a joint enterprise both if one looks at the actors involved, as well as one considers the interpenetration between commercial and industrial logics. In fact, both the theoretical discussion and the empirical evidence presented in this chapter – again, in combination with what argued in previous ones – support a view of the garment industry as defined by multiple industrial trajectories where different relations between production and circulation are at work. Without playing down their great diversity – as Banaji (2010) argues, the relation between commercial and industrial capital can hardly be reduced to a few typologies – an attempt is made here to categorize *some* ways in which these relations unfold, and their connection to processes of surplus extraction and the making of the sweatshop.

By looking at the trajectories of capital across the garment centres analyzed, at least four different typologies can be identified. Crucially, the co-existence of these different trajectories in an industry that has been largely dominated by mercantile castes and communities, particularly, albeit not only, by *Marwaris* and *Sindhis*, highlights the theoretical and analytical limitations of looking at merchant or industrial capital as separate, static categories, rather than in a relation of interplay and co-determination (Harriss-White, 2008). In the garment industry, production and circulation strongly intertwine at different levels and scales, as multiple global, regional and local actors fight to secure profitable economic opportunities in a context of great regional and global competition.

Indeed, the first way in which production and circulation combine is epitomized by the resilience and reproduction of putting-out systems of production. These are still at work in numerous parts of the Indian garment mall. In this case, circulation dominates over production in relation to processes of surplus extraction. Merchants sitting on top of these systems hardly merely buy cheap garment commodities from direct (petty) producers to re-sell them to buyers and retailers overseas. Some may only engage in trading; however, the tightening of competition works against these simpler 'buy-and-sell' practices. Those merchants who successfully manage to remain in business do develop some degree of control over production. They may do so either via advances, hence via the 'job-work model', or by simply banking on their gatekeeping role *vis-à-vis* final market access. As the analysis has shown, in export, putting-out systems of production are particularly resilient in Northern India and Kolkata, but present also in Mumbai's resident production, and in Tiruppur. Moreover, they are still widely dominant in domestic production. At a more general level of analysis, one could argue that these systems are more resilient where the product cycle is greatly fragmented, decentralized and composed of multiple different production realms and spaces of work. As illustrated in Chapter 2, in the context of this particular trajectory, labour may be subsumed into the capitalist relation both in real and formal ways, and the sweatshop appears as an extremely complex reality made by multiple spaces of work, social relations of production, and combinations of 'free' and 'unfree' labour.

The second way in which production and circulation combine in the industry involves instead the progressive primacy of industrial capital over commercial capital. In the industry, the evolution of merchants into industrial capitalists has taken place as a response to limited opportunities for accumulation along a more 'commercial' route. The rise of Bangalore as a key garment centre is a case in point. Clearly, the trading families who moved into garment production in Bangalore faced severe constraints in becoming successful exporters, particularly during the era of MFA quotas, when northern and western garment production and trading centres dominated. These actors needed to invest in manufacturing to carve their own space in the industry, and they did so by focusing on garment commodities and markets that, as we have seen, differ considerably from those monopolized nationally by northern exporters, and that instead could be efficiently realized through higher levels of manufacturing capacity and centralization of the production process in larger production establishments. In these cases, where labour is more likely to be subsumed into the capitalist relation in 'real' terms, the sweatshop mainly appears as a factory space and, as we have explored in Chapter 3, one inhabited by a greatly feminized workforce, who is subject to forms of social unfreedom that may exceed a mere focus on means of production or dispossession. It should be noted that, in many ways, this move from merchant to industrial capital could be considered largely in line with textbook examples of what the 'transition' towards more 'mature' forms of capitalist production should look like.

However, it should also be noted that the classic, stagist idea that the relation between circulation and production eventually, with time, always resolves in favour of the consolidation of industrial capital does not seem to hold in all cases analyzed here. Indeed, in the Indian garment industry also the opposite seems possible. If in some areas merchant classes have developed into industrial capitalists, like in Bangalore, in other areas, instead, industrial capital may resolve problems of profitability and increased regional competition by reinforcing its hold over processes of circulation. Arguably, this is what has happened in Mumbai, in the case of buyers–exporters backshoring production towards other garment-producing areas, based on their product specialization. In these contexts, the reality of the sweatshop depends upon the areas chosen for relocation. Backshoring practices represent a third way in which circulation and production may interplay and intersect in the industry, in which the former acquires a certain level of dominance, even in contexts where manufacturing capacity is still present. In these cases, in fact, industrial capacity appears as subordinated to the broader reach of what is essentially a commercial enterprise. This enterprise, which deploys strategies fully coherent and compatible with those of global retailers, may also increasingly reach out to these global retailers for different joint commercial agreements. Besides, circulation already dominates in other upper segments of the domestic industry, where a number of Indian giant retailers already operate. These domestic retailers have not only already concluded several commercial agreements with global buyers but also developed other partnerships with them, some even involving mergers and acquisitions. Overall, the cases reviewed in this analysis illustrate that we can neither capture the functioning principles of the garment industry and its composite regional chain nor those of its sweatshops by merely appealing to classic, modernist ideas of 'transition'. In fact, as already argued by Banaji (2010) in relation to the distinctiveness of national experiences, the idea of transition may be far too schematic and stagist to account for the great diversity of how capitalism has come to dominate the world economy. Indeed, the complexities at work in the sector analyzed here do not seem to represent at all different phases of a common transition, but rather different local trajectories of accumulation.

Notably, if in the three typologies depicted above the relation between production and circulation seem to 'resolve' in favour of one or the other process, we need to acknowledge that the two may also combine in ways that escape any easy characterization, giving rise to mixed or 'hybrid' organizational forms. These forms, which represent a fourth, complex group of relations between production and circulation, may be defined by the co-existence and co-determination of mercantile and industrial strategies at accumulation. In these cases, which are present across India, questions over the dominance of circulation or production remain open, and possibly unresolved. Let us consider garment exporters heavily relying on subcontracting practices. Do high levels of subcontracting always indicate the dominance of circulation over production? They do not, as some exporters, while heavily subcontracting their orders, may also as heavily invest in the production process, particularly in high fashion segments, where orders are far smaller, but FOB may peak at several hundred dollars. Obviously, this is not to say that in other cases, instead, high levels of subcontracting may not indeed indicate lower levels of investment in the production process. However, it is to say that it is hard to capture the great multiplicity of solutions adopted by exporters in this segment. These may vary based on orders, or indeed relations with different buyers across multiple markets.

Arguably, the acknowledgement of circulation as a key process impacting profoundly on processes of surplus extraction is also a fundamental step to study more in depth the relations through which labour is recruited, distributed and deployed across the different echelons and spaces of the local sweatshop. In fact, besides interplaying with production at multiple levels and scales to give rise to different organizational forms, circulation also appears to be a crucial, internal organizing principle at work *within* the production circuit, in relation to the movement of both commodities and labouring bodies. In particular, different typologies of labour contracting cover fundamental functions in processes of sweatshop creation. In fact, in many instances, and particularly in the context of highly decentralized and fragmented production systems, it is via contracting that labour 'lands' in the sweatshop. Indeed, contracting is crucial to establish those linkages, interconnections and corridors between rural and urban areas that renew access to reservoirs of cheap labour. Generally gathered in a rather homogenous bloc, under the blurred category of 'intermediation', also these internal forms of circulation may instead 'disguise' forms of surplus appropriation. It is to these issues that the analysis now turns its attention. For this purpose, however, we need to leave Mumbai, and move again up north, to visit one of the main labour contracting hubs of the northern region: Bareilly.

5 | The Broker and the Sweatshop

Labour brokers come in all guises ... Jobbers have not disappeared from the industrial economy; on the contrary, they are still emphatically present in the informal sector where they fill a key role.

(Breman, 1999, p. 413)

Sweatshop Corridors to the 'Global Village' and the Reserve Army of Homes

The world of the sweatshop is always a chaotic one. Production rhythms are hectic, delivery deadlines tight and all different garmenting activities need to be coordinated with careful precision. Everywhere in India – that is, across all the different floors of the India garment mall – this is a challenging task. Indeed, coordination is particularly crucial where the sweatshop is composed of multiple realms of production and work. In these cases, the local production chain or network is extremely composite and fragmented and the socio-economic and geographical boundaries of the sweatshop are extremely fluid and porous. Moreover, the movement of both garment commodities and labourers in and out of the local sweatshops analyzed may draw a much wider geography than that encapsulated by the main industrial site linked to final markets. Economic activities may be subject to processes of 'spatialization' that spans well beyond single production hubs. So far, our sketch of the Indian garment mall has mainly taken into consideration key garment-producing centres or 'clusters'; particularly those linked to export. However, the 'networks of accumulation and survival' (see Meagher, 2006, 2010, 2011) linked to these clusters may stretch across a constellation of different production sub-nodes.[57] Undoubtedly, garment-producing centres impact livelihoods far beyond their primary centre of gravity. For instance, in Tamil Nadu, the 'Tiruppur effect' had profound implications on livelihoods in surrounding

---

[57] The presence of both these types of networks in clusters in developing regions is a powerful reminder of the limitation of analyses over-emphasizing 'social' capital (for a critique of social capital, see Fine, 2010).

villages (Carswell and De Neve, 2013a; Heyer, 2013). There, the economic boom of the T-shirt town had indirect repercussions on wage rates as well as highly differential access to social mobility and new socio-economic opportunities (Heyer, 2012, 2013; Carswell, 2013). After all, many garment clusters crucially depend upon surrounding areas and subsidiary centres to sustain their process of accumulation (Mezzadri, 2014a).

Let us consider the NCR, for example. The high casualization of the factory workforce, mainly composed of male, rural migrants from UP and Bihar, clearly indicates that the accumulation of the centre is based on linkages and connections between villages scattered across these two states and the metropolitan industrial area. These villages offer to the NCR – as to many other garment centres – key reservoirs of cheap labour. In this sense, the 'global' aspirations of the regional capitalist garment elites are still stably anchored to 'the Indian village', which remains central to processes of accumulation in the sector. In fact, as we will explore in Chapter 6, it is often the same Indian village that may accommodate garment workers as they exit urban factories and workshops, both during lean season and at the end of their sweatshop experience. Moreover, employers' great reliance on different combinations of non-factory work for processes of value addition – embroidery, most of all – draws further connections between urban industrial areas and peri-urban and rural areas, where this type of work may be readily available, and at much cheaper rates (Mezzadri, 2008). All these non-urban sites increasingly represent a sort of huge, 'global village': central to all those processes that are projecting the 'made in India' in the global economy.

When asked about their value-addition activities and processes, a great number of NCR garment exporters answer that these take place either 'in the outskirts' or 'in the villages'. As illustrated in Chapter 2, these activities and processes are carried out at 'the periphery' of the main industrial areas that compose the NCR (see also Mezzadri, 2015b). However, in ladieswear production, the number of non-factory workers needed for value-addition activities may well exceed the reservoirs of labour available in and around the NCR urban industrial conglomerate. According to some informants, garment companies need three embroiderers for each tailor they employ in their factories. Briefly, they need a massive reserve army of homes and small workshops to meet their production needs. This is why – besides relying on different types of 'peripheral' non-factory labour in the NCR – employers also send their garments all the way to small towns or rural villages, particularly in UP. In doing so, they draw these towns and villages into the circuit of production of the NCR, as satellite centres.

This process of decentralization of activities and tasks from the NCR to satellite centres crafts corridors connecting urban and rural areas, which are crossed by many garments, as well as by many labouring bodies. Contrary to those established by formal, mega-projects aimed at shrinking economic space and tighten new forms of globalized governance (see, for instance, Dey and Grappi, 2015, on the Delhi–Mumbai Industrial Corridor), these are informal corridors, crafted by the different accumulation and survival strategies of the multiple actors crafting the sweatshop regime. Garments are 'pushed' from the NCR to peri-urban and rural satellite centres and back, sometimes loaded onto tracks, and some other times simply piled up in huge bundles fastened at the back of a two-wheeler. Indeed, the organization (or disorganization) of transport depends upon market segments. The same corridor is crossed by many workers, who move to the NCR from satellite centres for more or less short spells of employment. For the working poor, these corridors often represent a sort of revolving door between rural and urban livelihoods opportunities as well as regimes of work. Indeed, rural–urban migration often enables people to move across different poverty 'cycles', as argued by Jonathan Rigg (2006) in his study of South East Asia. In order to escape old, rural poverty traps, the migrant labourer may fall into 'new', urban ones. However, for many poor workers, the move is still well worth a try, given the substantially higher pay rates offered by the city. In many cases, the lives of the working poor remain entangled across these 'old' and 'new' poverty cycles, in the context of their highly mobile, multi-local livelihoods.

The multiple urban–rural corridors connecting different production sites and enlarging the spatial boundaries of the sweatshop are often shaped by the frantic work of a complex and highly diversified group of actors, vaguely labelled as labour 'contractors', 'jobbers' or 'brokers'. In many instances, in fact, these actors are in charge of providing the 'right' labourforce for each activity needed to complete the garment product cycle. In essence, they are in charge of processes of circulation *internal* to the sweatshop regime, and involving both commodities and labouring bodies. Despite being highly informal, the networks shaped by the contractor may be quite socially regimented. Indeed, for a large share of Indian workers, and not only in the context of garment sweatshops in fact, these networks define both the points of departure and arrival of the migration experience, often establishing a clear route back and forth. As argued by Jan Breman (1996, p. 233), in India, circular migrants are 'trapped in corridors running from their homes to the workplace and back again'. Generally, movements beyond such corridors are constrained by the same ties that made mobility possible in the first place (see also Breman, 2013).

Indeed, in the context of the highly composite sweatshops analyzed in this book, the study of labour contracting arrangements can shed further light on the different ways in which the sweatshop acquires its composite geography, and how different labouring classes – or 'classes of labour' (Bernstein, 2007) – 'experience' the sweatshop. It contributes to our understanding of the complex social and economic settings in which processes of surplus extraction unfold, and it further unveils the functioning mechanisms of the sweatshop regime as a 'joint enterprise' shaped at different levels and scales. In particular, the analysis below shows that contracting is not always only embedded in relations of 'intermediation'. Ultimately, the labour broker is an extremely complex figure, who escapes easy classification and covers multiple roles. He really comes 'in all guises' (Breman, 1999), an issue that is not necessarily addressed by studies focusing on global industries. Let us first analyze in detail these different possible 'guises' in the garment industry, before focusing on Bareilly. Known as the *zari* town, this is a key embroidery satellite centre for the NCR, and it is a city of contractors.

Contracting as a Disguised form of Capital Engaged in Interlocking

From the top-down vantage point of commodity studies and chain analysis, one may be tempted to club labour contractors altogether and primarily emphasize their intermediary, largely unproductive and even 'parasitic' role. Unsurprisingly, the debate on corporate social responsibility (CSR), which largely shares this vantage point, adopts this conceptualization and argues that today labour contracting is the major hurdle against improving labour standards globally. As argued by De Neve (2014b, p. 1303), this debate is currently creating the myth of the 'unscrupulous, rapacious contractor', who preys insatiably on the working poor. Admittedly, labour contracting has emerged as one of the 'Achilles' heel' of international labour standards and ethical trade initiatives (Barrientos, 2008). Labour contracting produces a process of disarticulation between the management of production and that of labour, which triggers processes of 'adverse incorporation' of labourers into production chains and circuits (Deshingkar, 2009), and makes monitoring labour laws and regulations extremely difficult.[58] However, arguably, this disarticulation is not always necessarily the outcome of contractors' intermediary or 'unproductive'

---

[58] See also Phillips (2011), building on the work of Hickey and du Toit (2007), Deshingkar (2009) and Mosse (2010).

role. On the one hand, anthropological studies reveal that it may be the product of workers' practices. In some cases, contractors may simply be 'aspiring workers', who struggle to climb the employment ladder (Picherit, 2009; Parry, 2013; De Neve, 2014b). On the other hand, however, contractors may instead actively participate in the 'joint enterprise' aimed at extracting labour surplus from the working poor not as mere intermediaries but as key players. In sum, contractors may not always be unproductive, mediating agents. And while some may indeed be 'aspiring workers', some others may instead be petty capitalists. Ultimately, a solid theorization of labour contracting networks, and of the role of 'the contractor', or 'the broker' in shaping them, can only start from the recognition of the great heterogeneity (Picherit, 2009) and differentiation of these networks.

Today, across many labour-intensive industries, there are indeed multiple forms of labour contracting at work, shaping a 'cascade system' of labour supply (Barrientos, 2013, p. 62). In fact, during its neoliberal phase, the process of globalization has determined an exponential rise in the deployment of 'external workers' employed through formal staffing agencies (Davis-Blake and Uzzi, 1993; Coe *et al.*, 2009; Barrientos, 2013). In highly informalized contexts – similar to the sweatshop regimes we have surveyed so far – the role of these formal staffing agencies is performed instead by unregistered agents, engaged in processes of hiring, supervising and organizing labour. Notably, formal and informal contracting are not mutually exclusive systems. In fact, John Chalcraft's study (2007) of Syrian migrant workers in Lebanon shows how trusted employees often work as informal labour contractors for formal staffing agencies. Similar arrangements are observed in the Gulf States where, for instance, armies of South Asian workers are deployed in the construction sector (Leonard, 2003; Jureidini, 2014) or are hired for domestic work (Kodoth and Varghese, 2011; Hanieh, 2011).

Given the multiple, diverse forms informal contracting can take, it could be helpful to differentiate between the different *functions* it can perform in contemporary, flexible, industrial systems. For instance, in factory and non-factory production realms, where the process of informalization plays out in different ways (see Mezzadri, 2008, 2012; Chang 2009b), different forms of contracting are at work. In factory realms, labour contracting functions as the key working mechanism through which the management of labour is decoupled from that of production. In these contexts, contracting involves the recruitment, supervision or organization of groups of workers inside the factory premises, in exchange for a commission on each of these workers. In non-factory realms, instead, labour contracting enables the subsumption of given economic activities into the orbit of a far wider production circuit. Here, contracting involves the full organization of some ancillary, labour-intensive economic activities, outside the factory realm. Both contracting systems may involve a broad spectrum of agents. Castells and Portes (1989) called the first practice 'in-contracting'. The second is here called 'out-contracting'. In India, both labour in-contracting and labour out-contracting are widespread. Agents engaged in them are all colloquially known as *thekedaars* in Hindi (Mezzadri, 2008; 2016).

Historically, in-contracting practices trace back to the *Sardar* and *Kangani* systems, at work during colonial times and deployed for the organization and management of Indian indenture labour in plantations, in the subcontinent as well as abroad (Roy, 2008; Kaur, 2014). This system survived and partially transformed and adapted in postcolonial India. For instance, it was deployed in the mills sector in Bombay (Chandavarkar, 1992), where it was hardly a 'relic' of a pre-capitalist past, but rather a device of late industrialization (see Chandavarkar, 1985; in Roy, 2008, pp. 976–978). Today, contracting still mediates the recruitment, management and supervision of a significant part of the Indian workforce in both factories and workshops (Srivastava, 2005). In the garment industry, interviews with employers reveal that they rarely know the exact number of workers in their factories. Instead, they always know the number of machines they possess. In Tiruppur, one exporter interviewed by Sharad Chari (2004) succinctly but rather effectively summarized that this is due to the fact that employers own the machines but 'not the work'. In fact, in Tiruppur the presence of contracting arrangements is significant. Also in northern sweatshops, factory realms are mostly characterized by the presence of contract workers, who, as we have shown in Chapter 2, are generally migrants from UP and Bihar. In the NCR, these workers are recruited through a vastly heterogeneous set of in-contractors (Singh and Kaur Sapra, 2007; Mezzadri, 2008; Barrientos *et al.*, 2010; Mezzadri and Srivastava, 2015). In-contractors perform a function that is primarily of intermediation, and whose main scope is disguising the labour relation between employers and workers (Mezzadri and Srivastava, 2015).

Out-contracting, however, is significantly different. Obviously, it can also take different forms and involve multiple agents, as labour outcomes in India are always crafted by a 'continuum' of informal relations (Lerche, 2010; Breman, 2013). However, its function far exceeds mere intermediation, and extends instead to the organization of entire segments of the production and labour process. This practice enables the incorporation of informal production and labour structures into wider industrial circuits, and allows producers, for instance, to source ancillary activities to specialized operators. Many of these activities, like embroidery, are linked to artisanal production, which organizes in petty commodity production and/or home-based work. Across the sweatshop regimes surveyed, petty producers and home-based workers generally work for out-contractors (Mezzadri, 2008; 2012, 2014a; Unni and Scaria, 2009).

A number of important studies highlight how realms of petty commodity production are characterized by combinations of capital and labour (Bernstein, 2007) and by complex social relations of oppression and power crossing both productive and reproductive realms (Harriss-White, 2014; Raju, 2013). Several of these studies have placed particular emphasis on the formal subsumption of petty commodity production into the capitalist relation; that is, they have emphasized how in many instances petty commodity producers are in fact disguised forms of wage labour (e.g. see Oya, 2007; Rizzo, 2013 on transport workers in Tanzania). In local sweatshops in Northern and Eastern India, our analysis in Chapter 2 has emphasized how this type of disguised wageworkers crowds the many spaces of work across non-factory realms of production. In areas like the NCR, they are one of many 'classes of labour'. However, the general literature on this subject has perhaps placed far less emphasis on the implications of this theorization for actors sitting on top of petty commodity production networks. Indeed, direct producers, while not dispossessed of their means of production, may still perform a role that is consistent with wage work. However, by the same token, one should also acknowledge that the dominant parties organizing their work might effectively engage in enterprising activities, even when they are not the direct owners of the means of production. In a nutshell, petty commodity production is not only characterized by the informalization of labour but also by the *informalization of capital* (see Harriss-White 2003; Breman, 1999, 2013).

Undoubtedly, in many instances, parties involved in forms of labour out-contracting at work across local sweatshop regimes should be conceptualized as representatives of India's informalized, petty capitalist classes. Their role, as already that of merchants and commercial enterprises discussed in Chapter 4, is strongly linked to processes of surplus extraction. In fact, in his discussion of the links between industrial and commercial capitalism, Banaji (2010, p. 304) also dedicates considerable time to petty forms of circulation and/or intermediation, which, through the provision of advances to subsistence producers, help to 'reconstitute the process of production', by 'enabling the reproduction of labour power' and 'of the means of production'. The advance, in this case, is 'an advance of capital', which 'does not lie within the scope of simple circulation' (Banaji, 2013, p. 9, quoting Marx, 1981, p. 676). Notably, through the provision of advances, dominant parties can 'attach' subordinates across multiple markets, significantly complicating relations of commodification and exploitation, which may become entangled with forms of oppression that are not necessarily only work related. In fact, within processes of informalization of capital, the labour market is only one of the numerous arenas where the subjugation of the working poor takes place.

Important insights in relation to the multiplicity of roles of capital in informal settings can be derived from the literature on *interlocking*. Primarily centred on agriculture, a segment of this literature adopts a clear neoclassical lens, and it focuses on market 'imperfections' in rural areas (e.g. Bardhan, 1980). In this conceptualization, dominant parties interlock subordinates across multiple markets simply as a result of some of these markets being 'missing' or 'imperfect' (see Srivastava, 1989). For instance, a landlord can provide credit to an agricultural tenant because formal credit provision is unavailable in rural areas. These studies do not necessarily unpack relations of domination and subordination, which remain locked into the 'black box' of the market (see Byres, 1998). On the contrary, as illustrated by Harriss-White (2008) in her study of West Bengal, rural markets are complex 'systems of circulation' permeated and moulded by power relations. However, a subset of studies on interlocking does centre the analysis around processes of surplus extraction and their complexities in rural settings. In particular, these studies shift the emphasis from markets to the process of exploitation. They highlight how surplus extraction involves interlocked modes of exploitation (Bharadwaj, 1974), where landlords reproduce their power by performing multiple roles at once. Landlords are often also merchants, or moneylenders. They do not simply provide land and work to subordinates, but they also craft market access for their goods and, crucially, provide credit. Overall, transactions between landlords and agricultural tenants and labourers are interlocked across land, labour, commodity and credit markets; a process reinforcing patterns of domination and subordination across all such markets (Bharadwaj, 1974, 1994; Bhaduri, 1983, 1986, 1999).[59]

In this characterization centred on social relations, the process of interlocking appears as primarily devoted to surplus extraction (Harriss-White, 2008), which the landlord aims at enabling in all possible ways while making sure subordinate parties are fully dependent upon him for all their basic needs, ranging from

---

[59] Studies on interlocked modes of exploitation (i.e. analyzing the political economy of interlocking) also present differences, for instance, in relation to the role of interest in interlocking (crucial for Bhaduri, and not for others), or in the conceptualization of 'backwardness' (see Byres, 1998). A discussion of these differences goes beyond the scope of this chapter.

work to credit. Empirical studies on the Indian countryside indicate that credit, in particular, performs at least a two-fold function. It guarantees subsistence, but it also enables the production process, as the two are inextricably linked in the lives of the rural poor. Only once a tenant or labourer obtains credit from the landlord he can survive, as well as labour. At any rate, in contexts characterised by high levels of poverty and dependence, subsistence credit may well always be production credit. Quite crudely put, it is the necessary pre-condition to make sure direct producers can be exploited; else, they would starve. In this sense, in many instances, credit provision is as crucial for the landlord as it is for his subordinates, as it makes surplus extraction possible at all. In his analysis of agricultural relations in UP, Srivastava (1989) clearly spells out this point, highlighting how interlocking 'enlarges the space in which surplus appropriation can take place, by making subsistence (of the producers) and production feasible in the first place' (Srivastava, 1989, p. 517).

Some of these insights on interlocking in rural agricultural markets can be expanded and deployed in analyses of contracting. In the context of our sweatshop regimes, in fact, many labour out-contracting networks are characterized by interlocked modes of exploitation, where labour contractors perform multiple roles. Obviously, these contractors are not landlords. They do not own land, and, unlike the owners of garment subcontracting units or workshops, they do not even own other type of fixed capital deployed in production, like, for instance, looms or stitching machines. However, like landlords, these labour contractors do actively try to interlock subordinates – in this case, petty commodity producers and home-based labourers – across labour and credit markets. Credit, in particular, is often crucial for these actors to reproduce their dominant position within specific segments of the sweatshop regime. Admittedly, this process is highly contested and negotiated; permeated by multiple pettier forms of intermediation that may be performed by the 'aspiring workers' Geert De Neve and others rightly refer to.

Successful contractors interlock subordinates through advanced payments. While, as argued in the previous chapter, the provision of advances is not necessarily systemic at the top of the garment chain, where the order placed by the buyer may in fact perform an interlocking function, this type of credit crucially shape the secondary networks of accumulation crossing the chain, and the processes of circulation internal to the sweatshop regime. Many studies centred on the Indian working poor highlight how labour contractors deploy advances to attach migrant labour, effectively creating relations of neo-bondage (Breman,

1996, 1999, 2013; Srivastava, 2005; Lerche, 2007; Picherit, 2009; De Neve, 2014b).[60] Specifically, within the out-contracting relations characterizing the sweatshop regime, advances should be considered as a form of investment through which contractors make sure 'their' labour will remain devoted to their business. Also in this case, as in the case of agriculture, it is an investment aimed at the subsistence of the direct producers, and at enabling them to produce for the contracting enterprise. In essence, advances play a crucial role in establishing a solid platform for the extraction of surplus, while at the same time they ensure high degrees of control over the labourforce.

Crucially, through the provision of this credit, labour discipline is not only interlocked across multiple markets, but it is also anchored to both reams of production and reproduction. This point is not explored in any depth by the literature on interlocking, as much of it *de-facto* conflates reproduction with the labouring experience. To some extent, it is true that for the working poor life is labour. However, reproduction always exceeds the labouring experience, even in settings characterized by extreme poverty. And in these settings, realms of reproduction are also crossed by relations of domination and subordination, which may coincide or not with those experienced through labour. Indeed, in some cases, the provision of advances in out-contracting networks may strengthen the hold of the contractor over the entire life of its labour. This said, in other cases, the relations of oppression already at work in the reproductive sphere may 'attach' some segments of the working poor and be simply strategically exploited by contractors, even without the need for credit provision. This is to say that processes of interlocking are always greatly facilitated and mediated by relations of domination playing across reproductive realms. However, the way in which this plays out cannot and should not be given for granted. Successful contractors are local patrons, who 'recruit' their subordinates in their direct neighbourhood and distinct kinship groups (Breman, 2013). They may find multiple different ways to benefit from their powerful position in (and their knowledge of) the local economy. Unsurprisingly, for instance, contractors generally adopt a fairly distinct strategy when it comes to the recruitment of men and women in their networks. For women, what Maria Mies (1982) defined as 'housewifization' already sets the boundary of their incorporation into the contracting employment ladder. In fact, as already discussed, gender norms construct a system of social unfreedom that

---

[60] The actual number of circular migrants in India is unknown. According to some estimates, they are at least 100 million (Deshingkar and Farringdon, 2009; Breman, 2010).

may make economic attachment redundant and unnecessary. Attachment, like debt, is always 'socially regulated' (see Guerin *et al.*, 2013).

Ultimately, in contracting networks interlocking works across three distinct fronts: across credit and labour markets, and across reproduction. This does not manifest in a contraposition between economic and extra-economic or 'customary' relations (see Bernstein's critique of Berry, 2004), but rather in a process of interplay between them. The outcomes of these processes are fluid and multiple, and depend upon contractors' ability to interlock as well as by the position of his subordinates within the socio-economic and reproductive ladder. Let us now analyze how these processes unfold in Bareilly, and how they reproduce distinct patterns of dependence and precariousness for different categories of workers there. The analysis of Bareilly allows for an in-depth exploration of the mechanisms through which exploitation takes place in the peripheral segments of composite sweatshop regimes. In short, it allows us to explore the very bottom of that 'joint enterprise' called sweatshop.

Bareilly, the Epicentre of a 'Global Village'

When buyers place their garment orders with suppliers based in urban industrial areas, they may claim they expect the order to remain in and around those areas, rather than travelling to peri-urban enclaves, small towns and villages around them. Many buyers sourcing from India have claimed so several times in the last decade; every time a hidden centre of home-based exploitation was discovered. For instance, the UK-based global retailer Primark, which in 2008 was named and shamed by a Panorama documentary broadcasted by the BBC (and fought hard to discredit the leading journalist), publicly swore it had no idea that some of the garments that were to carry its logo were manufactured in micro units in Tamil Nadu, where Sri Lankan refugees were employed.[61] However, the fact that Indian rural industries and homes have always been central to the globalization process is a truth already uncovered by Maria Mies (1982), in her seminal study on the lacemakers of Narsapur. Today, four decades after Mies' study, and with the exponential rise and establishment of fast fashion models of consumption in the West and in a number of emerging economies, these rural industries and homes

---

[61] The controversy generated by the documentary engaged both Primark and the BBC in a 3-year investigation, at the end of which Dan McDougall was found responsible for 'fabricating' footage. Notably, the accusation of fabrication referred to 45-seconds footage in the whole documentary that showed child labour. See The Telegraph (2011) and The Guardian (2011). See also Greenslade (2011).

are becoming more and more central to accumulation in the global garment industry. Besides, small town industrialization always played a crucial role in the making of 'Global' India (Harriss-White, 2003).[62]

The Indian garment mall needs dozens and dozens of Narsapurs, particularly in its northern floors, dedicated to highly embellished garment collections. In Northern India, Bareilly, a district in UP, is composed of many peri-urban enclaves and villages that traditionally specialize in embroidery. In particular, they specialize in *adda* work, which, as we have seen in Chapter 2, is crucial to the NCR garment product cycle. Therefore, Bareilly town, situated at 250 km from Delhi, has emerged as a key embroidery satellite centre for the NCR, thanks to its endless reservoirs of *adda* looms and hands. The urban–rural corridor running from the NCR to Bareilly and its surroundings is always busy. It can be crossed by road, either by bus or car, or also by train, as an increasing number of railway lines contribute to the intensification of exchange of goods and people between the NCR and the small UP town. Exchange is at the heart of the Bareilly economy. Despite its small size, the town's central market, *Bara Bazaar* (literally 'Big Market'), is quite famous, also thanks to the classic Hindi movie *Mera Saaya*, and its famous Hindi song, which narrates the story of a woman who loses her earring in the bazaar, following a spat with her lover.[63] Many stalls in the *Bara Bazaar* display some of Bareilly's key traditional crafts. One is bamboo furniture, for which the centre is renowned across India. The other is *adda* work, also locally known as *zari*. Many residents increasingly call Bareilly the *zari* town.

In fact, Bareilly is known for at least two types of embroidery work, carried out by Muslim communities. One, the oldest according to many artisans and merchants, is *zardosi* that traditionally involves the use of silk and silver thread. Its cost is considerable, and it is today practiced by a shrinking number of highly skilled artisans. Field findings reveal that the local merchants involved in the production and circulation of *zardosi* work often target the niche markets for religious articrafts, like cushions, tapestries or ropes worn by the clergy. Apparently, a booming market for these traditional Muslim articrafts is Israel, whose traders purchase *zardosi* goods for synagogues. The other type of embroidery work, widely available and practiced, considered a far simpler version of *zardosi* is *zari* – our

---

[62] In fact, this is also true in broader historical terms. See Haynes (2012) on 'Small Town Capitalism in Western India'.

[63] The name of the song is *Jumka gira re* (literally 'I have lost an earring').

adda work, also colloquially referred to as *hari*.[64] This is quite differentiated, entailing both simple and more complex designs realized with common threads.

The process of diversification of *adda* work started taking momentum in the 1980s. Until then, locally, *adda* work was practiced primarily to embroider *sarees, salwars* and *kurtas,* India's traditional clothing items. By the 1980s, however, the readymade garment export boom in northern garment clusters provided new avenues and business opportunities linked to the craft. According to many NCR exporters, this was the period when Bareilly started being 'discovered' as a key place to decentralise embroidery activities linked to export production. The export boom of the NCR, in particular, determined a rapid expansion of Bareilly's *adda* production, and resulted in the exponential growth of many 'newly made' artisans. In fact, while some exported garments did still require fairly intricate designs, hence placing a premium on high skills, others only needed simple work, which could be carried out by many 'neophytes' at the craft. From the 1980s onwards, together with the number of artisans, also the number of local labour contractors organizing the craft rose massively. Indeed, today, the *zari* town is also a town of *thekedaars*. As it happens in many of the myriad of artisanal clusters scattered across India's small towns and rural areas, the hierarchy of production is well known by people living around.[65] In any given neighbourhood where *adda* is going on, every auto-rickshawalla (driver) or tea staller knows who is the main local contractor. In fact, many, especially in peripheral neighbourhoods and enclaves, are *adda* subcontractors; that is, to say that they are already a secondary, subordinate contracting layer. Contrary to direct contractors, they have no access to final markets, either exporters or domestic traders. Their final market is the direct contractor himself, whom they work for.

In Bareilly, contracting agents share a common background and social profile in at least two respects. Almost all contractors – as well as subcontractors – belong to local Muslim communities. To an extent, this may be considered unsurprising, as *adda* is a traditional Muslim craft. However, in India, in many cases, those appropriating the labour of Muslim communities as well as that of lower castes are representatives of Hindu trading communities. In Bareilly's *adda* business, instead, both capital and labour share a relatively

---

[64] The terms are used interchangeably, although the analysis will mainly use the term 'adda work', as this is how the craft is also known in the NCR.

[65] A list of artisanal clusters in India appears on the website of the Development Commissioner for Micro, Small and Medium Enterprises (DCMSME, 2015).

common social fabric. This said, intra-community caste distinctions, too often concealed in discussions on Muslims in India, do apply. Field findings reveal that low-caste Muslims, like *Ansaris*, are greatly over-represented among labourers (see also Unni and Scaria, 2009). Upper Muslim castes like *Khans* or *Sheikhs*, instead, are only partially over-represented among contractors. This is to say that while some from the poorest local communities have experienced some degrees of social mobility, informal elites have hardly experienced any fall in their more privileged position.

Notwithstanding the relevance of intra-community distinctions, all contractors seem to have gone through the process of learning *adda* work. The majority of contractors interviewed in Bareilly report to have sat in front of a loom. They learnt the craft as children, and slowly moved up the ladder, with different degrees of success. They managed to obtain initial credit to start their business in multiple ways, but all linked to the family and neighbourhood economy. Some relied on their family to gather some savings; others used the help of the *thekedaar* they worked for initially. Some simply inherited the *adda* business from their family, or used family loans to start-up a unit. Contractors' life histories reveal the different social profile and background of their families. Contractors' family members were engaged in a variety of petty government jobs, construction work or farming. However, in all cases, contractors identified one relative, neighbour or close friend engaged in *adda* work, who introduced them to the secrets of the business.

While contractors' life histories may also suggest relative ease of entry and/or upper social mobility, this narrative should be challenged on at least two grounds. First, high social mobility characterized the boom period of the 1980s and 1990s when export orders flocked into town uninterruptedly. Today, instead, orders go by fits and starts, subject to the volatility of export markets, the many sweatshop scandals and the multiplication of financial crises. The global financial crisis of 2009 has ruined several contractors, particularly the smallest ones or those not strongly linked to the most reliable among Northern India garment exporters. However, it has also significantly enriched the largest contractors, wiping out local competition. Second, one should not forget that contractors are a highly diversified category. If it may still be possible for newcomers to access smaller contracting (or subcontracting) networks, it is indeed much harder to compete with established, larger contractors, those commanding the most significant and lucrative export orders. In fact, for large contractors, diversification is key to distinguish between proper businessmen and 'small fellows'. As powerfully spelt by a large contractor,

Baba Ansari, who works for many NCR and Jaipur exporters, the difference is considerable:

> 'Most people who claim to be *thekedaars* are actually labourers only. A *thekedaar* is one who does the management. Suppose we make a sample today on our *adda* here. After getting it ready, if we get the items prepared from 25 different people then who is the owner? *Bahin* (sister), I am the one who is getting orders and giving them further ahead. I am the one who is providing everything, payment, money, cloth materials! (...) All is mine (...). I am a *thekedaar*, and this will be accepted by the party working above me; but how can a small fellow be a *thekedaar*? (...) A *thekedaar* is someone who gets the work done from 100–400 people sitting beneath him. A person who gets work done from 2–4 people can't be a *thekedaar*.'

Indeed, Baba Ansari is right in stressing the multiple contracting layers and hierarchies at work in Bareilly. These host a vast pool of different actors and articulate across different production realms and spaces of work. Only leading contractors handle the entire system, as orchestra leaders, as they sit at the very top of the production network and its many echelons. Subcontractors help further enlarging the reserve army of labour that contractors can rely on. In fact, this reserve army is hardly the undifferentiated mass of workers who can easily move across sectors and jobs pictured by many classical and neoclassical economics accounts. It is highly segmented, differentiated and crossed by multiple social divisions, which provide it with differential mobility and access to work. However, let us first provide a full sketch of the functioning mechanisms of Bareilly contracting networks, starting from its masters, before moving the analysis all the way down to its subjects.

Large, *direct* contractors, that are those with access to final markets, generally own at least one *karkhana*, where they employ several artisans as informal wageworkers. The *karkhana* can be a physical, walled space, or simply a space of labour, like a spot on a street or in someone's home, where artisans gather to work for the contractor. The unit is often deployed for sampling purposes, design or checking, so that the artisans employed are generally highly skilled. The bulk of production is decentralized to subcontractors. The number of subcontractors handled by the contractor varies with the size of the contracting business. Some large direct contractors, albeit not all, also directly employ artisans working from their own dwelling. There are two types of home-based artisans. One type is represented by those artisans part of a full household unit, effectively a sort of family micro business that in India tends to be classified as self-employment or 'own-account' work. However, in this case, as in many others, it performs the role of disguised wage labour, as it lacks the autonomy necessary to develop proper entrepreneurial traits (see Breman, 1999). The second type is represented by individual home-workers sweating in their own dwelling, while other family members engage instead in other types of work. Hence, overall, Bareilly's *adda* contracting networks work through three different relations of proletarianization (Mezzadri, 2014a), and rely on three different types of labourers: informal, hired wageworkers (in real, or 'imagined' units); own-account, family workers (in households fully dedicated to *adda* work) and individual home-workers (in households where members engage in other types of work). Hired wageworkers are generally male. In family units, the work is organized by the husband and then distributed among household members. Women participate in family labour in different ways but always based on a harsh 'patriarchal bargain' (Kandiyoti, 1988), as secondary workers or 'helpers'. Individual home-workers are predominantly women (see also Unni and Scaria, 2009).

The organizational solutions adopted by the contractor also depend upon market segments. In fact, large direct contractors who work for high-end export production, and are linked to exporters working for well-known global buyers rarely employ home-based labour directly. Direct contractors working for smaller exporters, buyers and/or domestic producers instead do, especially when they cater to low-end markets. Notably, large contractors working for established exporters and renowned buyers may command extra *adda* units in Delhi, to deal with 'urgent' (or simply smaller) orders, or sampling (see also Mezzadri, 2008). When they do, they organize a flow of *adda* workers who circulate between Bareilly and Delhi. Artisans – all male, and generally quite young – leave in groups of 15 or 20, from the same village or neighbourhood. They arrive in the metropolitan area without their family and stay in Delhi for several months before going back, leaving the room to others who will replace them, from another neighbourhood or village. This politics of 'moving neighbourhoods' is crucial for the contractor, who can plan his labour inflows and outflows carefully. These artisans on the move are part of the million under-reported circular migrants of India.

If direct contractors may or may not directly employ home-based labour, subcontractors always do. In fact, their primary role is to reach out for less visible reservoirs of labour, often based in their own immediate geographical reach and local sphere of influence. Subcontractors have their own *karkhane*, and 'their' households and homes, and they manage them in ways that vary based on the orders and different market segments. While many contractors proudly boast about their 'exclusive' relation with their subcontractors (as Ansari does in the quote above), the latter often work for several parties. This is crucial to reduce risks and dependency on a single work provider, particularly during lean season. Also, many households may work for multiple parties; the diversification of livelihoods is crucial for those families who are fully dependent upon *adda* work for survival. However, their direct employers or managers are generally based in their same local area, as relations of production are fully embedded into the broader spectrum of social relations dominating artisans' everyday lives.

The complex networks of contractors and subcontractors sketched above unfold with a distinct spatiality, which stretches across urban- and peri-urban neighbourhoods and enclaves, also reaching many far away villages in the Bareilly district. A similar spatial reach may be found in other embroidery clusters, like the one centred in Lucknow, described by Wilkinson-Weber (1999). Production concentrates with particular density in the areas of Jagatpur, Nevada Shekan, Fike (or Fique) Enclave and Soofi Tola, in Bareilly town; in the peri-urban enclaves of Bindolia, Hararpur, Partapur and Partapur Jivan Sahai; and in the villages of Richola, Faridpur and Taha. By 2012, it was reaching the borders of the Philibit district (Figure 5.1). In each neighbourhood, enclave or village one finds a precise *adda* hierarchy; namely, a few leading contractors and/or subcontractors and a pool of labourers scattered in *karkhane*, family units and homes. This geography of production is fully embedded in local relations of domination also crossing the reproductive sphere. Locally, leading contractors are the main (or sole) employers in the *adda* colony. They often own the largest *karkhane*. In Taha, this is simply a space of work in the middle of a road, in front of the house of the leading local contractor, who can therefore watch over 'his' workers as he pleases. In the more distant neighbourhoods, enclave and villages, leading contractors may have their own subcontractors, or they may themselves be incorporated into broader contracting circuits starting from Bareilly town. Here, one can appreciate the extent of the control the contractor is able to exercise on 'his' subjects. In fact, he can enter and exit artisans' homes as he wishes. After all, these are homes he 'commands', and his control over them extends well beyond labouring time. In these highly informalized settings, there is hardly any separation between public and private sphere, and the contractor is generally able to extend his influence on both. Indeed, he often appeals to kinship or perceived kinship-based social hierarchies and relations. Many artisans may use familial appellatives to refer to

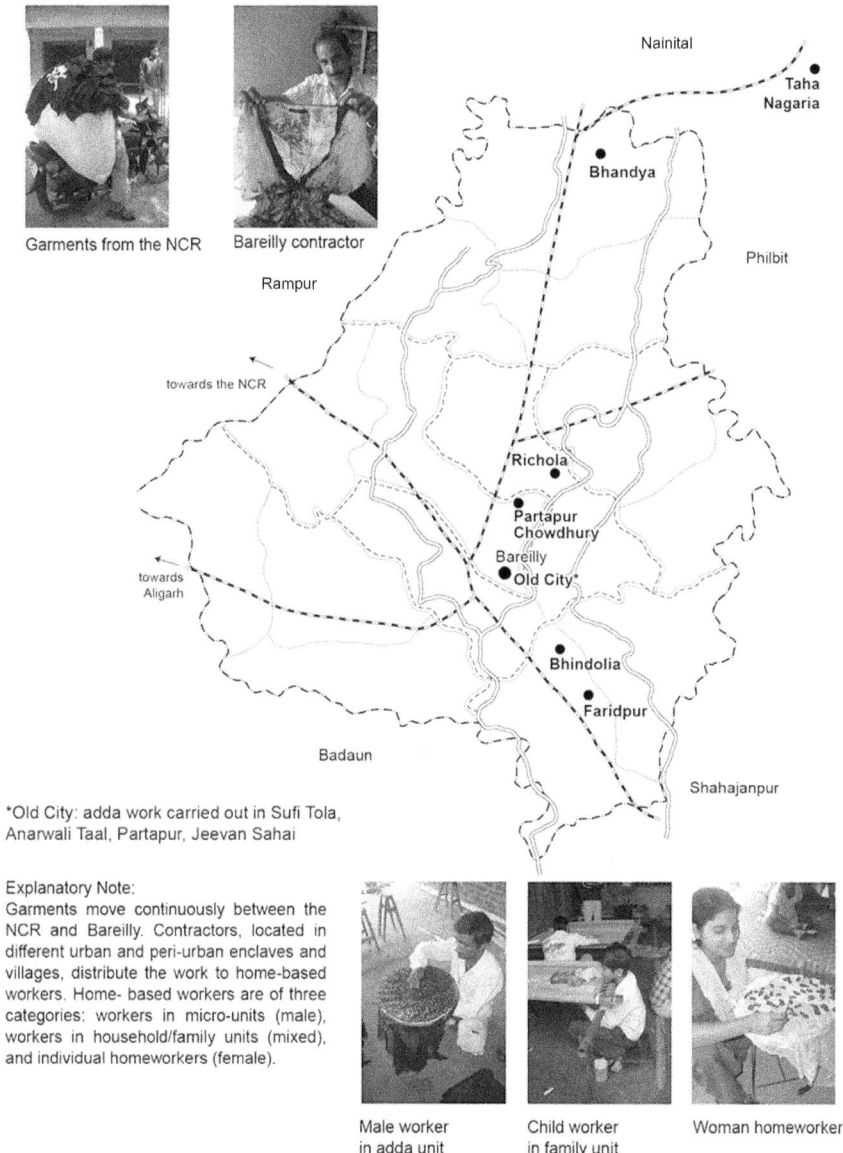

*Old City: adda work carried out in Sufi Tola, Anarwali Taal, Partapur, Jeevan Sahai

Explanatory Note:
Garments move continuously between the NCR and Bareilly. Contractors, located in different urban and peri-urban enclaves and villages, distribute the work to home-based workers. Home- based workers are of three categories: workers in micro-units (male), workers in household/family units (mixed), and individual homeworkers (female).

Garments from the NCR   Bareilly contractor

Male worker in adda unit   Child worker in family unit   Woman homeworker

Figure 5.1 Bareilly: The spread of adda work across the 'global village'

Source: Author's adaptation of the map provided by the Bareilly Development Industrial Unit Centre (execution by Edward Oliver)

him – obviously *chacha* (uncle) being the most common – although a *de-facto* blood tie may not exist. In many instances, artisans deploy these appellatives as a symbol of their subordination to the mechanisms of local patronage. The contracting hierarchy is so deeply embedded into local social structures of domination that business disputes may be resolved with the mediation of the local *Mukhiya*, who is the village headman (Mezzadri, 2014a).

Through the capillary organization analyzed here, *adda* work, decentralized from the NCR to Bareilly, is pushed further down, away from Bareilly town and towards more remote areas. By 2012, production stretched across the entire Bareilly district, which has indeed been turned into a 'global village'; a unique production conglomerate composed of myriads of tiny satellite sub-centres. This increasingly expanding geographical reach is intimately connected to the spread and evolution of export orders. The export boom has quite simply directly stretched the boundaries of production. While originally *adda* work mainly took place in Bareilly town, the rise in export orders has attracted countless new homes and hands into the orbit of export-based *adda* contracting networks. Moreover, with time, export has become increasingly volatile and risky for the contractors. In this sense, production has moved to many remote areas in order not only to find new reservoirs of labour but also to find new reservoirs of far *cheaper* labour. Here, contractors generally decentralize garments that need 'simpler' *adda* designs, and that can therefore be also embroidered by the newly made artisans scattered in more remote locations. Indeed, for the contractor, the socio-economic geography including Bareilly and surroundings is also a 'geography of skills', where different groups should be deployed for different tasks. However, skills are unsurprisingly socially constructed, and the rates paid by contractors mainly reflect opportunities and subordination. Village labourers, particularly women individual home-workers, generally perform simpler designs at cheaper rates. This said, they are not all necessarily less skilled than the many Bareilly-based male workers who manage to negotiate better deals with the contractor. Quite simply, at the very periphery of Bareilly's contracting hierarchy, and constrained by the practice of *purdah* (seclusion inside the household), these women have such limited alternative economic opportunities that the contractor can 'make' them into less skilled, cheaper workers.

The analysis above suggests that the core of *thekedaars'* business is based on the reproduction of highly diversified labour networks. However, it also suggests that this process hardly only entails intermediation. Notwithstanding the many different layers and hierarchies of contracting, the masters towering over this system engage in a vast array of activities, involving the tight organization of the overall network of sub-intermediaries; the organization of the labour process; and the provision of all necessary inputs (thread, cloth, breads, etc.) to subordinates. As artisans in Bareilly are indeed disguised forms of wage labour, subject to different relations of proletarianization, leading contractors represent disguised and informalized forms of capital. Intermediation, in this case, disguises a far more complex function contractors perform *vis-à-vis* processes of labour surplus extraction. Credit provision and payment systems are crucial to the reproduction of contractors' networks, as it is through them that contractors are able to attach – or, as we shall see, also eject – their many subordinates from their networks. The following section focuses on these aspects of the contracting relation.

The Unevenness of Economic and Reproductive Attachment

The great inequality and unevenness of the contracting enterprise is confirmed by the study of its payment systems, and of the role of credit within them. In order to ensure the reproduction of his labour networks, the contractor deploys different credit strategies. In general, one can say that he deploys advances to reproduce his dominant position in labour markets, through what is effectively a credit transaction. In fact, the advance interlocks the subordination of artisans to the contractor across multiple markets; namely, that of labour, and that of credit. Through the process of interlocking, the dominant position of the contractor is substantially reinforced. However, field findings reveal that the process of interlocking is highly uneven; specifically, the logics behind the provision of advances changes on the basis of different subordinates. For instance, the logics behind the provision of advances changes if these target subcontractors or labourers. Moreover, among labourers, some are effectively excluded from any access to credit.

The first type of advance found along contracting networks targets subcontractors. Advances to subcontractors are not necessarily regular, but fairly common, particularly in the context of time consuming or large orders. Wage rates are calculated on a piece rate basis that varies according to the complexity of the design and the time needed to complete it. Only once a rate is agreed with the subcontractor, the contractor provides the advance and production starts. In fact, in many cases, the ability to advance capital should be seen as one of the main differences between a contractor and a subcontractor. The subcontractor needs the advance in order to start the business, and in turn pay wages to labourers. Briefly, the advance is crucial to form the very platform necessary for the process of surplus extraction to become possible at all. Through the payment of the advance, the contractor draws the subcontractor into his business network, at least until the completion of the order. In some cases, the business relation between contractor and subcontractor is long-term and established, so that the subcontractor may work exclusively for that specific party. In this case, it is quite common for the contractor to refer to the *karkhana* of the subcontractor is if it was his own. This is because, as simply put by one of the contractors interviewed in Bareilly,

> If anybody is working only for you, then you must imagine that the karkhana is yours.

In other cases instead, the relation between contractor and subcontractors may be tenuous and not necessarily be of long-term. In this instance, the subcontractor will work for multiple parties, either openly or concealing his other business relations. In any case, he only needs to respect delivery times, rates and designs for each of the contracting arrangements. In domestic production, this type of less organized contracting networks dominate, while export tends to be based on more stable subcontracting relations, at the very least during peak season. However, the possibility for subcontractors to engage with multiple leading parties also depends upon their own size and their geographical location. In remote enclaves and villages, subcontractors may in fact have a very limited choice. Advances targeting subcontractors are clearly a form of productive investment, crucial to the very process of accumulation. They represent a clear indication of the enterprising nature of contracting.

A second type of advance, instead, targets labourers. Contractors can provide advances to the hired informal workers working in their own *karkhane*, as well as to households or home-workers. Also subcontractors may do the same. When asked about the practice, both groups of actors like to lament the great risks involved. In fact, labourers can technically escape with the money and may never come back. However, in practice, this is highly unlikely, as workers are severely disciplined by the tight social boundaries of the neighbourhood economy, where they live with their whole families. Escape would be a rather tricky business done at the expenses of those family members left behind, who may be left dealing with the contractor. The relations of attachment created by the advance may be considerably different from those shaped by older forms of debt bondage (see Breman, 1999). For instance, they hardly involve inter-generational obligations. Still, as local patrons, contractors may complicate the lives of the relatives of the 'fugitive' rather considerably. Notably, despite lamenting the risks involved, contractors stress the fact that the provision of advances to labourers is often a necessary practice to build 'trust' and to project themselves as worthy patrons. According to their narrative, if they are unable to provide advances, workers will move elsewhere, and find a contractor who can also act as a credit provider. However, this romanticized narrative centred on 'trust building' and reciprocity is considerably challenged by interviews and conversations with local labourers in Bareilly town and surroundings. Labourers hardly consider advances as that sort of 'labour right' contractors describe. Indeed, none of them has access to any type of formal credit provision. In this sense, for many the contractor represents the 'lender of last resort'. This said, not all of them can access advances, which are also often paid quite irregularly, and only based on contractors' strategic needs. Moreover, not all of them want to access them. In Bareilly, advance payments seem hardly embedded in relations of reciprocity. As underlined by David Graeber in his book *Debt* (2011, p. 121), 'During the time that debt remains unpaid, the logic of hierarchy takes hold'. This is largely incompatible with reciprocity.

Contractors generally are keen to provide advances to highly skilled workers, particularly those (all male) hired in their own *karkhane*. The contractor may benefit tremendously from attaching these workers to his network, as they are crucial to deal with more intricate and lucrative orders as well as samples. Flawless samples are crucial to obtain new orders from garment exporters. These are the workers contractors aspire to build 'trust' (read ties) with. Arguably, these workers know this all too well. Obviously, they remain highly subordinated in the context of the contracting networks; however, they are often the workers equipped with more options. Hence, they try their best not to accept advances; as if they do they know they will remain attached to the contractor until the advance is repaid, entering relations consistent with what Breman (1996, 2013) has described as 'neo-bondage'. During the entire period of attachment, they may be forced to accept lower rates for their work, a practice that effectively entails the presence of forms of disguised interest, not paid in money, but through the labouring service. Highly skilled male workers are also those who may choose to move to the NCR for short spells of migration. Interviews reveal that also in this case, as in the case of many other labouring activities (Breman, 2013; Srivastava, 2005; Deshingkar and Farrington, 2009), attachment and circulation are strongly intertwined. However, their relation may vary. Some workers move to the NCR to escape debt traps, and avoid accepting advances, which may temporarily curtail future wages. In the NCR, wages are substantially higher, and a few months work there can make a significant difference for workers' livelihoods. Some others instead move to the NCR to be able to repay advances, hence ending harsh relations of interlocking as soon as they can. This is to say that for the working poor, circulation may loosen or reinforce subordination, at once.

Advances are also offered more regularly to workers who work on more complex designs and need many days to embroider a batch of garments. These are order-based advances, and may also be offered to home-based workers. In particular, advances of this type are fairly common for households entirely dedicated to *adda* work, and who would otherwise starve. Field findings clearly indicate that contractors do not pay advances for simple designs, or for orders targeting low-end production. Cheaper peripheral workers at the margin of the global village generally work on these items. In many cases, these are also the poorest workers, those with less alternative employment opportunities. Moreover, they are generally women individual home-workers. Contractors hardly need to attach these workers via credit. Their remote geographical position and experience of patriarchy are already very potent devices at labour control. In this sense, these poor women home-workers are the least likely to be made 'unfree' via credit-based interlocking practices. However, this is only because they are already subject to patriarchal unfreedom, which reinforces their exploitation in labour markets.[66] Indeed, interlocking strategies not only play out across different markets, but they are also highly exclusionary and interplay with broader realms of social life.

The great unevenness of advances and the complex hierarchy of contracting work determine varying degrees of precariousness for labour in Bareilly. This unevenness is further reinforced by contractors' retention and expulsion strategies. These are a constant dilemma for the contractor, particularly if he works in export markets. These have become increasingly risky and insecure, since the financial crisis. Only few large contractors have long-term, export relations. The majority, instead, works under great uncertainty. Exporters not only represent huge profit opportunities for contractors but also possible ruin and bankruptcy. They may engage contractors in cutthroat competition; cheat them by placing the same orders with competitors, or reject impeccable and timely orders. Moreover, as contractors attach their subordinate and interlock them across multiple markets, in turn also

---

[66] In Lucknow, Wilkinson-Weber (1999) observes practices of payment retention targeting women home-workers engaged in less skilled type of embroidery (in this case, chikan work).

exporters may deploy credit as a way to attach contractors. They do so via payment retention rather than the provision of advances. By retaining payments, exporters turn contractors into subordinated agents within much wider production circuits; into a sort of 'bonded capital', which can be disposed of. In this instance, extremely common in global commodity chains and production networks, interlocking takes place across commodity and credit markets. Ultimately, as argued by Breman (1999), different forms of attachment may discipline both capital and labour in the informal economy.

Due to these increasing levels of risk, the contractor must 'own' a network that is flexible enough to allow for labour retention and expulsion to occur at the same time. The network must be stable enough so that production could immediately start once orders arrive. However, the same network must also ensure the easy expulsion of workers during lean season, and when orders dry up. This dual need is satisfied through the deployment of combinations of different typologies of labour, subject to a fairly different employment strategy. On the one hand, skilled workers, who represent the core of contractors' business, must be retained at all costs. In order to keep them busy throughout the year, during lean season many contractors engage in domestic production. Domestic markets are massively expanding in the subcontinent; they pay higher rates than export, although they only guarantee limited volumes. Export-based contractors increasingly deploy these markets as a safety net to minimize the risks of engaging in global markets. On the other hand, non-core workers, instead, must be expendable, and easily retrenched. This is why many contractors are increasing the composition of peripheral workers in their labour network, a practice that is further expanding the already porous boundaries of the global village, by pushing production towards the frontier with Uttarakhand.

The 'Home' of the Sweatshop Regime

At the very bottom of the sweatshop regime, a joint enterprise formed at multiple levels and scales, capitalist relations may appear in disguise. Indeed, labourers, who primarily work in home-based settings, in many instances may appear as self-employed, while performing functions consistent with wage labour. While this issue has already been partially discussed in Chapter 2, when discussing the architecture and the dual 'materiality' of the sweatshop regime, here the analysis has further dwelled into the mechanisms through which this process takes place in settings emerging as crucial reservoirs of peri-urban and rural labour for the sweatshop. On the one hand, the analysis has focused in depth on the ways in which petty commodity producers are made into wageworkers, an issue discussed by several scholars in other parts of the world and/or sectors (e.g. Bernstein, 2007; Oya, 2007; Rizzo, 2013). On the other hand, however, the analysis has also placed under the microscope those who organize this type of labour, namely labour contractors. In fact, in highly informalized settings, also their role and function may appear in disguise. Much less studied than workers, and generally clubbed into the undifferentiated category of 'intermediaries', labour contractors may instead perform functions that considerably exceed mere intermediation. They may participate in the making of the sweatshop regime as proper petty capitalists, rather than simply as mediators between capital and labour. Moreover, these contractors also participate in the making of the sweatshop regime by expanding its reach and its spatiality, effectively stretching commodity chains and production networks far beyond the main urban production nodes where garment production generally takes place. Labour contractors – at least the kind analyzed here, namely out-contractors – establish crucial corridors between urban, peri-urban and rural areas, effectively expanding the scope and trajectories of accumulation, and annihilating the fictitious divisions between 'global' and 'traditional' India and between industry and craft production. These actors work around the clock to bank from the tight articulation between these divides.

A traditional figure in India as well as in other part of the developing world, linked to the colonial enterprise and to the many guises of indenture labour (Roy, 2008, 2010; Kaur, 2014), today, in the context of the sweatshop regime, the labour contractor also performs, paradoxically, a very modern function. He disarticulates the management of production from that of labour; he participates in reproducing the segmentation of the production process and its polarization in core and ancillary activities, and he organizes parts of the production process in full. Most of all, he further develops commodity chains and production networks whose flexibility is inexorably centred on making labour cheap across an increasing variety of spaces of work and realms of production. Today, this contractor is hardly only a remnant of a traditional past, but rather also an agent of a neoliberal future, no less than the myriads of head-hunting agencies increasingly crowding our supposedly more 'formalized' labour markets. He is the broker as well as the entrepreneur of contemporary working poverty.

Towering over huge reservoirs of home-based units and micro units, labour contractors strengthen their domination over the lowest echelons of the working poor producing our clothes by interlocking subordinates across different markets and across markets and broader realms of reproduction. They deploy credit – advances in particular – to carefully reproduce labour networks. Their domination through advances successfully subjugates both those who access credit and those who do not, as already attached to contracting relations by other structures of oppression at work in the reproductive sphere. In this sense, contractors crucially contribute to the reproduction of the sweatshop regime as based on and crossed by multiple differences and 'unfreedoms'. In Bareilly, the contractual 'unfreedom' of the male worker hired in a *karkhana* and circulating between his enclave or village and Delhi to pay back advances co-exists with the social 'unfreedom' of the woman home worker at the periphery of the global village, who is 'attached' to the contracting network by harsh patriarchal relations who block her within the thick walls of the household.

Notably, contractors also participate in strengthening the correspondence between the physical and social materiality of production across given sweatshop regimes. On the one hand, through the work of the contactor, also at the very bottom of sweatshop regimes characterized by a strong presence of non-factory labour different labouring bodies are subject to the uneven and unequal process of distribution of different activities and tasks. These activities and tasks are distributed based on workers' 'skills', may these be real or perceived, due to their social profile. As the analysis has shown, in Bareilly, different embroidery designs are unevenly distributed to different labourers placed across the different echelons of the global village. On the other hand, in the case under scrutiny, the availability of the huge non-factory, home-based sector handled by the contractor also strengthens regional patterns of specialization banking on artisanal work. Bareilly, in this light, crucially adds to the ability of the NCR to remain a key centre for ladieswear, embellished production.

Arguably, placing contracting networks under the microscope, a number of over-simplistic policy recommendations appear as quite problematic. Recently, and again linked to the many sweatshop scandals the garment industry has faced, one of these recommendations has focused on 'cutting the middleman'. However, this is hardly an easy option in contracting networks like the one characterizing the Bareilly embroidery sector. This is because these supposed 'middlemen' are in fact petty capitalists; employers, rather than mere intermediaries. Severing the ties between the NCR and satellite ancillary centres like Bareilly can hardly be depicted as a progressive, pro-labour policy, as it would simply increase the already significant patterns of unemployment or underemployment many home-based workers face in peri-urban and rural areas. In fact, unemployment and underemployment have emerged as one of the key problems faced by labourers in many non-factory-based realms of production across the entire NCR and beyond (Mezzadri and Srivastava, 2015).

Overall, the analysis carried out so far and based on a complex empirical journey across the many export-oriented garment-producing areas of India – the NCR, Ludhiana, Jaipur, Kolkata, Chennai, Bangalore, Tiruppur and Mumbai – have managed to unveil the architecture of the sweatshop, its regional variations, its patterns of labour control and the multiple sets of power relations at the basis of its reproduction. It has highlighted the strong relation between processes of production and circulation, shaping both the external and internal social boundaries of different sweatshop regimes, which can therefore be characterized as a complex joint enterprise. Adding to this, the extension of our empirical journey to Bareilly, a key satellite centre for one of the main garment-producing areas, the NCR, has allowed us to further appreciate the complexity of this joint enterprise, and to better grasp the multiple layers of contracting blurring the separation between industrial and traditional garment activities and tasks, and producing different degrees of precariousness experienced by different labouring bodies. Ultimately, so far the analysis has shown that the sweatshop is better characterised as a regime because it entails a multiplicity of capital–labour relations where power, social differences, subordination and unfreedom appear in combinations that are as varied as the many seams of the clothes we wear. In the next chapter, the analysis will add a final layer to the complex picture drawn so far, by shifting the emphasis to the impact of the labouring experience on the bodies of the different garment 'classes of labour'. In this sense, the sweatshop will finally also appear as an unforgivingly depleting regime, able to consume workers' bodies in many different ways before expelling them, exhausted, in its endless quest to find new recruits.

6 | The Body and the Sweatshop

> If we allow the politics of health to do no more than follow the shifting
> effects of the structural contradictions in the labour-reserve system ...
> then, indeed, we do no more than accept the boundaries of suffering.
>
> (O'Laughlin, 2013, p. 194)

Poor Health, Lack of Safety: The Depletion of the Labouring Body Inside the Sweatshop

The labouring body is always central to the production and reproduction of the garment sweatshop. Indeed, as a regime based on interplays between physical and social materiality, crossed by multiple forms of difference and unfreedom and shaped by the joint work of many global and regional masters, the sweatshop provides a price tag to workers' bodies no less than to the many garment commodities it continuously churns out. It assigns these bodies to different segments of the product cycle. It orders them on a complex employment ladder, where, as illustrated in this analysis, wages, entitlements, rewards and duties are greatly socially regimented. Effectively, the sweatshop nurtures processes of labour fragmentation also through a capillary 'body-politics', aimed at commodifying as well as exploiting each and every social feature of workers' distinct corporality. In this sense, the body of workers emerges as the primary 'raw material' to be deployed in sweatshops to achieve and reproduce sources of comparative advantage.

Arguably, however, in this process the body is also the primary raw material *depleted* by the sweatshop, consumed as bolts of cloth or bundles of thread going through a stitching machine. Undoubtedly, the devastating effects the sweatshop may have on workers' bodies have been all too clearly shown by the Rana Plaza disaster of 2013. In fact, this entailed the destruction of over a thousand of these bodies – trapped, broken, burnt to ashes, gone in a few moments. The broadcasted images of torn up garments and wreckages of stitching machinery scattered across the ground zero of the industrial disaster only provided a pale if already painful glimpse into the far more sinister and heart-breaking reality of all the lives lost in the collapse. As chillingly described by Jeremy Seabrook (2015, p. 21) in his *Song of the Shirt*, the bodies of the workers recovered and laid out one after the other in front of the ruins "stretched hundreds of meters in the dust and debris".

The magnitude of the Rana Plaza horror finally brought a considerable degree of attention on the potentially greatly violent nature of the sweatshop, and on the unacceptably high social costs of current models of consumerism. Unsurprisingly, the case triggered a huge upsurge in national and international campaigning in favour of Bangladeshi garment workers, and many buyers, under huge public pressure, 'agreed' to compensate their 'fashion victims' and their families. Two international agreements were immediately elaborated to prevent another Rana Plaza from ever happening again. The first was the EU retailers-led Accord on Fire and Building Safety in Bangladesh (Kumar and Mahoney, 2014, p. 203). The second, a weaker, US retailers-led counterpart of the Accord, is the Alliance for Bangladesh Worker Safety, which remains voluntary even once signed (Gunther, 2013). Serious campaigning was also paralleled by more controversial forms of what Richey and Ponte (2011) would call 'Brand-Aid', with celebrities racing to wear T-shirts inside out for 'Fashion Revolution Day', under the widely popularized slogan 'it is what is inside that counts' (see Jacob, 2014 in *Metro*; and Khatun, 2014, in *The Huffington Post*).

However, despite the great public uproar and attention triggered by the event, to what extent are the bodies of garment workers worldwide much safer today, 2 years after Rana Plaza? Not substantially. First, with time, the Rana Plaza disaster seems to have been slowly reconceptualized as a sort of 'exceptional' event, an unpredictable disastrous outcome, and one mainly concerning Bangladesh, despite the fact that, as argued in Chapter 1, other sweatshop scandals and 'minor' tragedies have continued hitting the industry. As expressly noted by the CSR regional manager of a world renowned American brand, whom I interviewed in Delhi 2 days before the Rana Plaza collapse, garment production in the country was always undermined by significant 'infrastructural problems', although ironically, he reported these as 'improving' at the time. Needless to say, one can be sure that he, like many others, soon wished his company never sourced from Bangladesh in the first place. Second, current debates on health and safety seem to increasingly focus on infrastructure and on avoiding factory collapses – briefly, they seem to focus on the rather modest agenda of keeping workers alive. This weak approach is marred by at least two problems. On the one hand, by reinforcing ideas of exceptionality, it risks representing infrastructural issues as delinked from the overall labour conditions and relations in the sector, which instead, are greatly exploitative as a whole, and not only in Bangladesh. On the other hand, this approach is hardly sufficient to take into consideration all the different ways in which garment work depletes the bodies of workers. Even in the absence of major so-called disasters, garment work has profound implications for the health and wellbeing of workers. It imposes a slow but inexorable tax on their labouring bodies, and, once it has absorbed their working potential and consumed them as a source of competitiveness, it simply discards them like a sort of 'human waste'. This is especially true where large reserve armies of labour are available, like across the Indian garment mall, which can still massively benefit from slack labour markets, and the millions and millions of informalized workers composing the great majority of India's labourforce (again, see the estimates in NCEUS, 2007, and WTO and ILO, 2009). In these contexts, in fact, capital can consume workers' bodies without major concerns for profitability. After all, upon the depletion of some, others can be made available at the same cheap rates. The production of cheap labour, as this analysis has shown, is all but an easy endeavour. However, the same analysis has also shown that it is an endeavour successfully realized through complex but systemic processes of labour subjugation at work across India's sweatshop regime.

Building on this analysis, but also drawing from the work of Bridget O'Laughlin (2010, 2013) on the production of affliction, and Silvia Federici's (2004, 2012) insights on the 'making' of the body under capitalism, the following sections further develop these arguments. Then, they analyze the ways in which the sweatshop regime at work in India systematically promotes processes of depletion of workers' bodies, across both factory and non-factory settings. For this scope, the analysis will discuss evidence on wages, working rhythms, labour circulation, occupational safety and daily reproduction as reported by garment workers in the NCR. Before discussing the empirical evidence, the analysis also returns to and expands on a critique of international labour standards, which are not only largely irrelevant in systematically addressing the reality of the sweatshop and its severe impact on workers' health and livelihoods, but, in many cases, also greatly participate in 'dumping' health and safety responsibilities onto workers themselves. This point is illustrated by making reference to recent CSR and/or ethical trade projects, in the NCR and Bareilly.

The 'Unexceptional' Production of Disasters and the Externalization of Reproduction

Despite attempts to represent Rana Plaza as a tragically, 'exceptional' case of infrastructural failure, the garment industry is hardly new to death and destruction. In fact, comparing the Dhaka events with those that unfolded in 1911 in New York City, when the Triangle Shirtwaist factory fire consumed the bodies of over one hundred workers, one finds chilling similarities. The first is obviously the social profile of those at work in the factory and who lost their lives to the sweatshop. The Triangle Shirtwaist factory was crowded with young immigrant women, Jewish and Italian in particular, in the same way in which Rana Plaza hosted hoards of first-generation industrial workers, mainly young female migrants labouring to escape the hardship of rural poverty. The second similarity concerns instead the modality with which the events unfolded. In both cases, in fact, and despite a time lapse of over 100 years, garment workers were locked into the industrial premises, and could not escape as the fire and collapse started. This is to say that in both these cases of supposed industrial 'infrastructural failure', although sharply separated in time and space, the terrible social costs paid were first and foremost the outcome of the specific social practices enforced on the shop-floor, and of the regime of discipline and control imposed on garment workers. In New York, as in Bangladesh, the shop-floor was organized in ways that entailed long shifts, during which it was simply standard practice to lock workers inside the industrial premises. In India, interviews with employers reveal how this practice, fairly common across sweatshops worldwide, may respond to different aims, like forcing workers to finish their shift; ensuring they do not steal anything; concealing overtime from labour inspectors or 'protecting' workers – mainly women in this case, whose work is subject to patriarchal, paternalistic control (e.g. Kabeer, 2000; Caraway, 2005; Wright, 2006; Ruwanpura, 2011) – against unspecified threats they may face outside the factory gates. Whatever the (many) justifications provided, in factories, garment workers are often literally stuck at their workstation until employers and/or supervisors decide it is time to stop production and go home. Arguably, practices effectively bounding workers to their space of work represent yet another of the many different forms of unfreedom at work in the industry.

Overall, infrastructural failure in the garment industry always had clear social connotations. It was always rendered more lethal by the harshness of the sweatshop regime. In fact, one could argue that it has always been part and parcel of such regime. And once the poor health and safety record of the garment industry is considered as yet another defining aspect of the sweatshop regime, events like Rana Plaza stop appearing as 'exceptional' moments of rupture in the otherwise linear, positive development of industrial relations in the sector. They simply epitomize, if tragically, what having a garment job – precarious, informalized, poorly paid and unsafe – may entail. Dying is by all means a possible option when employed in the sweatshop.

Overall, processes of labour informalization are generally accompanied by a fall in health and safety provisions. For instance, it is amply documented how these processes often severely constrain access to health services, particularly for the most vulnerable categories of workers, like migrants, ethnic minorities and obviously women (Gideon, 2007; see also Dreze and Sen, 2014). In fact, even in the absence of major catastrophic events, labouring in a sweatshop also entail multiple, 'minor' forms of sickness and injuries; a sort of low-intensity epidemic engaged in a systematic and relentless attack on the labouring body. Admittedly, this is true for garment work as well as for many other labour-intensive jobs (e.g. Chan *et al.*, 2014 on the automotive industry). As vividly reported by Tansy Hoskins (2014, p. 68) in her *Stitched Up: The Anti-Capitalist Book of Fashion*, 'in the Pearl River Delta, 40,000 fingers are severed each year in work-related accidents'. Undoubtedly, also work-related injuries and illnesses, as already factory fires and collapses, should be understood in relation to the overall social relations and labour practices at work in the industry. They illustrate how given patterns of accumulation may wage a proper war on the labouring body, and how the development of capitalism may imply a complete disregard for the social reproduction of the workforce, at least in the absence of a serious threat to profitability and – even more crucially – in the absence of legal limits to exploitation. As noted by Karl Marx himself (1990, p. 381) "Capital…takes no account of the health and the length of life of the worker, unless society forces it to do so". If left unchecked, capital's power can consume the workforce to its death, devouring 'its physical strength, mental development, and ability to live' (Marx, 1855, in Anderson, 2010, p. 18).[67]

Building on Marxist insights and reflecting on what she defines as the 'production of affliction' in Southern Africa, Bridget O'Laughlin (2013) convincingly shows that poor health outcomes – while obviously reflecting lack of access to formal health provisioning – are first and foremost produced by the conditions of labour. In particular, these outcomes are produced by capital's struggle

---

[67] Neveling (2017), for instance, highlights how this has always been the case in EPZs, since their early origins.

'to externalize responsibility for the reproduction of its workers' (O'Laughlin, 2013, p. 175). The spread of various forms of disease afflicting the working poor during both colonial and post-colonial times can only be fully understood in relation to the specific moments of capital accumulation in the region, and their manifestation in the establishment of specific labour regimes. In her thorough analysis, O'Laughlin highlights how the spread of tuberculosis in the first decades of the twenty-first century in South Africa was due to the organization of mine labour, and particularly to the system of labour recruitment at work. By the same token, the rise and rapid spread of malaria across Swazi sugar estates was strongly connected to the use of casual workers from non-infested areas. This strategy aimed at expanding the reserve army of labour while fragmenting the workforce, hence ensuring the minimization of costs and potential labour troubles. Along similar lines, again, the development of Konzo paralysis in Mozambique was triggered by excessive consumption of unprocessed or poorly processed cassava, introduced as a staple food to cheapen the cost of social reproduction of the labourforce in the rising textile sector. According to O'Laughlin, even the current spread of HIV-AIDS in post-apartheid South Africa should be understood in relation to the shifts in the movement of migrant labour and its new flexible living arrangements. In order to understand this pandemic, there is the need to stress its 'bio-social' dimension (O'Laughlin, 2015). Indeed, in all cases, health outcomes appear as inextricably linked to processes of accumulation, and the social relations of production they entailed. They should not be considered as isolated, disastrous – or 'exceptional' – moments in the history of the region (see also O'Laughlin, 2010).

Obviously, by stressing health and safety 'failures' as directly connected to specific processes of capital accumulation, one also indirectly questions the core assumptions of modernizing ideas celebrating instead what Marx, in the *Grundrisse*, defined as the 'civilizing influence' of capital (see Federici, 2004). Arguably, it is exactly based on a fetishization of such modernizing ideas that simplistic conceptualizations in 'praise' of cheap labour as a first, unfortunate but temporary stage of industrial development still persist (see Cawthorne and Kitching, 2001). Today, this process of fetishization also influences other debates, like for instance the one on 'land grabbing', represented by stagist, hyper-modernizing scholarship as potentially beneficial despite counter-evidence suggesting their potentially catastrophic effects (see McMichael, 2012).

Stagist narratives seem to always propose the same mantra, and one largely based on the highly problematic assumption that taking from the poor will eventually be good for the poor in the 'long-run', an issue we shall discuss in the conclusions of this book. On the contrary, focusing on the effects of the 'influence' of capital on the labouring body, the picture emerging is all but rosy. The feminist literature, in particular, has contributed greatly to this debate. As argued by Silvia Federici (2004), the establishment of the capitalist relation is hardly only a revolution as a production technique, that is, in relation to the structuring of a specific labour process. It is also a revolution for the body itself, which is submitted to an external 'order' (Federici, 2004, p. 135). In fact, the first hurdle for capital is the creation of individuals that are 'willing' – that is forced by their need of survival – to work for a wage. This involves a process of transformation of the body into the mere 'container' of labour power. In this sense, 'the human body, and not the steam engine, and not even the clock, was the first machine developed by capitalism' (Federici, 2004, p. 146). Notably, the body does react to this submission to the capitalist order and the process of alienation it implies, particularly when such order involves particularly harsh rhythms. At given working rhythms, the process of extraction of labour power from its 'container' – the body – is an overly debilitating experience, that can produce extreme reactions and even be confused or compared with possession by evil spirits or by the devil itself, as the work of anthropologists like Michael Taussig (1980) or Aiwa Ong (1988) has shown. In this light, sickness, injuries and exhaustion epitomize, at once, the attack by capital against the labouring body as well as the rejection of the capitalist order by the body itself; its ultimate attempt to escape the dictatorship of the new order of survival. Obviously, the harshness of working rhythms is always higher when capital is not forced to internalize the costs of the reproduction of the workforce, that is in contexts – as argued by O'Laughlin – where large reserves armies of labour are available. Processes of externalization of costs of reproduction by capital and of serious depletion of the labouring body often go in tandem, reinforcing each other. Indeed, this seems the case across the global garment sweatshop, where both a process of systematic externalization of costs related to the reproduction of the workforce and a continuous attack to workers' labouring body are simultaneously at work. Here, the negative consequences of the presence of a vast reserve army of labour are further exacerbated by a rhetoric accepting the ever-falling prices of commodities in the world market as a 'lamentable but inescapable reality' (Prentice, 2014).

Crucially, understandings of health and safety embedded in the social relations of production characterizing the sweatshop also inform debates on global labour standards. In particular, they illustrate the reasons behind the failure of corporate approaches to standards, like CSR and ethical trade interventions, which have proliferated in the garment industry since the 1990s, remaining, however, largely unable to address the poor health and safety record of the industry. In fact, one could argue that, in many instances, these interventions have further reinforced processes of externalization of costs concerning the social reproduction of the workforce and their negative impact on the labouring body.

Unexceptional Failures of Regulation

Since the 1990s, the debate on global labour standards and their effectiveness has been a rather prolific one. In fact, as already outlined in Chapter 1, the 1990s were the decade when, following processes of global outsourcing of manufacturing production, different consumer movements around the world started increasingly focusing on denouncing the poor working conditions of the labourers employed in the new 'global' factories (Frank, 2003; Bair and Palpacuer, 2012). Effectively, the 1990s were also the decade of corporate response to such international consumer pressure. In the garment industry, following the 'year of the sweatshop' (see Klein, 2000), all major global buyers and brands started elaborating their codes of conduct for labour, to be deployed in factories producing their goods worldwide (Jenkins *et al.*, 2000). Today, after decades of CSR initiatives, policies and projects, there is finally a growing consensus recognizing the limitations of corporate approaches to labour standards. Critical voices against the CSR model have focused on multiple, different issues. Some have stressed the imperialist nature of codes that are imposed by the 'West' on the 'Rest' and reinforce patterns of neo-colonialism in the global economy, while supporting 'protectionism with a human face' (see Kabeer, 2000). Along similar lines, others have highlighted the ways in which CSR has been increasingly institutionalized as yet another disciplining mechanisms subjecting regional and local suppliers to the diktats of global governance (De Neve, 2009; Taylor, 2011). A third, fruitful line of criticism has indicated the pernicious effects of mainstreaming corporate voluntarism as the way forward to enforce – and monitor – the 'right' social standards, a process substantially subverting the balance of power between business and civil society (Jenkins, 2005; Blowfield, 2005), promoting the 'moralization' of market outcomes (O'Laughlin, 2008) and paving the way to processes of 'commodification of ethics' (Mezzadri, 2012). Finally, numerous applied studies have illustrated the practical failure of corporate approaches to labour standards and ethical trade initiatives in different sectors and geographical areas (e.g. Barrientos and Smith, 2007; Nadvi, 2008;

Blowfield and Dolan, 2008; Lund-Thomsen *et al.*, 2012; Lund-Thomsen, 2013). The garment industry has often been the object of these studies (e.g. Kabeer and Mahmud, 2004; De Neve, 2009, 2014b; Ruwanpura, 2011, 2013; Ruwanpura and Wrigley, 2011; Pun, 2005; Mezzadri, 2012, 2014a, b).

Arguably, a focus on health and safety and the labouring body can contribute significantly to these critical debates on corporate standards (see Prentice and De Neve, 2017). In particular, understandings of health and safety outcomes anchored to the functioning mechanisms of the sweatshop regime help debunking the mythology of 'exceptionalism' also in relation to the failure of alleged pro-labour interventions. In fact, as one should reject portraits of Rana Plaza as an 'exceptional' case in the history of the garment industry, by the same token one should also severely question a view that represents the Savar tragedy as a case of 'exceptional failure' of regulation. If something, this tragedy quite graphically epitomizes, perhaps more than any other criticism, the sheer inadequacy of corporate-based labour regulations in ensuring the health and safety of garment workers worldwide. Indeed, through the lens of regulations, one would have expected far less continuities between industrial disasters in the history of the garment sector. Let us remember that the Shirtwaist factory fire in New York City took place in a period when tuberculosis was still also widely informally known as 'tailor's disease' (Hoskins, 2014). Garment work took place in filthy, unsafe dungeons, where the health and lives of the workers were always severely at risk. Today, instead, as major retailers, brands and global manufacturers boast about the fairness of their labour practices – by now, each and every website of major clothing giants has a dedicated section on CSR practices and ethical sourcing guidelines – one would hardly expect garment work to involve similar levels of health and safety risks for the labouring bodies engaged in it.

The lack of impact of CSR interventions – in both their 'classic' guise of company-based codes of conduct and in the new avatar of *ad-hoc* ethical trade projects – on reducing levels of risks associated with garment work is even more striking once one reflects on the nature of such interventions over the last decades. Quite ironically, in fact, before Rana Plaza one of the main criticisms moved to the practical functioning of corporate approaches to labour standards in the garment sector was their over-emphasis on health and safety regulations *vis-à-vis* other potentially more sensitive areas of concern (e.g. Barrientos *et al.*, 2010; Ruwanpura, 2013, Mezzadri, 2014a). Indeed, anyone doing field-based research in the garment industry can testify to the fact that buyers – as well as regional suppliers, for that matter – have always been more at ease in discussing health and safety regulations than issues like wages, labour contracts, type of employment, or social entitlements and contributions. This is also because suppliers generally adopt the rather standardized practice of owning a 'show-piece' for compliance purposes; namely, a factory that presents itself as neat and clean, in line with health and safety regulations, and which buyers can audit at all times (e.g. Mezzadri, 2009a). In this sense, demonstrating compliance with health and safety norms is always perceived as a relatively manageable task by brands, buyers' inspectors, and suppliers, as well as an easy way to be able to claim engagement in socially responsible business practices. Instead, norms based on an in-depth understanding of labour relations would necessarily be a far more costly and time-consuming objective to achieve – besides being largely counterproductive for both buyers and suppliers. Interventions on wages or social entitlements, for instance, could not but raise the cost of labour, undermining the neoliberal diktat on how to achieve competitiveness in labour-intensive production.

Hence, one could argue that, notwithstanding the complex hierarchical nature of the politics of social compliance (De Neve, 2009; Taylor, 2011), its great emphasis on health and safety norms seems to have worked as a useful compromise between buyers and suppliers. Undoubtedly, this approach has satisfied their mutual need of protecting competitiveness, while producing credible and tangible indicators of social compliance. After all, health and safety standards should be universally valid. However, this approach is problematic. First, as convincingly illustrated by Kanchana Ruwanpura (2013, p. 102) in her study of Sri Lankan garment factories, one should be wary of over-emphasizing the universalistic nature of health and safety norms. As any other form of regulation, these norms 'travel across uneven production spaces', possibly leading to a distinct, irregular – and at times erratic – application. Moreover, and more crucially for the argument developed here, these norms attempt to provide technicistic solutions to what is instead a complex social problem; namely the functioning of the sweatshop regime and the ineluctable process of depletion of the labouring body it generates.

The elaboration of health and safety norms as a technical exercise may have been quite productive for both buyers and regional suppliers. However, it has definitely failed workers. It has left the core of the sweatshop regime and its many relations of subjugation and oppression largely untouched, and has exposed workers to great levels of danger and insecurity. The Rana Plaza collapse has tragically called off this bluff and shown the great inadequacy of the current ways in which health and safety standards are elaborated and implemented. Besides, also in areas that have not been hit by major disasters or catastrophes, like India, the sweatshop reveals a poor health and safety record. Also here, garment work remains a greatly taxing work with seriously depleting effects on the labouring body. In fact, in India, in a context of extremely low social provisions, and greatly ineffective labour regulations and corporate initiatives, employers continue engaging in systematic processes of externalization of health and safety concerns and provisions. Pushed outside factories and spaces of work, these concerns and provisions are effectively 'outsourced' to households and homes. Overall, they are socialized by realms of social reproduction, where workers therefore appear as subsidizing employers. Paradoxically, and in line with what already suggested here, some current CSR interventions may be even reinforcing these processes, rather than substantially ameliorating working conditions. The following sections illustrate how such processes unfold by further expanding on the analysis of working and living conditions of garment labourers in the NCR, and by discussing one of the ethical initiatives that has relatively recently targeted home-workers in Bareilly.

The Externalization of Health and Safety Provisions and Concerns in the NCR

The different classes of labour at work in the Indian garment mall and its sweatshops are indeed subject to harsh working and living conditions. As illustrated in detail in this analysis, the changing regional architecture of the sweatshop regime at work across this mall is based on an inextricable correspondence between garment commodities and composite social processes of production banking on multiple social divides, differences and patterns of unfreedom. Through these processes, distinct labouring bodies become subject to the sweatshop, and experience its harshness in different ways. Undoubtedly, notwithstanding the varied ways in which the sweatshop acquires specific local or regional connotations, as described in Chapters 2–4, all Indian garment workers seem exposed to high level of risk and insecurity. Employers, across the entire Indian garment mall, are able to minimize their responsibility towards their workforce, through strategies changing on the basis of different industrial needs set by localized patterns of product specialization, and which have systematically managed to undermine in various ways national or international pro-labour interventions (see Mezzadri, 2012, 2014b).

In particular, in garment-producing areas characterized by a product specialization targeting niche markets of different types, where the sweatshop appears as shaped by complex factory and non-factory production realms, employers manage to bank on processes of systematic externalization of costs related to the social reproduction of the workforce. This clearly emerges from field trips as well as from interviews with both employers and labour activists. It also more fundamentally emerges from what reported by labourers themselves, whose bodies so often 'wear' the depleting effects garment work entails. Crucially, these effects may change based on workers' different positioning across the varied, multiple echelons of the sweatshop.

A survey of over 300 factory-based workers sampled across 35 garment companies and of 70 home-based workers labouring in the NCR, carried out between 2012 and 2013 (see CDPR, 2014a, b; Mezzadri and Srivastava, 2015), provides a solid platform for in-depth reflections on the level of health and safety provisions in the industry, as well as on the impact of the sweatshop regime on the labouring body. Processes of externalization of costs related to the social reproduction of the workforce emerge by looking at processes of labour circulation. In fact, a closer look at how labour circulation unfolds in a greatly complex, industrial social formation like the NCR indicates the need to further break down this analytical category into at least three distinct typologies; one capturing the yearly pace of internal migration (as analyzed in depth by the literature; e.g. Breman, 1996, 2013; Deshingkar and Farrington, 2009), one expressly linked to the labour process and the last one signalling the exit of the labouring body from the sweatshop. Let us first start from a general analysis of the social profile characterizing the NCR garment proletariat, to then identify and analyze the ways in which these distinct types of labour circulation at work affect the politics of health and safety in this corner of the Indian garment mall.

Similar to many other garment-producing countries and as already suggested in Chapter 2, over 90 per cent of the NCR garment workers, in factories and workshops, who are mainly composed of OBCs, come from rural areas. Crucially, around 70 per cent of all of them still own some land back in their place of origin. For over 40 per cent of these workers (43 per cent), this land is considered as a crucial part of overall livelihood income. However, workers also identified different forms of informal wage employment as crucial to their subsistence and reproduction (Srivastava, 2015). This is to say that while the majority of workers do indeed survive across the rural–urban divide, as highlighted in our briefer sketch of the NCR, the way in which this survival is guaranteed is quite complex. In fact, it seems to vary in relation to workers' other means of survival – or with the degree of freedom or unfreedom workers 'possess' as measured against the means of production they still command at their place of origin. Notably, while land ownership emerges as a relatively important indicator, highlighting how the garment proletariat is not yet exposed to full dispossession, the land workers own in their village may or may not be deployed for agricultural activities. Obviously, this significant percentage of land ownership goes hand in hand with the greatly circulatory nature of garment labour in the NCR.

If labour circulation, together with the recruitment patterns it entails, has already emerged as a key feature of the sweatshop regime at work in the NCR (e.g. Singh and Kaur Sapra, 2007; Mezzadri, 2008, 2012, 2014a; Barrientos *et al.*, 2010), evidence provided by workers helps further understanding its complex nuances. While a significant part of the workforce reports to be circulating between the NCR and their place of origin on a yearly basis, and in correspondence of holidays or lean season, a far more significant proportion also reports circulation *across the NCR*. Attrition rates, that is rates of labour turnover, are rather staggering, and overall 60 per cent of workers report to work for the same unit for less than 1 year. This is to say that even in cases where migratory labour may be of a less circulatory nature, it remains primarily circulatory in relation to the labour process. This is a key point, as it implies that the prevention of the formation of a cohesive working class in the NCR is not merely due to 'incomplete' dispossession. It is mainly due to the labour deployment strategies of employers and their representatives. In this sense, modernizing ideas identifying factory work as eventually leading to a stable inclusion of the workforce and to the internalization of its social reproduction simply remain an illusion, in the NCR. Here, capital's 'civilizing influence' (Marx, in Federici, 2004) and its alleged 'liberating' potential still seem nowhere to be found.

Focusing on patterns of recruitment, once again workers' experiences crucially complement information already available on the vast presence of labour contracting in the industry (see Singh and Kaur Sapra, 2007; Barrientos, 2013), as part of capital's strategies at labour cost minimization (see Mezzadri, 2008, 2012). Quite puzzling at first, interviews with employers seem to reveal higher degrees of labour contracting than those suggested by workers' questionnaires (see Mezzadri and Srivastava, 2015). In fact, workers report a wide range of recruitment options. In particular, through the eyes of labour, contracting appears as a greatly segmented order, and arguably a rather chaotic one. Keeping in mind the discussion developed in Chapter 5, which has introduced the multiple, different 'guises' in which 'the broker' can manifest (see Breman, 1999), the more organized, factory segments of the sweatshop regimes appear as dominated by in-contracting practices aimed at disguising the wage relation. Contractors may either be in an internal or in an external relation with garment companies or factories; that is, they may be directly employed by them, or instead work for them based on formal or informal agreements (see Srivastava, 2015). Also, contracting may involve the management and supervision of the workforce on the shop-floor, or instead simply impose an extra layer of intermediation between the employer and the worker. In the first case, the role of the contractor, who may at times be a key worker like a master tailor or shop-floor supervisor, presents clear continuities with old forms of intermediation of indenture labour like the *Sardar* or *Kangani* systems, as already discussed in Chapter 5 (see Roy, 2008; De Neve, 2014b). The second case, instead, epitomizes the 'neoliberal modernization' of the contracting enterprise. After all, under globalization, contracting – albeit in more formal ways – is also becoming increasingly spread across developed regions (see Barrientos, 2013).

Notably and despite these important differences, contracting complicates the 'external order' the labouring body is subject to when entering the sweatshop, through a process of multiplication of the masters workers need to respond to. Importantly, workers' responses also indicate the relevance of direct recruitment, operated at factory gates. However, due to the many contracting options at work in the industry, the relationship between contracting and direct recruitment seems blurred at best. Overall, quantitative and qualitative evidence based on both employers' and workers' responses seems to possibly indicate that workers themselves may not necessarily know whom to consider their primary employer; a clear victory for capital. Unfortunately, current legislation allowing contracting in core business functions of the industry is likely to further boost the complexity of contracting practices and their ability to conceal primary employers (Mezzadri and Srivastava, 2015).

Combined together, labour circulation, labour-process-based circulation (or 'industrial circulation') and the multiplicity of contracting practices at work across the NCR sweatshop regime offer employers the possibility to systematically eschew their responsibility towards the workforce. Besides, in a context where the lion share of the workforce stays in the same industrial unit for less than 1 year, the factory hardly internalizes the costs of its social reproduction. If this point clearly emerges in relation to employment patterns, it is further reinforced by considerations over the daily social reproduction of labour in the industrial area. The analysis of living arrangements reveals that workers either live in colonies close to the main industrial areas or deploy a variety of informal living arrangements, renting rooms in nearby slums. In all cases, five to eight labouring bodies generally share a tiny living space for the whole period in which they are hosted in the metropole and deployed in its sweatshop. In one of the most 'infamous' of the

NCR labour colonies, Kapashera, in southwest Delhi, close to Gurgaon and the Haryana border, workers live in miserable conditions. Piles of rubbish and an unbearable stench welcome the visitor to the colony, where access to water and sanitation is a luxury, and workers share filthy common toilets located at the entrance. The colony, as many others hosting endless crowds of India's working poor, is 'managed' by the many housing contractors and landlords who thrive in the slum economy (Mezzadri, 2015d).

The chaotic overlap between multiple types of mobility of workers, in and out of the NCR and across its units, enables a process of capital accumulation that does not entail the internalization of costs related to the social reproduction of the workforce. This is obviously extremely helpful to employers, who in fact continue engaging in practices that reproduce this complex labour geography. However, it would be wrong to assume that this geography is only drawn by capital, and that labour is simply a passive spectator. In fact, even in the absence of organized resistance, like in the case analysed here – an issue that we shall discuss at the end of this chapter – workers always strategize, adapt and show an incredible resilience in moulding their actions in ways apt to resist capital's disregard for their livelihoods. And in so doing, they participate in crafting their own labour geography (see Carswell and De Neve, 2013a). If this process can be seen as reactive, it should nevertheless be taken into account. In particular, in the NCR the great endurance of processes of labour circulation need to be seen also in the light of workers' own strategies at survival. Here, for instance, at times workers themselves are hardly interested in remaining at work in the same unit. First, the rising demand for labour in the industry means that they will always find garment work once they return from their villages. In brief, 'break in service', lamented by several employers, is an option workers feel they can afford. In some respect, it may also be a sort of sabotaging strategy against 'bad' employers. Second, workers do not necessarily see some units as providing more desirable work than others, in the NCR. While many studies of global garment production generally insist that first-tier, larger units tend to pay higher wages and offer better employment conditions (see Barrientos *et al.*, 2010), evidence on wage levels suggests otherwise. Quite surprisingly, take-home wages, or wages excluding social contributions, are extraordinarily similar in the NCR, across categories of industrial units (small, medium, large) and even contractual positions (direct employment and contract employment) (see CDPR, 2014b; Srivastava, 2015). This also further explains why workers seem to hardly develop a particular attachment to a specific employer. Notably, adding to our reflections on the current nature of factory work in the industry, these findings deconstruct ideas of large capital as necessarily being a provider of better salaries.

Focusing on non-factory-based labour that, as discussed in Chapter 2, is heavily present in ancillary activities taking place in micro-enterprises and home-based realms of production, and that is greatly socially differentiated, field findings indicate interesting trends. While confirming the ways in which (unfree) self-employment is systematically proletarianized and subsumed into the capitalist relation as a form of wage labour, workers' interviews reveal that the division between informal micro-units and homes is becoming increasingly ambiguous and blurred. Particularly, in metropolitan settings, home-based production units may be turning into a luxury newcomers cannot afford, given the price of real estate and rents. It is not a case, in this respect, that the government of India (GoI) has reclassified the unit of analysis defining homework to include home-based unit, home-based work, but also home-based-like units (see Raju, 2013). In fact, our survey reveals that, quite tellingly, once regularity of employment – guaranteed only in 11 per cent of cases – is taken into consideration, own-account, allegedly self-employed workers individually earn a very similar income than that of the migrant wageworkers labouring in micro-units. Only female home-workers, who are generally engaged in either *adda* or *moti* work, systematically earn significantly less (less than half, and in some cases, less than one third) than other categories of non-factory labour at work at the periphery of the NCR industrial formation (see CDPR, 2014a; Mezzadri, 2015b).

Also across the most informalized segments of the sweatshop regime, the majority of workers are rural migrants. Although only 16 per cent own some land back home, the majority still consider their village as their primary residence and home (Mezzadri, 2015b). Non-factory-based labour is always recruited by contractors, who are, however, in line with our discussions of out-contracting networks, considered proper employers. In fact, they organize the entire segment of the product cycle in which non-factory labour is involved. Often, they are kinfolks or relatives, coming from the same place of origin of non-factory workers. In some cases, they may command their labour both in the NCR and back home. In *adda* networks, contractors often set wage rates before migrants, many of whom come from Bareilly, start their journey to the NCR. They also often retain payments, a practice which adds to the many ways in which relations of neo-bondage (see Breman, 2013) may be crafted in the sector. Living arrangements, for non-factory labour, vary considerably, ranging from own-dwelling (for the self-employed) to informal housing in colonies or slums. Many migrant workers in micro-units simply sleep in the contractor's unit (Mezzadri, 2015b, 2008; see also Singh and Kaur Sapra, 2007). In no case, neither in factory-based nor non-factory-based production realms, we ever found workers in dormitories, unlike what is reported by studies focusing on labour-intensive industries elsewhere. In China, or in Vietnam, for instance (see Pun and Smith, 2007; Cerimele, 2016), the full commodification of the time and space of workers' daily social reproduction is a fairly widespread practice, aimed at strengthening control over labour in the context of tight labour markets. Crucially, this commodification often only targets individual workers, and not their family (see also Pearson and Kusakabe, 2012). In the NCR, instead, neither employers nor the state bear any of the costs of workers' daily social needs, and it is up to workers to find suitable living arrangements to join the sweatshop.

In terms of health and safety provisions, only one-fourth of all garment workers sampled in the surveys reported to have access to emergency medical facilities or routine medical check-ups through their employers. Access is always linked to work-time in a given unit (Srivastava, 2015). As over 60 per cent of the workforce stays on in the same unit for less than 1 year, the internalization of health costs per worker borne by employers is minimal, as it is the impact on company-based health services on workers' lives. High levels of labour-process-based circulation greatly undermine the already limited health and safety provisioning by the industry. The other key provision of healthcare by employers should be via social security contributions and particularly, in India, via the payment of ESI (Employee State Insurance) and PF (Provident Fund) contributions. These should also provide access to public clinics and medical facilities. However, only 40–50 per cent of workers reported to be entitled to ESI and PF in factory settings, and none in non-factory settings. Notably, entitlement does not necessarily mean access. Again, the latter largely depends upon working for the same company over some time, which is hardly the case in the NCR. In a context of lack of portability of social contributions, once workers move across units, social contributions simply go wasted. This explains why 80 per cent of them declare to have no entitlement in relation to both injury compensation or retirement benefits (Srivastava, 2015). In non-factory settings, we had to explain what we meant with work-related social benefits during interviews. None of the workers is covered under any scheme. Across all the different echelons of the sweatshop, workers generally pay privately when experiencing health problems, by accessing local private clinics (Mezzadri and Srivastava, 2015). In effect, workers systematically subsidize the sweatshop in looking after their own health.

The Inexorable Depletion of the Labouring Body and its Ejection from the Sweatshop

The field findings of the combined surveys on factory and non-factory labour in the NCR clearly show the great intensity of the sweatshop regime. Across both factories and more 'organized' workshops, the labouring experience entails extremely long working shifts.[68] On average, the majority of workers – 51 per cent of all workers in factories and 67 per cent in workshops – work for 10–12 hours per day. One-third of sweatshop workers employed in workshops even works 13–16 hours per day. In 'peripheral', non-factory spaces of work instead, labour intensity changes based on patterns of un(der)employment. Circular migrants always work more than 12 hours per day, while female home-workers at the bottom of the sweatshop regime work far less, as their time is claimed by reproductive activities (Mezzadri and Srivastava, 2015).

In the NCR, the disregard of the sweatshop regime towards the social reproduction of its workers is paralleled by its harsh, depleting effect on their labouring body. Focusing specifically on indicators of patterns of occupational health and hazard, one-third of all workers reported to experience back pain, while one-fifth also referred to allergies, particularly to the dust generated by cloth particles. Exhaustion was also reported as a key problem. In large units, this has to do with the stress of working against set targets or production quotas, entailing highly standardized, alienating and intense working rhythms. During an interview, the former production manager of the largest garment manufacturer of the NCR reported that he left the post due to the great number of workers fainting on the shop-floor. He found the sight of all these people simply dropping down like flies unbearable. He now works for a medium-large employer instead. While also his current company breaches labour regulations in a number of ways – for instance, in relation to hire and fire practices or overtime – it does not deploy similarly 'inhumane' working rhythms, mostly needed when dealing with giant buyers placing massive orders with overly strict time deliveries. Notably, waves of fainting in the garment industry are hardly new, as explained by Julia Wallace (2014) in her brilliant article in the *New York Times*, ironically titled *Workers of the World, Faint!* Indeed, fainting is one of the possible violent reactions experienced by the labouring body when subject to great levels of pressure, its way of fighting

---

[68] The term 'organized' is deployed only to differentiate more 'visible' workshops from micro-units of less than 10 workers, clubbed instead in the universe of 'peripheral', home-based (or 'home-based-like' work). See Mezzadri and Srivastava (2015).

against the intensity of processes of extraction of labour power. Different forms of physical and mental stress and anxiety often characterize the lives of the garment proletariat (Prentice 2015; see also Mezzadri 2015d; Ashraf; and Hewamanne; in De Neve and Prentice, 2017). For workshop workers, and for peripheral workers in micro-units and homes, the majority of health and safety issues are related to eyestrain and loss of eyesight. This is particularly the case for those engaged in embroidery work.

If each of the health issues reported above is relevant in its own right, it is their combination that overall wears out workers' labouring bodies. Tellingly, across both factory and non-factory realms of production very few workers still labour past the age of 30. Findings from our surveys indicate that 58 per cent of factory and workshop labourers were between 21 and 30 years of age, while 12 per cent were younger than 20. Only 21 per cent was above the age of 30, and a staggeringly low 5.9 per cent above the age of 40. Workers above the age of 50 were less than 2 per cent (Srivastava, 2015). Generally, in fact, this handful of older workers can mainly be found in supervisory positions. Also in non-factory, peripheral settings, the average age of the garment proletariat was quite young, with only 6 per cent of workers – generally own-account workers – older than 40 (Mezzadri, 2015b). This means that the industrial experience remains only a temporary, transitory moment in the lives of garment workers. This is the case not only in India, but also in other countries like Cambodia, Bangladesh itself, and China, where similar findings are reported (e.g. respectively, Cambodian Centre for Human Rights, 2014; War On Want, 2011; Pun *et al.*, Report, 2015). By the age of 30, workers' labouring bodies are so greatly impacted by the intensity of the sweatshop regime that this regime ejects them, in order to welcome instead a new, young stitching platoon. The old one marches back home, often, as mentioned in Chapter 5, to the villages where workers were originally from. In his accounts of circular migration, Jan Breman (2013, p. 57), highlights how once the labouring stamina of workers is fully exhausted and depleted, these cannot but return home as 'suck oranges'. Indeed, this is what happens across the garment sweatshop, as neither the employers nor the state cater for the survival of the garment proletarians once they are separated from the clothes they have produced. Therefore, the village – and realms of reproduction in general – must play the role of informal social security cushion, and absorb back the workers initially donated to the sweatshop. In fact, this process of ejection of the labouring body from the sweatshop represents a third and final act of labour circulation. It signals the end of the cycle of labour circulation. Altogether, all the three processes of labour circulation analyzed here – yearly labour circulation, labour-process-based (or 'industrial') circulation and life cycle labour circulation – are crucial functioning mechanisms of the sweatshop. They enable the externalization of costs related to the social reproduction of the workforce, while also ensuring the discard of depleted labouring bodies – a sort of 'human waste' the sweatshop regime disposes of incessantly – and their substitution with 'new' ones. The analysis of what happens to the garment proletariat once it is ejected from the sweatshop – without substantial access to either social contributions or retirement benefits – is one of the most compelling future research agendas labour studies should start focusing on, to deepen our understanding of the long-term impact of the sweatshop on livelihoods. Crucially, the development of this agenda would necessarily mean expanding definitions of working conditions and work-related wellbeing (or certainly un-wellbeing) far beyond narrow interpretations only focusing on technicistic measures, or decoupling labour outcomes from the overall workings of the sweatshop regime. Unfortunately, instead, it is this narrower and compartmentalized understanding that seems to inform the majority of interventions supposedly in favour of garment workers, particularly when they are part of the CSR agenda.

Bringing Health and Safety 'Home' in Bareilly, and the Paradoxes of Ethical Projects

The systematic externalization of health and safety provisions by the industry and the depleting effects of garment work on workers' labouring bodies have been hardly challenged by corporate approaches to labour standards or ethical trade initiatives, despite their rhetoric of bringing positive social change. In fact, in some cases, these even reinforce the status quo, participating in decentralizing responsibilities on work-related wellbeing, shifting it onto workers themselves. This is particularly evident in home-based settings, which gather greatly vulnerable segments of the sweatshop regime. Arguably, there is no better way to demonstrate the limitations of CSR and of the ethical trade mantra than to analyze which type of projects they have entailed in practice. Notably, the analysis of such projects also further illustrates the unexceptionality of failures in regulation.

One cannot say that the NCR has not been the target of multiple CSR initiatives, particularly in the aftermath of the sweatshop scandals concerning the region. In particular, scandals involving the presence of child labour have even led, for a period, to the blacklisting of India by the US department of labour, which still mentions garment among activities at risk of including indenture or forced labour (see Bureau of International Labour Affairs, 2014). The Indian government has increasingly realized the crucial role CSR plays in relation to strengthening competitiveness. The adoption of the CSR Bill should be also seen under this light (Sharma, 2013). In fact, as argued in Chapter 1, also the AEPC has increasingly entered the CSR game, for concerns over competition. Through the development of DISHA (2013), the AEPC code of conduct for labour, the council hopes to regain control over social compliance and boost the competitiveness of India's SMEs (Mezzadri, 2014b). All these developments have multiplied the number of corporate, allegedly pro-labour initiatives in the region, and complicated substantially the local politics of social compliance. Today, in the NCR, social compliance is a highly segmented business and an arena characterized by the proliferation of third party monitors, local compliance agents, and evaluators of various sort. Different employers adopt distinct measures and initiatives based on their size, exposure to international markets, and engagement in specific market segments (Mezzadri, 2015a). At the top of the social compliance business, large employers linked to giant, renowned buyers must necessarily adopt the codes of conduct imposed by the latter, and subject themselves to buyers' inspections. Average or small employers, who do not target top-market segments, instead, can get away with adopting minor initiatives or general systems of certification that are not always less costly, but surely less demanding. So far, DISHA seems to be placed at the very bottom of this second set of compliance interventions and forms of certification. Due to the increasing diversification of CSR models, during interviews many NCR employers like to lament their 'survey fatigue', triggered by the multiple ways in which they are asked to respect the so-called social clause. In reality, with time, many buyers have joined multi-stakeholder initiatives to ensure the respect of minimum labour standards. Through these initiatives, sizeable groups of buyers adopt the same code of conduct, arguably simplifying the work of suppliers. Notably, the raise of these collective forms of business engagement may have further strengthened business' ability to impose voluntarism as the way forward for the elaboration of meaningful social standards. In the NCR, through these initiatives, the CSR model has partially evolved towards a wider focus on ethical trade. To their credit, one could say that some of these initiatives have tried to overcome an overly narrow focus on single factories and the relation between single buyers and suppliers, to consider instead a number of systemic, regional problems associated with garment work. Some initiatives attempt, moreover, to create tripartite platforms where business, labour NGOs and unions should, in theory, negotiate the focus of compliance. Adopting this model, the Ethical Trade Initiative (ETI), for instance, has focused on non-factory work (ETI, 2006, 2013), given its staggering presence in the NCR and the embroidery centres – like Bareilly – incorporated into its vast, decentralized production network.

However, despite their attempt to overcome CSR limitations, also many of these new ethical initiatives reproduce the failings of classic corporate codes of conduct (Mezzadri, 2014a). In particular, they mainly focus on 'visual issues' (see Barrientos *et al.*, 2010), while leaving the balance of power between capital and labour largely untouched. Moreover, like already many classic CSR practices, these initiatives seem to place a lot of emphasis on issues of health and safety. However, in their efforts, they seem to fall into the trap to simply accept the process of externalization of responsibility for health and safety provisions, while focusing on households and homes as the main locus where health and safety matters should be addressed. In short, also these initiatives, despite well-meaning intentions, seem to assume that workers are ultimately responsible for looking after their own health and safety, and protecting their labouring bodies from the pernicious effects garment work may entail.

This point clearly emerges from the analysis of one of these ethical trade interventions in Bareilly, aimed at ameliorating the working conditions of its many home-workers. Created by the ETI, in Bareilly this initiative has led to the formation of an association of contractors, the Bareilly Homeworkers Group (BHG), later renamed as the Handwork Foundation (HF).[69] The association should have worked with a local branch of SEWA, the Self Employed Women Association, India's famous union targeting female informal workers. The project also financed SEWA's work in the area, under the assumption that the two bodies would have cooperated for the wellbeing of workers. However, field findings in Bareilly indicate the greatly hierarchical nature of the project, and its problematic take on health and safety. In Bareilly, the role of HF was simply to facilitate SEWA's work, and namely 'allowing' SEWA activists to work in the homes commanded by contractors. As illustrated in Chapter 5, control over home-workers is so tightly regimented by the mechanisms of contracting and by the power of contracting agents that it is hard even to talk to home-workers if their 'masters' do not agree and collaborate. All the ethical content of the project, however, was provided by SEWA. Locally, SEWA was asked to offer health and safety training to artisans in their homes,

---

[69] This followed the creation, in Delhi, of the National Homeworkers Group (NHG). See Mezzadri (2014a).

and make sure artisans liaised with the local state to benefit from state-sponsored social security schemes. Two schemes, in particular, could be locally available to home-workers; the Rajiv Gandhi Shilpi Swasthya Bima Yojana, approved within the 11th Five-Year Plan, which guarantees medical insurance for artisans, their wives and two of their children, and the Khadi Karighar Janashree Bima Yojana, aimed at providing life insurance to members of vocation/occupation groups below the poverty line or marginally above it (DCMSME, 2013; Development Commissioner for Handicraft, 2013). Moreover, SEWA also run a medical camp for home-workers and their families. In fact, despite SEWA's efforts, interviews with over 100 home-based workers in Bareilly reveal that these poor labourers do not subscribe to any state-sponsored scheme. They are also not covered by any other form of social security, like already non-factory workers in the peripheral echelons of the NCR. In fact, as we have illustrated in Chapter 5, many (mainly young and male) *adda* artisans engage in short spells of circular migration to the NCR to complement their meagre income through the substantial wage increment available in the metropolis (Mezzadri, 2014a, 2015b).

Field findings indicate that, in Bareilly as in the NCR, no local contractor and certainly no NCR exporter – let alone international buyer – offers any health and safety provision to home-based workers. Overall, across the whole sweatshop regime, the logic of subcontracting enables the entire chain of garment employers and contracting agents to transmit risks 'upstream', towards households, homes and workers. Moreover, in home-based settings, due to the overlap between productive and reproductive realms and rhythms, capital can fully externalize all costs for workers' wellbeing and safety even during work-time. Indeed, the complex process of proletarianization at work in Bareilly does not come with any social entitlement. The ethical initiative set up by ETI hardly challenged the *status quo*; rather, it was fully embedded into the relations of domination at work across 'the global village'. In fact, one could argue that the project further institutionalized these relations, by reinforcing the role of the home as the main *locus* where social compliance must be ensured and delivered. Workers were asked to internalize lessons concerning their wellbeing, particularly in relation to posture and use of light during work-time, in order to mitigate the strenuous effects embroidery work can have on their back and eyesight. In essence, workers were asked to become managers of their own labouring body, and were made in charge of protecting it against the harshness of their toil for others. Notably, this push towards self-regulation is also in line with the rise of the culture of self-entrepreneurship that characterizes neoliberal India (Gooptu, 2013). However, such mild measures are unable to contrast the strain experienced by the labouring body over time. As in the NCR, only few home-based workers work beyond the age of 30, almost none beyond 40. Many will become supervisors of their children's work, despite their wishes for a different future for their offspring. Notably, the lack of health and safety provisions greatly contributes to chaining workers to their traditional occupations. In fact, health emergencies, socialized by the households, are one of the most common reasons pushing home-workers in relations of debt and exposing them to the harshness of interlocking practices. Women, in particular, are those more likely to remain chained to embroidery work, as they generally bear the brunt of the socialization of costs related to social reproduction (see Raju, 2013). None of these processes can be challenged by simplistic interventions, which expect somewhat 'ethical outcomes' on the basis of measures leaving all the harsh processes of exploitation home-workers are subject to untouched, and asking home-workers themselves to fight against the depleting signs of the sweatshop regime on their bodies.

The Bodily Traits of the Sweatshop Regime

By the end of this chapter, the last one of the book, our long journey into the world of India's sweatshop regime has progressively moved from its relation to the global chain to how its effects are 'worn' by the bodies of its workers. In so doing, the analysis has revealed the correspondence between the sweatshop as a complex regime, whose social architecture is shaped by the commodities produced and the multiple social relations of oppression shaped by the joint work of different masters, and the ways in which it is experienced by workers. As argued and documented here, this experience is an extremely harsh one, involving ineluctable processes of depletion of workers' labouring bodies, in a context where employers are able to systematically decentralize costs of social reproduction outside their remit and responsibility, dumping them onto workers' shoulders. In this sense, while the attention placed on recent tragedies like Rana Plaza constructs a narrative of exceptionalism to interpret industrial disasters, an understanding of health and safety outcomes anchored to the overall functioning mechanisms of the sweatshop regimes and its implications for the labouring body deconstructs such a narrative, showing instead the tragic banality and unexceptionality of disastrous events. Indeed, these events remain the most tragic manifestations of what having a garment job in the sweatshop may entail. However, they are hardly isolated moments in the development of industrial relations of the garment industry. And even in the absence of disastrous events, the labouring body is always subject to 'minor' but continuous attacks that hit and deplete it as forms of low-intensity epidemic. Crucially, the unexceptionality of poor health and safety outcomes is paralleled by unexceptional failures in regulation. In the last decades, these regulations, particularly in the form of corporate approaches to labour standards, which have progressively taken centre stage in the attempt of tackling poor working conditions, have largely failed to address the poor health and safety record of the industry, as they have tended to isolate health and safety concerns from the overall exploitative labour relations dominating the sector. Instead, only a systemic attack to the sweatshop and its functioning mechanisms can improve workers' health and safety entitlements and provisions.

Evidence from the NCR and Bareilly, analyzed here, clearly illustrates how these processes unfold in practice in India, while also revealing the great limitations of CSR approaches to labour standards, as well as new forms of ethical trade interventions, technically aimed at mitigating workers' hardship. Field findings reveal that in factory-based realms, multiple processes of labour circulation undermine the factory as an arena of work-related social protection. They also clearly indicate how the factory remains only a transient moment in the complex history of workers' livelihoods. As the majority of workers quickly enter and exit industrial areas and units, circulating endlessly between the urban–rural divide as well as across the different spaces of work composing the labour process, employers remain able to eschew their responsibility towards the workforce, a responsibility which is also not internalized by the state, which in India remains an agent of informalization (see Basile and Harriss-White, 2010; Mezzadri, 2010). If the labouring strain is experienced differently by workers located across the distinct echelons of the sweatshop regime – sometimes involving fainting spells on the shop-floor, other times chronic fatigue or permanent loss of eyesight – it always quickly consumes the working potential of all workers, pushing them out of the sweatshop when they are still young. The move out of the sweatshop is yet another way in which labour circulation manifests in the sweatshop, and a process that further minimizes employers' responsibility towards its labour. Overall, the process of extraction of labour power from the labouring bodies of garment workers appears as a violent act, involving different mechanisms and stages.

In this context, corporate approaches to health and safety have largely failed. Their technicistic approach to health and safety, and their tendency to shy away from fighting against the relations of power at work in the sweatshop, make them largely irrelevant for workers' lives. In fact, in many cases, CSR and ethical projects may have further reinforced the relations of domination at work in the sweatshop, like in the case illustrated here. Overall, under the sweatshop regime, its low wages and social security provisions, health and safety outcomes cannot but remain highly problematic. O'Laughlin (2010, p. 5, building on Wilkinson, 1996) rightly observes how 'unequal societies are literally sick societies'. By the same token, the highly iniquitous production system and relations of domination and oppression shaping the sweatshop regime can only produce a sick and unsafe reality for all those fighting to make a livelihood at the bottom of this regime, consuming their body while cutting, stitching and embroidering our clothes.

Conclusions

The Resilience of the Sweatshop Regime across Time and Implications

At the end of our long journey into the world of the Indian sweatshop and its multiple regional manifestations in India, we cannot but appreciate the great complexity of the social questions paving its foundations. Despite endless scandals and attempts at regulation aimed at improving labour and living standards, the great resilience of the sweatshop across time appears as the final outcome of processes that go well beyond the responsibility of single actors. This resilience, in fact, appears as the overall outcome of the structuring of the sweatshop as a complex regime of exploitation and oppression, organized in a joint enterprise shaped and commanded by multiple global, regional and local lords that link processes of surplus extraction to different realms of social reproduction of the labourforce. The forms of exploitation and oppression at work in the sweatshop change based on the commercial dynamics and on the physical characteristics of the garments produced. If the seams and features of our jeans, T-shirts, shirts, sweaters or jackets are all manufactured through the heavy toil of the millions who produce our clothes today, they also conceal different stories of exploitation, social oppression, labouring and unfreedom. The process of manufacturing different garments for the global economy also does produce a greatly different garment proletariat, decomposed in multiple 'classes of labour' shaped by numerous social differences and divides. The sweatshop is experienced in different ways across the NCR and Bareilly, in Ludhiana, Jaipur, Kolkata, Bangalore, Chennai, Tiruppur or Mumbai. It is experienced differently by the army of UP and Bihari male migrants sweating and circulating across the NCR, by the endless numbers of home-based workers of Bareilly, by the thousands of women factory workers of Bangalore and Chennai. In fact, the ways in which these different classes of labour live the labouring reality of the sweatshop vary based on their social traits and wider conditions of social reproduction, both at their place of origin and across the industrial areas where they find work. The sweatshop constructs a social reality where commodity fetishism effectively comes to life and workers themselves are fetishized into distinct 'raw materials' to be deployed in different activities and tasks. The organization of global industries (or chains) can only be fully captured by engaging with the tremendously diverse social and economic life that characterizes them and ensures their reproduction.

It is through the sum of all these complex processes of 'making' things as well as cheap labouring bodies – often consumed as quickly as fast-fashion items – that many developing regions continue producing and reproducing their comparative advantage in cheap labour. Indeed, it is through these complex processes that India is currently ensuring and defending its place in the world economy as a key garment producer and exporter that can bank on many patterns of product specializations. These many specialization patterns, which today shape India into a massive, giant garment mall crossed by complex circuits of production and circulation of clothing items, continue banking on the distinct social traits dividing and fragmenting India's working poor, 'assigning' them to different echelons of the sweatshop. The analysis of India's sweatshop regime not only reveals the great social costs that lie behind the design of 'Global India', built on the shoulders of the working poor, but it also unveils how different categories of working poor are assigned distinct roles in the completion of such a design.

Moreover, the analysis of the sweatshop regime also highlights the precarious and temporary nature of the harsh service demanded of the working poor, who, despite their centrality in the process of production for global markets are then easily ejected from the world of the sweatshop, once their labouring ability is considered exhausted and their labouring body inexorably depleted. Paradoxically, the working mechanisms of the sweatshop create a rapidly revolving door between the incorporation of the working poor in a supposedly 'modern' industrial sector and their sudden ejection from the world of industrial labour and potential compulsory return to non-industrial livelihoods. As concluded in Chapter 6, the reality of post-work in the garment sector as in many other labour-intensive industries should be one of the key concerns of both labour and development studies, which should start taking a careful look at what happens to workers once they march out of factories and workshops, as a sort of human waste, to join again the reserve army of labour. In India, this is undoubtedly likely to become an increasingly crucial issue, considering the rising culture of self-entrepreneurialism that has accompanied processes of (neo)liberalization (see Gooptu, 2013), and the labour agenda of the current Modi government. Heavily framed around self-regulation, this agenda risks curtailing social entitlements and transfers even further, while hiding behind the rhetoric of socially 'empowering' labouring masses (see Bhowmik, 2015). The significance of this point, however, lends itself to broader generalizations.

Indeed, moving from the concrete case studied here to an understanding of the sweatshop as an instantiation of the workings of contemporary capitalism, the analysis presented in this book bears important implications for a number of key theoretical and policy debates in the broader field of development. Studying contemporary capitalism through the lens of the sweatshop regime, first, warns against facile modernizing narratives. Second, it significantly contributes to debates on 'modern slavery'. Third, it suggests a number of important lessons for the debate on ethical consumerism and ethical trade interventions. The following concluding sections discuss the ways in which such lens sheds light on these three different theoretical and policy debates.

The Sweatshop Regime Against the 'Modernization Fetish'

While ideas of the 'civilizing influence of capital' have resisted over time, from the early development models based on Rostow's stages of economic growth or Arthur Lewis' 'dual-sector' model (see Preston, 1996) to current stagist accounts of sectoral 'industrial upgrading' in the world economy developed by commodity studies (for a critical review of these see Selwyn, 2013), once labour and labouring are placed at the centre of the analysis of contemporary capitalism the picture emerging is a substantially different one.

The sweatshop regime debunks the mythology of 'good development' embraced by many modernizing narratives. In fact, the great resilience and harsh working mechanisms of the sweatshop regime raise crucial questions in relation to the effectiveness of these narratives, well beyond the Indian case. The case of the sweatshop defies the fictitious promises of benign accounts of industrial modernization, as still mainstreamed in many development policy circles. Clearly, the sweatshop escapes the supposedly 'natural' laws that should ensure a virtuous cycle of industrial development, eventually leading to a systemic amelioration of working conditions and standards. The story of the sweatshop reveals these narratives for what they are: (at best, well-meaning) constructs.

The survival and resilience of the garment sweatshop does not happen because the process of industrial modernization has not yet taken place. On the contrary, in all its disquieting aspects, the sweatshop regime *already is* our industrial modernity. As processes of labour informalization become increasingly rampant also in the 'West', that ultimately is by now following the 'Rest' in creating a world shaped by rising patterns of labour vulnerability and inequality (Breman, 2013; Breman and van der Linden, 2014), the garment sweatshop seems definitely here to stay. It is further expanding and 're-spatializing' across the rural areas of many developing regions, while also travelling back towards our own backyards, in the underbelly of many metropolitan areas and towns in countries like Italy (Lan, 2014), Spain or the UK (Kabeer, 2000; Hammer *et al.*, 2015), which host many impoverished migrant communities. Its potentially disastrous effects have already travelled all the way from NY to Rana Plaza, over a span of more than 100 years (see also Seabrook, 2015).

Clearly, in the case of garment – and garment across Asia, I should add – the continuous reproduction of working poverty across time and space can hardly be ascribed to 'insufficient globalization', as many modernizers do (see Kiely, 2008). After placing the sweatshop regime under the microscope, narratives like Paul Krugman's praise and defence of cheap labour (see Cawthorne and Kitching, 2001), as many other growth-obsessed accounts (e.g. Powell, 2014), only appears as informed by some sort of 'hope economics' systematically moving the social urgency of the labour question ahead in time to an unclearly defined future. The same goes for Marxist stagist accounts still heavily inspired by the work of Bill Warren (1973).[70] By over-emphasizing the role of productive forces in poverty eradication (e.g. Sender, 2016 on South Africa), they systematically subordinate the organization of labour to that of capital, endlessly postponing discussions on resistance and social justice, and effectively divorcing Marxism from political practice.[71] However, while waiting for the happy future portrayed by modernizing narratives, the sweatshop will continue exhausting, depleting and consuming whole generations, while not even significantly changing its working logic, as this delivers just fine to its many masters.

---

[70] Crucially, mainstream and stagist Marxist accounts would accept the social costs of modernization for different reasons. The former for the greater good of development and the second as a 'necessary step' towards class struggle (see Warren, 1973).

[71] Sender recognizes the need to also propose policies mitigating the crushing effects of capitalist agriculture (e.g. on women). He also acknowledged the potential relevance of movements. However, they are both subordinated to the primary role productive forces play in producing positive processes of social transformation. See Wilson (2011) for a different reading of the South African case, for instance, in relation to patterns of inequality and their socio-economic effects.

Undoubtedly, placing labour and labouring at the very centre of the analysis of industrial processes reveals the cracks in this type of economic analyses. Particularly, from this vantage point, their (many) Achilles heel(s) are exposed: the linearity of 'time' in their accounts; the sharp contraposition they propose between the worlds of industrial and non-industrial work; and their obsession with industrial size.

First, these analyses do not contemplate the possibility of an industrial future worse than or not considerably different from the past for the labouring masses. This is to say that industrialization is only and always considered a force for good since the start, and the time and process of 'transition' towards it is generally considered worth the final result. However, as stressed by many sectoral accounts, 'industrial upgrading' and 'social upgrading' may follow divergent paths and timing (Rammohan and Sundaresan, 2003), with the former betraying promises of necessarily leading to the latter (Barrientos *et al.*, 2011), which is also too often quite narrowly defined (Selwyn, 2013).

Second, modernizing narratives generally see the entry into industrial work as the (happy) ending of the story for the labouring poor, who, even when significantly exploited within the factory, would still be considerably better off than in non-industrial occupations, for instance, in the informal sector. However, the analysis of the sweatshop regime reveals that industrial work and non-industrial work are strongly connected moments in the lives of the working poor, and not necessarily in a pre-defined order that does not leave space for any 'return ticket'. Often, for the sweatshop worker, the factory remains only a transient experience, after which s/he may go back (or indeed move forward) to engage in other types of (often informal) activities. Overall, the extreme complexity and ever-changing temporalities of livelihoods across the sweatshop regime crucially undermine narratives suffering from the 'modernization fetish'.

Third, while such fetish generally comes with considerable faith in the ability of large industrial units to deliver better working conditions, the analysis presented in this book poses serious questions on the validity of this assumption. Across the regional manifestations of India's sweatshop regime, large factories are not necessarily providers of better working conditions. Employers often engage in systematic processes of externalization of all costs related to the social reproduction of the workforce, like in the NCR, or in practices aimed at twisting and bending the meaning of permanent worker status effectively circumventing labour regulations and their potentially positive effects, like in Bangalore (see also Mezzadri, 2012). Evidence from the NCR also shows that, for workers, working in 'large' or 'small' units may matter up to a point, in a context where wages are quite similar (see Srivastava, 2015), and where significant levels of labour circulation and labour-process-based industrial circulation undermine access to social security contributions even for those (few) who should technically be in the position to claim them (Mezzadri, 2015d). In fact, the broader relevance of circulation in paving processes of accumulation and labour surplus extraction is often completely ignored by modernizing narratives, which instead generally merely focus on single production units.

Hyper-modernizing accounts, finally, must also be set against debates on unfreedom. The analysis of India's sweatshop regime has revealed how workers always take their socio-economic chains with them, both those who sweat from their homes, and those who walk through the door of the garment factory. From a Marxian perspective, 'full dispossession' is not a defining trait of the garment proletariat. From a feminist perspective, as discussed in detail in Chapter 3, workers' social chains, as linked to realms of reproduction, are hardly simply related to their space of work. Hence, simplistic assumptions on how to deliver 'liberation' should be avoided. Rather, this should remain a question for empirical investigation and, obviously, struggle. As argued by Federici (2004, in Federici, 2012, p. 95), liberation would hardly simply come 'through the machine', or via mere increases in productivity. These organize capital, *not* labour. On the contrary, the study of the sweatshop regime has revealed that unfreedom, exploitation and social oppression interplay in complex ways, which cannot be captured by narrow debates on industrial transition or industrial size. Left unchallenged, oppression neither does have an expiry date nor disappears simply because it lands in a larger venue.

From Modern Slavery to Global Neo-bondage and 'Development as Unfreedom'

If, on the one hand, the analysis of the sweatshop regime is a useful warning against overly optimistic accounts stressing the benign (or the troubled but ultimately necessary) nature of current processes of industrialization, it also informs debates on 'modern slavery'. Often represented as lying at the opposite end of the spectrum from modernizing narratives, accounts stressing the rise of new slavery underline the similarities between the harsh labouring conditions of today's proletariat and that of slaves. On the one hand, the debate on 'new', 'modern' or 'modern-day' slavery, greatly inspired by the work of Kevin Bales (1999; 2005), is clearly marred by a number of analytical and methodological problems, besides lending itself to selective interpretations (Davidson, 2015) that may even be politically dangerous. On the other hand, it may also open up fruitful avenues for the (re)development of a systematic discussion on the ways in which different forms of unfreedom do not simply 'survive' under capitalism. Rather than being at the margins of processes of proletarianization, they have always been central to capitalist development (Banaji, 2003, 2010) and have significantly expanded during its current neoliberal phase (Lerche, 2007; LeBaron and Ayers, 2013). Let us first assess the limitations and strengths of the debate, and then highlight how the analysis of the sweatshop regime developed in this book may contribute to it.

There is little doubt that the escalation of the debate on modern slavery has developed in the context of a rising number of reports on human right abuses, human trafficking and 'extreme forms of exploitation' (loosely defined), which nowadays also figure prominently on major national newspapers. *The Guardian*, for instance, today hosts a whole column on modern slavery. Reports have covered considerably different stories of extreme toil, brutal exploitation and oppression. Some of these stories have focused on the actual sale of labouring bodies (like in the case of the Thai shrimp industry, see Lawrence's report in *The Guardian*, 2015); a process that meets the general traits of slavery as a system of full commodification of the body. Others, instead, have portrayed the extreme measures deployed to severely limit the personal freedom of international migrant workers across a vast range of sectors and geographical areas. In these cases, the correlation or difference with slavery is far more complex. Considerable attention has been paid, for instance, to South Asian workers deployed in the Gulf (e.g. see Pattison's report in *The Guardian* on Qatar's World Cup 'Slaves', 2013). Many reports also increasingly focus on the Mediterranean, where, in countries like Italy, undocumented migrants sweat across 'new' agricultural plantations. They are paid as little as 3 euros per day, and they are violently controlled under the system of '*caporalato*' (Italy's own system of indenture labour; see Muzi's report in *The Guardian*, 2014; Ciccarello, 2012, in *Il Fatto Quotidiano*). According to the Global Slavery Index (2014), today across the world economy 35.8 million people live in some form of modern slavery.

Despite the well-meaning nature of many of these reports, their largely uncritical deployment of the world 'slavery' for different forms of abuse, their representation of such abuses as lying at the margins or outside the otherwise 'normal' pace of processes of capitalism, and their tendency to identify 'leading culprits' to pursue, signal their analytical limitation. The main problem of these takes on modern slavery lies in their implicit deployment of 'methodological individualism' (Le Baron and Ayers, 2013, p. 874), in a schema where unfreedom and unfree labour as a category within it are 'typically understood and portrayed as an individual relationship of domination', and represented as outliers or 'excesses' of the world economy.[72] In fact, the whole poverty debate is broadly dominated by this 'anti-relational habit', and poverty outcomes are often 'exceptionalized' and turned into 'abnormal or pathological, rather than everyday, social processes' (Mosse, 2010, pp. 1158–1159).

This view poses serious dangers, as it can be instrumentalized in all sorts of possible ways. If, on the one hand, reference to slavery can be instrumentally deployed in targeted campaigns to raise public opinion successfully (see the iSlave campaign in China, SACOM, 2011), in other cases, it can be deployed in regressive ways, through political arguments hardly in favour of the supposed 'new slaves'. The recent abuse of the slavery debate to justify the closure of European borders to migrants and refugees, portrayed as the helpless victims of a handful of trafficking warlords is a case in point (for how this position dangerously 'twists the lessons of history', see Beyond Slavery Column, 2015; see also De Noronha and Anderson, 2015).

Yet, the great noise increasingly caused by this debate can be used as a platform to develop – or perhaps simply revamp? – far more fruitful understandings of the ways in which 'slavery', or indeed unfreedom, may reproduce across modes of production, phases of capitalist development and regimes of wage work (Mezzadri, 2015c). While rejecting methodological individualism, these understandings should *re-focus* instead on the systemic embeddedness of unfreedom in economic life under capitalism, so as to avoid the risk of creating multiple narratives of 'exceptions', either existing at the margins of the world economy, or representing, at best, only its darkest fringes. Re-focusing on such embeddedness means building upon a number of key contributions on the continuity between forms of freedom and unfreedom within capitalism (starting from Banaji, 1977, 2003, 2010), which have strongly inspired this narrative, and which offer precious tools to engage in the modern slavery debate. Let us rehearse some of their arguments, placing them now in direct conversation with the debate on modern slavery.

Despite many representations equating capitalism with the emergence of 'free' (read wage) labour, unfreedom has always been a key feature of capitalism as a

---

[72] This focus on 'excesses' is analyzed by Novak (2015) in relation to refugees. Recently, Mathew (2016) has convincingly disproved prevalent ideas that even trafficking and smuggling necessarily operate 'outside' capitalism.

mode of production across its different phases (Banaji, 2003). This has hardly been an 'anomaly' (see Miles, 1987). The generation of unfreedom does not lie outside processes of proletarianization (indicating, for instance, 'de-proletarianization', see Brass, 1990; see also Manzo, 2005, on Africa), but it has instead always been strongly related to such processes. Admittedly, dispossession from the means of production and survival is only one of the ways in which unfreedom manifests. Others can only be captured by focusing on realms of social reproduction where social structures and social differences and inequalities create different 'cages' and 'walls' reproducing the oppression and greatly limited room of manoeuvre for many vulnerable groups (Harriss-White and Gooptu, 2001). Women, but also children, ethnic minorities or, in India, lower castes experience unfreedom in ways that clearly exceed a mere focus on economic dispossession. Rather, these may include social subjugation or even 'stigma' (see John, 2013). For women, questions of dispossession have always interplayed inextricably with harsh forms of patriarchal control (Mies, 1982, 1986). If indeed, neoliberalism seems to have accelerated the production of forms of unfreedom (Lerche, 2007; Le Baron and Ayers, 2013), it has done so thanks to processes of de-regulation that have opened the way for alternative forms of social regulation to strengthen their hold and control over the labourforce worldwide (Mezzadri, 2009b). This is to say that many of these forms of unfreedom were already endemically present in many regions; neoliberalism has simply further unleashed their potential as a source of economic competitiveness (Mezzadri, 2008). For instance, the 'tremendous flexibility' in which caste in India has interplayed with liberalization is amply discussed (Harriss-White, 2003; Deshpande, 2000; 2011; Shah and Harriss-White, 2011).

Examining these dynamics through the lens of the sweatshop, as argued in this book, evidences the presence of multiple forms of unfreedom. This is one of the key features that characterize the sweatshop as a regime. Undoubtedly, these forms of unfreedom escape definitions that are exclusively based on productive realms; rather they intersect with the reproductive sphere and on its multiple social divides. A woman factory worker exposed to verbal and physical abuse, or increasingly subject to severe limitations of her personal freedom once swallowed by the employer's dormitory; a male rural circulatory migrant trying his fortune in the factories of the NCR before returning to his village for harvesting; or a self-employed adda worker trying to put together a wage in Bareilly while experiencing the harshness of the interlocked modes of exploitation imposed by the local contractor, all experience unfreedom in distinct ways. Paradoxically, if there is one thread weaving their labouring lives together, this has more to do with their very limited 'freedom'. In fact, they are all 'free' to stitch or starve (Mezzadri, 2015c). They are free from a dignified existence (Breman, 2013) and most of all often 'free' from reproducing themselves as anything but individual labourers, compartmentalized across the different echelons of the sweatshop (Mezzadri, 2015c). In the context of the current industrial paradigms and global production circuits, as epitomized by the sweatshop, it is hard to conceive 'development as freedom' as once envisaged and advocated by Amartya Sen (1999). Rather, the intensification of the neoliberal logic is increasingly delivering *development as unfreedom*.

In India, the debates on unfreedom and forced labour have been particularly prolific and productive, far before the debate on modern slavery acquired its current connotations as a global problem and concern. It is not a case that many of the most important early contributions that shaped this debate come from scholars focusing on the subcontinent. India is still the country showing the highest percentage of bonded labour (Lerche, 2007, 2010, 2012), with forms of 'neo-bondage' further significantly inflating these estimates (Breman, 2013).[73] In fact, overall, neo-bondage may perhaps be the most useful term to capture the different modalities of unfreedom experienced by the Indian garment proletariat, as this always involves hardship crossing both productive and reproductive realms (Breman, 1996, 2013). As these patterns of unfreedom and neo-bondage become increasingly subsumed within the logic of the sweatshop, and deployed for manufacturing its multiple and distinct cheap labouring bodies as well as 'global' garments, they are also increasingly projected into the world market. They are globalized and tightened to the pace of international competition. Crucially, while the rise of this 'global neo-bondage', or indeed unfree labour in general, should be understood in relation 'to the re-organization of production and social reproduction that has been integral to neoliberalism' (Le Baron and Ayers, 2013, p. 880), one should hardly stop at global explanations. Instead, the analysis should also include considerations over the political economy of specific regions, and attention to the many actors who reproduce the unfreedom, exploitation and oppression of labouring classes in practice. In countries like India, an emphasis only stressing the neo-colonial roots of workers' social and economic chains would simply not work. In fact, the analysis of India's colonial and post-colonial experience reveals the key role played by regional and local lords in shaping trade and production routes (Roy, 2013) and subjugating the labouring masses

---

[73] Unsurprisingly, the Global Slavery Index (2014) ranks India first in terms of incidence of modern slavery.

through processes of production and circulation (Banaji, 2010). These trends have continued in post-colonial India (Breman, 1996, 2013). In line with this, the study of India's sweatshop regime has also revealed the many masters steering the joint enterprise of the sweatshop, and jointly reproducing unfreedom and neo-bondage within globalized circuits through processes of production and circulation. In the Indian sweatshop, unfreedom is in fact clearly anchored to and generated through both these processes.

This is to say that if we do need to return the debate of modern slavery to political economy, where it belongs, we also need to make sure we embed this debate in the complex socio-economic history of given countries. Their history is no secondary complication to the way in which the neoliberal design manifests, reproduces and, sadly, thrives. Else, not much differently from modernizing narratives, also debates on modern slavery would simply reproduce homogenizing visions of development, albeit in this case not as a force for good, but as manifesting in ever similar relations of dependence.

Finally, the debate on modern slavery and unfreedom should also start to more systematically report on the 'voices' of the supposed slaves it aims to 'rescue'. Their accounts, in many cases, significantly complicate our categories of analysis. As mentioned in the Introduction of the book, it is only in Bareilly, and from the bottom of the sweatshop, that this started appearing for the complex regime that it is. By the same token, the accounts of sweatshop labourers – women, men, migrant factory workers or home-based workers – crucially unveil the traits of 'lived' unfreedom, so that one can appreciate their nuances and differences. Workers' life stories of toil, exploitation and oppression must be systematically included in accounts of labour and labouring, and in debates of freedom and unfreedom. Unsurprisingly, these voices are often dissonant and contradictory, but hardly more than the complexity of contemporary capitalist transformations. If something, they provide a crucial glimpse into the contested nature of the latter.

For example, for some workers, the language of freedom or unfreedom is associated with opportunities as shaped by social norms; for others, it relates to the possibility of snatching some moments of leisure time. As argued by the (real life) protagonist of Aman Sethi's brilliant book *A Free Man*, perhaps one of the most vivid accounts of Delhi's casual, contract labour markets and rhythms, *Azadi* – which in Hindi literally means 'freedom' – is for many male rural migrants one of the most crucial aspirations. Azadi represents the freedom to tell the contractor to get lost, as he 'owns our work. He does not own us' (Sethi, 2012, p. 19). For many male households' heads in Bareilly, instead, this is hardly the case. Many of them have a conceptualization of '*mazdoor*' (labour) that is already largely incompatible with freedom, which they often seek through circular migration to the NCR, although there they will most likely squat on the floor of the contractors' workshop, which is at once a living and working space. Women rarely identify themselves as *mazdoor*, despite engaging in exactly the same activities as men. Their usual self-representation as *Karighar* (artisans), however, is at times a positive account, in other instances, instead, betrays the pain of being confined to the asphyxiating walls of the household. In several occasions, when asked directly and collectively, members of the same household enter heated discussions in relation to their self-representation, as either (wage) 'labourers' or (self-employed) 'artisans', with positions greatly varying based on gender lines, age and position within the family.

Indeed, the debate on free versus unfree labour, through workers' eyes and voices, is often ultimately one about aspirations and perceived opportunities (or, indeed, the lack thereof). Many workers, despite greatly limited options, fight extremely hard to avoid the most severe traps posed by unfreedom, particularly those potentially leading to the spiral of debt. Overall, while enduring harsh labouring conditions, many of these workers really are tireless *unfreedom fighters*.

More problematic, perhaps, is the assessment of freedom and unfreedom for workers trapped into industrial hostels. In India's sweatshop regime, as we have illustrated, these are mainly women, many of whom are vulnerable, as young rural migrant. In some areas, like Bangalore or Tiruppur, India may be in the process of catching up with China's dormitory labour system (Smith and Pun, 2006). Here, instances bordering bondage, as in the case of the so-called *Sumangali* girls discussed in Chapter 3, co-exist with situations where women workers sabotage the assembly-line abandoning a factory life that swallows their full daily reproduction beyond work time (see Ruthven's recent report on *The Guardian*, 2015). However, in all cases, freedom and unfreedom always interplay in different ways that escape polarising and simplistic representations focusing on 'extremes', and should instead be represented as placed along a 'continuum' (Lerche, 2007, 2010; Breman, 1996, 2013).

The main point that arises from an examination of these multiple voices, in sum, is that the deployment of the word 'slave' necessarily ends up in concealing their differences. It hides the complex nature of workers' agency in globalized circuits (see Carswell and De Neve, 2013), which, even in contexts not characterized by organized resistance, often entails many forms of everyday resistance and resilience, through sabotage, absenteeism, delay in production or 'cheating' the boss whenever possible (see Katz, 2004; see also Chari, 2003).

Ultimately, the deployment of this term should always be informed by a clear political strategy, respond to a clear political goal, and take into consideration the risks of its potentially dangerous re-appropriation by anti-labour forces. Only in these admittedly *ad-hoc* terms, it seems to me, the use of the expression modern slavery may result effective, and politically meaningful. Else, it would risk remaining a narrative of victimhood, linked to a growing 'rescue industry' (Quirk, 2015) and emptied of political meaning as mainly embedded in a politics of guilt. There are already far too many of these narratives focusing on the sweatshop, as there are many top-down interventions aiming at 'fixing' the problems of these victims through quick solutions.

This is, perhaps, one of the traps that also current ethical consumerism should avoid. It is with no doubt one of the main pitfalls of contemporary forms of corporate, ethical trade interventions. Some reflections on the current trajectory of ethical consumerism and ethical trade, both in general and with reference to India, are developed below, as final remarks of this analysis. These reflections stress the need to retune debates on ethics to the sound of sweatshop workers' own demands, whose echo, if still at a distance, seems to be finally mounting.

The Utopia of Ethical Consumerism Against the (not so) Distant Echo of Resistance

When the early consumer campaigns in favour of people sweating in the 'tailoring business' started in the US, many of them were partially influenced by a politics of guilt and focused, for instance, on what they considered the most extreme forms of exploitation, like child labour (Boris, 1994; Prugl, 1996). However, many consumer campaigns also strongly articulated with labour demands, so that the politics of consumerism soon became greatly differentiated, polarized between conceptualizations privileging either ideas of 'consumer–citizens' or of 'consumer–customers' (Frank, 2003). The former evolved along far more progressive lines, as they established productive connections between labour-centred politics and consumer-politics, giving rise to efforts that bridged progressive forces in society. The rise of global outsourcing, accelerated by neoliberalism and the 'export' of the sweatshop around the world, has obviously severely tested these early attempts at building broader forms of solidarity, as it has undermined the relevance of the national sphere as the crucial platform where such forms of solidarity could be imagined and played out. Since then, the reconstitution of the anti-sweatshop movement as a globalised one, albeit still significantly shaped by national politics and the evolution of different 'varieties of activism' (see Bair and Palpacuer, 2012), has been marred by the obvious contradictions of trying to overcome multiple social divides.

The global divide between production and consumption in which the movement started to operate was further exacerbated by a widening class divide between anti-sweatshop activists (often middle-class) and beneficiaries (the working poor), particularly in a context where organized labour started playing a far more modest role (Frank, 2003; Bair and Palpacuer, 2012). These contradictions have been magnified by the rise of the CSR model as a corporate response to consumer pressure. This model – which today represents a fundamental aspect of how governance is exercised in globalized production circuits (De Neve, 2009) – is certainly contested (Bair and Palpacuer, 2015), but it also forcefully counters the more radical demands of the anti-sweatshop movement.

For instance, the proliferation of many shared platforms where business, NGOs, labour organizations and unions come together in forms of tripartitism is mainly taking place on 'business terms', under an agenda aimed at systematically neutralizing the more radical content of labour activists' demands. While many of these platforms claim to organize according to the logics of past experiences of collective bargaining, they are also often also heavily financed and therefore influenced by business actors, risking to reproduce a highly unequal distribution of power over negotiating a better deal for workers. Moreover, these platforms hardly overcome the logics of 'consent', where brands and retailers must necessarily 'come on board', confirming the inexorable alignment of states with capital during the neoliberal era. This market-based approach many activists had to embrace to oppose sweatshops may have had the 'paradoxical effect of increasing the symbolic power of global lead firms as regulatory institutions' (Palpacuer, 2017). Even the recent *Accord on Fire and Building Safety in Bangladesh*, heralded by global unions as signalling 'the end of voluntarism' (see Kumar and Mahoney, 2014) and the return to international mandatory regulations, must be joined by buyers first, before becoming legally binding. Besides, while focusing on one country, it is not mainstreamed to other garment sourcing areas: buyers can behave 'well' (or better) in Bangladesh, and still poorly in other regions.

Briefly, CSR has systematically attempted to and partially succeeded in colonizing the politics of consumption, redirecting it towards conceptualizations of ethical production and trade that are non-threatening for corporations in their quest for searching new sources of profits. Obviously, the many progressive fringes of the global anti-sweatshop movement, like *Labour behind the Label* or *War on*

Want, are fighting these developments, and reach out for progressive, pro-labour regional partners who have fought against their local sweatshop for a long time. In India, the work of unions and labour organizations or NGOs like NTUI, GATWU, GLU, SEWA, Cividep, or SAVE, amongst others, should be similarly acknowledged.

However, if the rise and deepening of 'corporate' activist models (see Dauvergne and Le Baron, 2014) is not systematically opposed, many progressive organizations may increasingly find themselves with little room for manoeuvre. In the UK, for instance, funding is already shrinking for organisations seen as too 'militant' in their labour politics. These are dangerous developments, as a progressive politics of consumption can only be imagined as strongly connected to a progressive labour politics; not merely to a politics of guilt or one aspiring to squeeze the few concessions capital may be willing to make to clean its own image.

Crucially, if suppliers have long lamented the imposition of CSR as yet another governance tool re-proposing their subordination into given globalized networks, the current rise of giant contractors (Appelbaum, 2008; Merk, 2014; Mezzadri, 2014b) from key emerging economies may be determining a shift from contestation to co-optation. Undoubtedly, India seems to have learnt its CSR lesson well. While the top layer amongst the regional lords of India's sweatshop regime still laments the 'western' imposition of codes of conduct, it is also organizing to appropriate CSR tools and re-elaborate them in its own terms and under its own control. This is, ultimately, what the DISHA project seems to be about so far (Mezzadri, 2014b), although close monitoring of its evolution is still needed. These developments are taking place against a general background of intensification of broader pro-capital interventions in India, many of which seem to be also adopting a largely 'India-centric' CSR framework. In its current elaboration, for instance, there is little doubt that India's new CSR Bill is likely to reproduce the old model of community-based charitable work done by corporations to show the social commitment of business (Mezzadri, 2015a). It is unlikely, however, to increase the control by the state on business for the development of a serious politics of accountability of corporations towards Indian citizens. Ultimately, the evolution and internalization of the CSR agenda in the Indian case suggests that even where perhaps a more equal redistribution of global gains may be in sight for Indian capital, this is unlikely to be the case for labour. As these processes unfold, supposed 'ethical' interventions continue only scratching the surface of India's sweatshop regime, as a clear outcome of the pro-capital nature of their conceptualization.

These interventions, as illustrated in this book, particularly with reference to the NCR and Bareilly, seem to simply sit on the complex relations of power and subordination shaping the sweatshop across India, without affecting any of its key working mechanisms. Once again, while lamented by sweatshops' regional and local masters, these interventions hardly touch the core of their operations and power, leaving their aggressive processes of labour surplus extraction connecting production and circulation across both productive and reproductive domains largely unchallenged. Instead, interventions should aim at challenging the working mechanisms of the sweatshop regime. Given the great diversity of the different echelons of the sweatshop, this might entail different forms of policy intervention. For instance, in areas where exploitation heavily interlocks across markets and reproductive realms, interventions only focused on single labour markets may not be sufficient (Mezzadri, 2014a).

So far, in India, the lords of the sweatshop seem to proceed largely uncontested in their exploitation of the working poor. Episodes of resistance are mostly sporadic and spontaneous, as it is the case across all economic activities characterized by the predominance of informal labour (Breman, 2013; Bhattarcharya, 2014). They are nevertheless significant as they indicate the potential social traits that could characterize struggle in the future (see Agarwala, 2013). Confirming the relevance of both processes of commodification and exploitation at work in the sweatshop regime, and the possible convergence between 'Polanyian' and 'Marxist struggles' (see Chhachhi, 2014), these episodes suggest that struggles should involve both realms of production and reproduction.

Strikes have taken place in the NCR, an area that has been recently also involved in various forms of protest in more capital-intensive sectors like automobile (Monaco, 2015), in relations to conditions of work. Recently, in Okhla, 350 garment workers successfully negotiated a higher bonus with their employer (Yadav, 2015). Other strikes targeting wages and benefits have taken place in Bangalore, led by the NTUI-affiliated union GATWU (Kumar and Mahoney, 2014), or by GLU. Unorganized and spontaneous labour revolts have also ignited against forms of oppression and domination at work in the sweatshop regime far exceeding low salaries. Over 3,000 workers employed by Orient Craft, one of India's giant garment company, set fire to the fabric store inside the plant once rumours spread that some workers had been electrocuted inside a plant elevator (Yadav, 2015). While these rumours turned out as unfounded, workers' extreme reaction cannot but be understood in relation to the violence of the sweatshop regime as a body-depleting enterprise, where incidents and even death are daily realities for labour. Areas like Kapashera, offering workers inhumane daily living conditions, are only likely to become possible cradles for workers' resistance, in the context of state absence and minimal employers' contributions. In the context of harsh working and living conditions, labour struggles cannot but also increasingly become struggles over reproduction. This is also what seems to be emerging from a look at the global landscape of workers-led anti-sweatshop protests across the world. In China, for instance, dormitories, key sites of labour control, have also already turned into key sites for resistance (Pun, 2007).

From Cambodia to Bangladesh, from China to Vietnam, workers are raising their voices and are starting to fight hard against the brutality of the sweatshop in all its different facets, in factories as well as outside. They are refusing to become a 'permanently redundant mass' (Breman, 2002, p. 13) to be confined to a *Planet of Slums*' (Davis, 2006), marginalized from that world economy they helped building. Hopefully, their voices will become increasingly audible across the complex sweatshop echelons of the NCR, in the factories of Bangalore and Chennai, in the knitwear units of Ludhiana and Tiruppur, all the way to sweatshop outposts like Bareilly, and will be joined by those of the Indian garment proletariat. Obviously, their demands are likely to be addressed to different masters and/or focus on distinct issues, as their exploitation and social oppression vary significantly. However, it is only through an articulation of their multiple social struggles that the complex joint enterprise of the sweatshop can be jointly fought. Ultimately, it is only workers' rising voices that will show us the long road towards ethical consumption. May the mounting echo of these voices finally crack the thick walls of the sweatshop, in both its most visible and most remote chambers.

Pictures from the Sweatshop Chambers

Picture 1 Men factory workers in the NCR

Picture 2 Woman adda homeworker in the NCR

Picture 3 Woman moti worker in the NCR

Picture 4 Children adda workers in the NCR

Picture 5 Men adda workers in a 'street unit' in Bareilly district

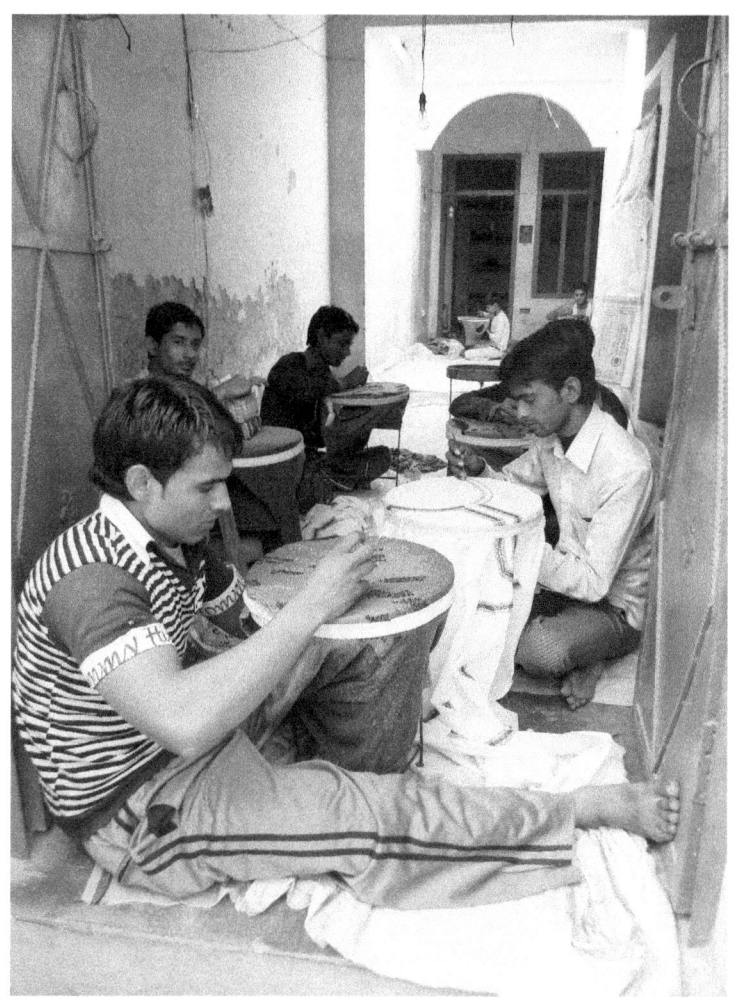

Picture 6 Men adda workers in a contractor-run unit in Bareilly district

Picture 7 Women adda homeworkers in Bareilly district

Picture 8 Women adda homeworkers in Bareilly district

Picture 9 Men workshop workers on the shopfloor in Jaipur

Picture 10 Men workshop workers on the shopfloor in Mumbai

Picture 11 Men workshop workers on the shopfloor in Kolkata

Picture 12 Women factory workers on the shopfloor in Bangalore

Picture 13 Women factory workers on the shopfloor in Chennai

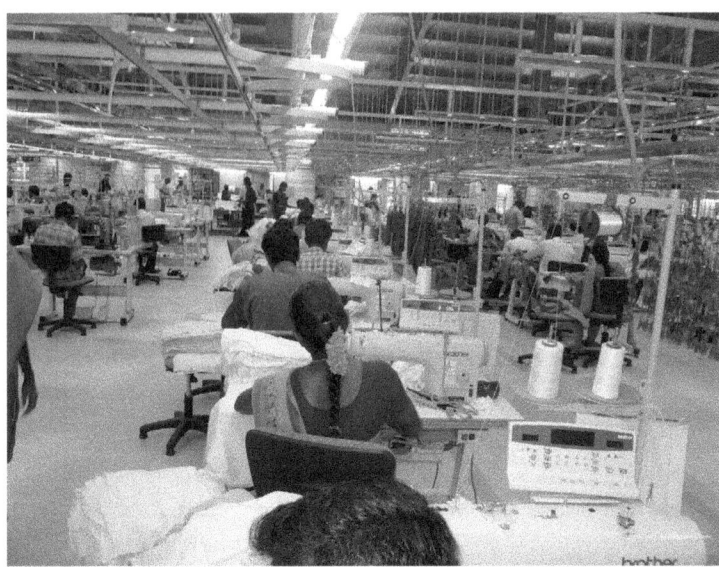

Picture 14 Men & women factory workers on the shopfloor in Tiruppur

Picture 15 Men & women factory workers on the shopfloor in Coimbatore district

Source: All pictures are taken by the author, with the exception of picture 14 (Tiruppur), courtesy of Grace Carswell.

References

Abraham, V. 2013. 'Missing Labour or Consistent "De-Feminisation"?' *Economic and Political Weekly* 48 (31): 99–108.

AEPC. 2004. *Handbook of Export Statistics* (Data from 1983–2003, Various Issues). New Delhi: Apparel Export Promotion Council.

_____. 2009. *Indian Apparel Clusters*. New Delhi: Apparel Export Promotion Council.

_____. 2013a. *DISHA Brochure*. New Delhi: Apparel Export Promotion Council.

_____. 2013b. *Handbook of Export Statistics (Electronic)*. New Delhi: Apparel Export promotion Council.

Agarwala, R. 2013. *Informal Labor, Formal Politics, and Dignified Discontent in India*. New York: Cambridge University Press.

Alam, G. 1992. *Industrial Districts and Technological Change: A Study of the Garment Industry in Delhi*. Mimeo, New Delhi: Centre for Technological Studies.

Ambekar Institute of Labour Studies. 1980. *Problems of Clothing Industry in India – A Trade Union View*. Report Presented at the International Labour Organisation Second Tripartite Technical Meeting for Clothing Industry, Geneva, 23 Sep–2 Oct 1980. Mumbai: Ambekar Institute of Labour Studies.

_____. 2005. *Textile and Clothing Industries in India and Phasing Out of MFA – A Study Report*. Internal report. Mumbai: Ambekar Institute of Labour Studies.

Anderson, K. B. 2010. *Marx at the Margins: On Nationalism, Ethnicity and Non-Western Societies*. Chicago: Chicago University Press.

Andrijasevic, R. and D. Sacchetto. 2014. 'Made in the EU: Foxconn in the Czech Republic'. *Working USA: a Journal of Labor and Society* 17 (3): 391–415.

Anner, M. 2015. 'Labor Control Regimes and Worker Resistance in Global Supply Chains'. *Labor History* 56 (3): 292–307.

Appadurai, A. 1986. 'Introduction: Commodities and the Politics of Value'. In *The Social Life of Things – Commodities in Cultural Perspective*, edited by A. Appadurai. New York: Cambridge University Press.

Appelbaum, R. P. 2005. *TNCs and the Removal of Textile and Clothing Quotas*. Global and International Studies Program, paper 38, University of California, Santa Barbara. New York and Geneva: UNCTAD.

_____. 2008. 'Giant Transnational Contractors in East Asia: Emergent Trends in Global Supply Chains'. *Competition & Change* 12 (1): 69–87.

Appelbaum, R. P., and N. Lichtenstein. 2014. 'An Accident in History'. *New Labor Forum* 23 (3): 58–65.

Arizpe, L., and J. Aranda. 1981. 'The 'Comparative Advantages' of Women's Disadvantages: Women Workers in the Strawberry Export Agribusiness in Mexico'. *Signs* 7 (2): 453–73.

Arnold, D., and J. R. Bongiovi. 2013. 'Precarious, Informalizing and Casualizing Labor: Transforming Concepts and Understanding'. *American Behavioural Scientist* 57 (3): 289–308.

Arnold, D., and J. Pickles. 2011. 'Global Work, Surplus Labor, and the Precarious Economies of the Border.' *Antipode* 43 (5): 1598–1624.

ASK. 2001. *Basic Information on Regional Labour Conditions in the Garment Industry in the Region of Mumbai*. Report. New Delhi: ASK.

Atzeni, M. 2013. 'Introduction: Neo-Liberal Globalisation and Interdisciplinary Perspectives on Labour and Collective Action.' In M. Atzeni (ed.) *Workers and Labour in a Globalised Capitalism: Contemporary Themes and Theoretical Issues*. London: Palgrave McMillan.

Azmeh, S., and K. Nadvi. 2013. 'Greater Chinese' Global Production Networks in the Middle East: The Rise of the Jordanian Garment Industry. *Development and Change* 44: 1317–40.

Bair, J. 2005. 'Global Capitalism and Commodity Chains: Looking Backward, Going Forward.' *Competition and Change* 9 (2): 163–80.

_____. 2009. *Frontiers of Commodity Chain Research*. Stanford: Stanford University Press.

_____. 2010. 'On Difference and Capital: Gender and the Globalization of Production.' *Signs: Journal of Women in Culture & Society* 36 (1): 203–26.

Bair, J., and F. Palpacuer. 2012. 'From Varieties of Capitalism to Varieties of Activism: The Antisweatshop Movement in Comparative Perspective.' *Social Problems* 59 (4): 522–43.

_____. 2015. 'CSR Beyond the Corporation: Contested Governance in Global Value Chains.' *Global Networks* 15: S1–S19.

Bales, K. 1999. *Disposable People: New Slavery in the Global Economy*. Berkeley, Los Angeles and London: University of California Press.

_____. 2005. *Understanding Global Slavery: a Reader*. Berkeley, Los Angeles and London: University of California Press.

Banaji, J. 1977. 'Modes of Production in a Materialist Conception of History.' *Capital and Class* 1 (3): 1–44.

_____. 2003. 'The Fictions of Free Labour: Contract, Coercion, and So-Called Unfree Labour.' *Historical Materialism* 11 (3): 69–95.

_____. 2010. *Theory as History: Essays on Modes of Production and Exploitation*. Leiden and Boston: Brill Academic Publishers.

_____. 2013. 'Seasons of Self-Delusion: Opium, Capitalism and the Financial Markets.' *Historical Materialism* 21 (2): 3–19.

Banerjee, N. 1999. 'How Real is the Bogey of Feminisation?' In *Gender and Employment in India*, edited by T. S. Papola, and A. N. Sharma, 299–317. New Delhi: Vikas.

Barboza, D., and P. Meller. 2005. 'China to Limit Textile Exports to Europe.' *New York Times*, 11 June. Accessed September 20, 2015. http://www.nytimes.com/2005/06/11/business/worldbusiness/11textile.html.

Bardhan, P. 1980. 'Interlocking Factor Markets and Agrarian Development: A Review of the Issues.' *Oxford Economic Papers* 32 (1): 82–98.

_____. 2002. 'The Political Economy of Reforms in India.' In *Facets of the Indian Economy*, edited by R. Mohan, New Delhi: Oxford University Press.

Barrientos, S. 2002. 'Mapping Codes Through the Value Chain: From Researcher to Detective.' In *Corporate Responsibility and Labor Rights-Codes of Conduct in the Global Economy*, edited by R. Jenkins, R. Pearson, and G. Seyfang, London: Earthscan Publications.

_____. 2008 'Contract Labour: The 'Achilles Heel' of Corporate Codes in Commercial Value Chains.' *Development and Change* 39 (6): 977–90.

_____. 2013. 'Labour Chains: Analysing the Role of Labour Contractors in Global Production Networks.' *Journal of Development Studies* 49 (8): 1058–71.

Barrientos, S., and S. Smith. 2007. 'Do Workers Benefit from Ethical Trade? Assessing Codes of Labour Practice in Global Production Systems.' *Third World Quarterly* 28 (4): 713–29.

Barrientos, S., K. Mathur, and A. Sood. 2010. 'Decent Work in Global Production Networks.' In *Labour in Global Production Networks in India*, edited by A. Posthuma, and D. Nathan, 127–145. Oxford and New Delhi: Oxford University Press.

Barrientos, S., G. Gereffi, and A. Rossi. 2011. 'Economic and Social Upgrading in Global Production Networks: A New Paradigm for a Changing World.' *International Labour Review* 150: 319–40.

Basi, J. K. T. 2009. *Women, Identity, and India's Call Centre Industry*. London: Routledge.

Basile, E. 2013. *Capitalist Development in India's Informal Economy*. London: Routledge.

Basile, E., and B. Harriss-White. 2000. *Corporative Capitalism: Civil Society and the Politics of Accumulation in Small Town India*. QEH Working Paper 38. Accessed September 20, 2015. http://www3.qeh.ox.ac.uk/pdf/qehwp/qehwps38.pdf.

_____. 2010. 'Introduction.' Special Issue on India's Informal Capitalism and Its Regulation. *International Review of Sociology* 20 (3): 457–71.

Becattini, G. 1990. 'The Marshallian Industrial District as a Socio-Economic Notion.' In *Industrial Districts and Inter-firm Cooperation in Italy*, edited by F. Pyke, G. Becattini, and W. Sengemberger. Geneva: International Institute for Labour Studies.

Beckert, S. 2015. *Empire of Cotton. A New History of Global Capitalism*. UK: Allen Lane, Penguin.

Beneria, L., and M. Roldan. 1987. *The Crossroads of Class and Gender: Industrial Homework, Subcontracting, and Household Dynamics in Mexico City*. Chicago: University of Chicago Press.

Benjamin, S. 1996. *The Neighbourhood as Factory: The Influence of Land Development and Civic Politics on an Industrial Cluster in Delhi, India*. Unpublished PhD thesis submitted to MIT, Cambridge, MA.

_____. 2000. 'Governance, Economic Settings and Poverty in Bangalore.' *Environment and Urbanization* 12 (1): 35–56.

Bequele, A., and J. Boyden. 1988. *Combating Child Labour*. Geneva: ILO.

Berger, S. 1980. 'Discontinuity in the Politics of Industrial Societies.' In *Dualism and Discontinuity in Industrial Society*, edited by S. Berger, and M. Priore, 129–141. Cambridge: Cambridge University Press.

Bernstein, H. 2004. 'Considering Africa's Agrarian Questions.' *Historical Materialism* 12 (4): 115–44.

_____. 2007. *Capital and Labour from Centre to Margins* – Keynote Address for Conference on 'Living on the Margins, Vulnerability, Exclusion and the State in the Informal Economy', Cape Town, 26–28 March 2007. Accessed September 20, 2015. http://www.povertyfrontiers.org/ev_en.php?ID=1953_201&ID2=DO_TOPIC.

_____. 2010. *Class Dynamics of Agrarian Change*. Canada: Fernwood, Pluto and University of Michigan Press.

Bernstein, H., and L. Campling. 2006. 'Commodity Studies and Commodity Fetishism I: Trading Down.' *Journal of Agrarian Change* 6 (2): 239–64.

Berry, S. 1993. *No Condition is Permanent. Social Dynamics of Agrarian Change in Sub-Saharan Africa.* Madison: University of Wisconsin Press.

Beyond Slavery Column. 2015. 'Twisting the 'Lessons of History' to Authorise Unjustifiable Violence: The Mediterranean Crisis.' *Open Democracy, Beyond Trafficking and Slavery* 20 May 2015. Accessed September 20, 2015. https://www.opendemocracy.net/beyondslavery/twisting-"lessons-of-history"-to-excuse-unjustifiable-violence-mediterranean-refugee-c.

Bezuidenhout, A., G. Khunou, S. Mosoetsa, K. Sutherland, and J. Thoburn. 2007. 'Globalisation and Poverty: Impacts on Households of Employment and Restructuring in the Textiles Industry of South Africa.' *Journal of International Development* 19 (3): 545–65.

Bhaduri, A. 1983. *The Economic Structure of Backward Agriculture.* New Delhi: Macmillan.

_____. 1986. 'Forced Commerce and Agrarian Growth.' *World Development* 14 (2): 267–72.

_____. 1999. *On the Border of Economic Theory and History.* New Delhi: Oxford University Press.

Bharadwaj, K. 1974. *Production Conditions in Indian Agriculture.* Cambridge: Cambridge University Press.

_____. 1994. 'A View on Commercialisation in Indian Agriculture and the Development of Capitalism.' In *Accumulation, Exchange and Development*, edited by K. Bharadwaj, 206–228. New Delhi: Sage.

Bhattarcharya, S. 2014. 'Is Labour Still a Relevant Category for Praxis? Critical Reflections on Some Contemporary Discourses on Work and Labour in Capitalism.' *Development and Change* 45 (5): 941–62.

Bhowmik, S. 2015. 'The Labour Code on Industrial Relations Bill 2015: Tough Times Ahead for Labour in India.' *Global Labour Column* 207. Accessed September 20, 2015. http://www.global-labour-university.org/fileadmin/GLU_Column/papers/no_207_Bhowmik.pdf.

Blake, S. 1993. *Shahjahanabad: The Sovereign City in Mughal India 1639–1739.* Cambridge South Asian Studies Series. Cambridge: Cambridge University Press.

Blowfield, M. 2005. 'Corporate Social Responsibility: Reinventing the Meaning of Development?' *International Affairs* 81 (3): 515–24.

Blowfield, M. E., and Catherine S. Dolan. 2008. 'Stewards of Virtue? The Ethical Dilemma of CSR in African Agriculture.' *Development and Change* 39 (1): 1–23.

Bonacich, E., and R. Appelbaum. 2000. *Behind the Label.* Berkeley, CA: University of California Press.

Bonacich, E., L. Cheng, N. Chinchilla, N. Hamilton, and P. Ong. 1994. *Global Production: the Apparel Industry in the Pacific Rim.* Philadelphia: Temple University Press.

Boo, C. 2012. *Behind the Beautiful Forevers. Life, Death and Hope in a Mumbai Slum.* London: Portobello Books.

Boris, E. 1994. *Home to Work: Motherhood and the Politics of Industrial Homework in the United States.* Cambridge: Cambridge University Press.

Boserup, E. 1989. 'Industry: From the Hut to the Factory.' In *Women's Role in Economic Development,* 106–118. London: Earthscan Publications (Originally published in 1970).

Brass, T. 1990. 'Class Struggle and the Deproletarianisation of Agricultural Labour in Haryana (India).' *Journal of Peasant Studies* 18 (1): 36–65.

Braudel, F. 1981. *The Wheels of Commerce: Civilization and Capitalism: 15th–18th Century*. London: Collins.

Braverman, H. 1974. *Labour and Monopoly Capital: The Degradation of Work on the Twentieth Century*. New York: Monthly Review Press.

Breman, J. 1977. 'Labour Relations in the "Formal" and "Informal" Sectors: Report of a Case Study in South Gujarat, India. Part 2.' *Journal of Peasant Studies* 4 (4): 337–59.

_____. 1985. 'Between Accumulation and Immiseration: The Partiality of Fieldwork in Rural India.' *Journal of Peasant Studies* 13 (1): 5–36.

_____. 1995. 'Labour, Get Lost: A Late Capitalist Manifesto.' *Economic and Political Weekly* 30 (37): 2294–300.

_____. 1996. *Footloose Labour: Working in India's Informal Economy*. Cambridge: Cambridge University Press.

_____. 1999. 'The Study of Industrial Labour in Post-Colonial India. The Informal Sector: A Concluding Review.' *Contributions to Indian Sociology* 33 (1&2): 407–31.

_____. 2002. *The Labouring Poor in India: Patterns of Exploitation, Subordination, and Exclusion*. New Delhi: Oxford University Press.

_____. 2010. 'Neobondage: A Fieldwork-Based Account.' *International Labor and Working-Class History* 78 (1): 48–62.

_____. 2013. *At Work in the Informal Economy of India, A Perspective from the Bottom-Up*. New Delhi: Oxford University Press.

Breman, J., and M. van der Linden. 2014. 'Informalizing the Economy: The Return of the Social Question at a Global Level.' *Development and Change* 45: 920–40.

Brenner, R. 1977. 'The Origins of Capitalist Development: A Critique of Neo-Smithian Marxism.' *New Left Review* I/104: 25–92.

Brooks, A. 2015. *Clothing Poverty*. London: Zed.

Brusco, S. 1982. 'The Emilian Model: Productive Decentralisation and Social Integration.' *Cambridge Journal of Economics* 6: 167–84.

Burawoy, M. 1985. '*The Politics of Production: Factory Regimes Under Capitalism and Socialism.*' London: Verso.

_____. 1998. 'The Extended Case Method.' *Sociological Theory* 16 (11): 4–33.

_____. 2001. 'Manufacturing the Global.' *Ethnography* 2 (2): 147–59.

_____. 2010. 'From Polanyi to Pollyanna: The False Optimism of Global Labour Studies.' *Global Labour Journal* 1 (2): 301–13.

Burawoy, M., J. A. Blum, S. George, Z. Gille, and M. Thayer. 2000. *Global Ethnography: Forces, Connections and Imaginations in a Postmodern World*. Berkeley and London: University of California Press.

Burchielli, R., D. Buttigieg, and A. Delaney. 2008. 'Organizing Homeworkers: The Use of Mapping as an Organizing Tool.' *Work, Employment and Society* 22 (1): 167–80.

Burchielli, R., A. Delaney, J. Tate, and K. Coventry. 2010. 'The Fair Wear Campaign: An Ethical Network in the Australian Garment Industry.' *Journal of Business Ethics* 90 (4): 575–88.

Bureau of International Labour Affairs. 2014. List of Products Produced with Forced or Indenture Child Labour. US: United States Department of Labour.

Burke, J. 2012. 'Weaves of Change.' *The Hindu* (March 25). Accessed September 20, 2015. http://www.thehindu.com/todays-paper/tp-features/tp-sundaymagazine/weaves-of-change/article3221661.ece.

Business Standard. 2013. Trent plays catch-up. Accessed May 20, 2016. <http://www.business-standard.com/article/management/trent-plays-catch-up-110091300044_1.html>.

Byres, T. J. 1998. *Inter-Linked Rural Markets/Modes of Exploitation*. Lecture notes on Agriculture and Economic Development. London: Department of Economics, SOAS. Copy given by the author.

Cerimele, M. 2016. *Informalising the Formal: Work Regimes and Dual Labour Dormitory Systems in Thang Long Industrial Park* (Hanoi, Vietnam). Working Paper, copy given by the author.

Cambodian Centre for Human Rights 2014. *Workers' Rights are Human Rights. Policy Brief: The Garment Industry in Cambodia*. Phnom Penh: cchrcambodia.org.

Caraway, T. L. 2005. 'The Political Economy of Feminization: From "Cheap Labor" to Gendered Discourses of Work.' *Politics and Gender* 3: 399–429.

Carr, M., M. A. Chen, and J. Tate. 2000. 'Globalisation and Home-Based Workers.' *Feminist Economics* 6 (3): 123–42.

Carswell, G. 2013. 'Dalits and Local Labour Markets in Rural India: Experiences from the Tiruppur Textile Region in Tamil Nadu.' *Transactions of the Institute of British Geographers* 38 (2): 325–38.

Carswell, G., and G. De Neve. 2013a. 'Labouring for Global Markets: Conceptualising Labour Agency in Global Production Networks.' *Geoforum* 44 (1): 62–70.

_____. 2013b. 'From Field to Factory: Tracing Bonded Labour in the Coimbatore Powerloom Industry, Tamil Nadu.' *Economy and Society* 42 (3): 430–54.

Castells, M., and A. Portes. 1989. 'World Underneath: The Origins, Dynamics and Effects of the Informal Economy.' In *The Informal Economy: Studies in Advanced and Less Developed Countries*, edited by A. Portes, M. Castells, and L. A. Benton, 11–37. Baltimore: John Hopkins University Press.

Castree, N. 2003. 'Commodifying What Nature?' *Progress in Human Geography* 27 (3): 273–97.

Cawthorne, P. 1992. 'The Labour Process Under Amoebic Capitalism: A Case Study of the Garment Industry in a South Indian Town.' *Milton Keynes Development Policy and Practice Series* Working Paper no. 23. Milton Keynes: Open University.

_____. 1995. 'Of Networks and Markets: The Rise and Rise of a South Indian Town, the Example of Tirupur's Cotton Industry.' *World Development* 23 (1): 43–56.

Cawthorne, P., and G. Kitching. 2001. 'Moral Dilemmas and Factual Claims: Some Comments on Paul Krugman's Defense of Cheap Labor.' *Review of Social Economy* 59 (4): 455–66.

CDPR. 2014a. 'The Oppressive Labour Conditions of the Working Poor in the Peripheral Segments of India's Garment Sector.' *Development Viewpoint* 81. London, SOAS: CDPR. Accessed September 20, 2015. http://www.soas.ac.uk/cdpr/publications/dv/file93820.pdf.

_____. 2014b. 'Surveying Informalised Labour Conditions in India's Organised Garment Sector.' *Development Viewpoint 79*. London SOAS: CDPR. Accessed September 20, 2015. https://www.soas.ac.uk/cdpr/publications/dv/file93801.pdf.

Centeno, M. A., and A. Portes. 2006. 'The Informal Economy in the Shadow of the State.' In *Out of the Shadows*, edited by P. Fernandez-Kelly, and J. Shefner, 22–48. Pennsylvania: Pennsylvania State University Press.

Chalcraft, J. 2007. 'Labour in the Levant.' *New Left Review* 45: 27–47.

Chamberlain, G. 2010. 'Gap, Next and M&S in new sweatshop scandal.' *The Observer* (August 8). Accessed September 20, 2015. http://www.theguardian.com/world/2010/aug/08/gap-next-marks-spencer-sweatshops.

Chan, J., N. Pun, and M. Selden. 2013. 'The Politics of Global Production: Apple, Foxconn and China's New Working Class.' *New Technology, Work and Employment* 28 (2): 100–15.

Chan, A., Y. P. Chen, X. Yuhua, W. Zhao, and C. Walker. 2014. 'Disposable Bodies and Labor Rights: Workers in China's Automotive Industry.' *Working USA, The Journal of Labour and Society* 17: 509–29.

Chandavarkar, R. 1992. *The Origins of Industrial Capitalism in India: Business Strategies and the Working Classes in Bombay, 1900–1940*. Cambridge: Cambridge University Press.

Chandrasekhar, C. P., and J. Ghosh. 2015. *Growth, Employment Patterns and Inequality in Asia: A Case Study of India*. ILO Asia-Pacific Working Paper Series. Bangkok: ILO Regional Office for Asia and the Pacific. Accessed September 13, 2015. http://www.ilo.org/wcmsp5/groups/public/---asia/---ro-bangkok/documents/publication/wcms_334063.pdf.

Chang, D. 2009a. *Capitalist Development in Korea: Labour, Capital and the Myth of the Developmental State*. London: Routledge.

_____. 2009b. 'Informalising Labour in Asia's Global Factory.' *Journal of Contemporary Asia* 39 (2): 161–79.

Chang, H. J. 2003. *Kicking Away the Ladder*. London: Verso.

_____. 2012. *23 Things They Don't Tell You About Capitalism*. London: Penguin.

Chari, S. 2003. 'Marxism, Sarcasm, Ethnography: Geographical Fieldnotes from South India.' *Singapore Journal of Tropical Geography* 24 (2): 169–83.

_____. 2004. 'Fraternal Capital: Peasant-Workers, Self-Made Men, and Globalization in Provincial India.' New Delhi: Permanent Black.

_____. 2010. 'Fraternal Capital and the Feminisation of Labour in South India.' In *The International Handbook of Gender and Poverty: Concepts, Research, Policy*, edited by S. Chant, 446–51. Cheltenham: Edward Elgar.

Chatterjee, S., and R. Mohan. 1993. 'India's Garment Exports.' *Economic and Political Weekly* 28 (35) (Review of Industry and Management): M95–119.

Chen, M. 2012. *The Informal Economy: Definitions, Theories and Policies*. WIEGO working paper. Accessed September 20, 2015. http://wiego.org/sites/wiego.org/files/publications/files/Chen_WIEGO_WP1.pdf.

Chhachhi, A. 2014. 'Introduction' to the Special Issue on 'The Labour Question.' *Development and Change* 45 (5): 813–1218.

Ciccarello, E. 2012. 'Caporalato e mafie: "700mila schiavi nell'agricoltura italiana"'. *Il Fatto Quotidiano* (10 December). Accessed September 20, 2015. http://www.ilfattoquotidiano.it/2012/12/10/caporalato-e-mafie-700mila-schiavi-nellagricoltura-italiana/441656/.

CIVIDEP and SOMO. 2009. *Richer Bosses, Poorer Workers: Bangalore's Garment Industry*. Netherlands: Somo.

Coe, N. M., and M. Hess. 2013. 'Global Production Networks, Labour and Development.' *Geoforum* 44: 4–9.

Coe, N. M., P. Dicken, and M. Hess. 2008. 'Global Production Networks: Realizing the Potential.' *Journal of Economic Geography* 8 (3): 271–95.

Collins, J. 2003. *Threads: Gender, Labor, and Power in the Global Apparel Industry*. Chicago: University of Chicago Press.

Coronil, F. 1997. *The Magical State*. Chicago and London: University of Chicago Press.

_____. 2001. 'Towards a Critique of Globalcentrism: Speculations on Capitalism's Nature.' In *Millennial Capitalism and the Culture of Neoliberalism*, edited by J. Comaroff, and J. L. Comaroff, 63–87. Durham and London: Duke University Press.

Cross, J. 2014. *Dream Zones*. London: Pluto.

De Noronha, L. and Anderson, B. 2015. 'Interview: Bridget Anderson on Europe's 'violent humanitarianism' in the Mediterranean.' *Ceasefire*. Accessed May 20, 2016. https://ceasefiremagazine.co.uk/interview-bridget-anderson/.

D' Monte, D. 2002. *Ripping the Fabric: The Decline of Mumbai and Its Mills*. New Delhi: Oxford University Press.

D'Costa, A. P. 2011. 'Globalisation, Crisis and Industrial Relations in the Indian Auto Industry.' *International Journal of Automotive Technology and Management* 11 (2): 114–36.

Damodaran, H. 2008. *India's New Capitalists – Caste, Business, and Industry in a Modern Nation*. Basingstoke: Palgrave Macmillan.

Damodaran, S. 2013. 'New Strategies of Industrial Organization: Outsourcing and Consolidation in the Mobile Telecom Sector in India.' *Capturing the Gains, Economic and Social Upgrading in Global Production Networks*, Working paper 32. Accessed September 20, 2015. http://www.capturingthegains.org/pdf/ctg-wp-2013-32.pdf.

Das, K. 2005. *Industrial Clusters: Cases and Perspectives*. Aldershot: Ashgate.

Dasgupta, R. 2014. *Capital: A Portrait of 21ˢᵗ Century Delhi*. New Delhi: Fourth Estate.

Datta, K., and R. Abraham. 2005. 'Private Mills to Contest Public Interest Litigation.' *Business Standard* (March 28). Accessed September 20, 2015. http://www.business-standard.com/article/economy-policy/private-mills-to-contest-public-interest-litigation-105032801028_1.html.

Dauvergne, P., and G. Le Baron. 2014. *Protest Inc.: The Corporatization of Activism*. London: Polity.

Davidson, J. O. 2015. *Modern Slavery: The Margins of Freedom*. New York: Palgrave Macmillan.

Davis-Blake, A., and B. Uzzi. 1993. 'Determinants of Employment Externalisation: A Study of Temporary Workers and Independent Contractors.' *Administrative Science Quarterly* 38 (2): 195–223.

Davis, M. 2006. *Planet of Slums*. London: Verso.

DCMSME. 2013. *Khadi Karighar Janashree Bima Yojana*. GoI website. Accessed September 2015. http://msme.gov.in/msme_ jby.htm.

_____. 2015. *List of SME industrial clusters in India*. New Delhi: GoI. Accessed September 20, 2015. http://www.dcmsme.gov.in/clusters/clus/smelist.htm.

De Angelis, M. 2000. *Trade, The Global Factory and the Struggles for New Commons*. Paper presented at the CSE conference 'Global Capital and Global Struggles: Strategies,

Alliances, and Alternatives', London 1–2 July 2000. Accessed May 10, 2015. https://libcom.org/files/NewComm.pdf.

_____. 2007. *The Beginning of History: Value Struggles and Global Capital*. London: Pluto.

De Neve, G. 2005. 'Weaving for IKEA in South India: Subcontracting, Labour Markets and Gender Relations in a Global Value Chain.' In *Globalizing India: Perspectives from Below*, edited by J. Assayag, and C. J. Fuller. London: Anthem.

_____. 2008. 'Global Garment Chains, Local Labour Activism: New Challenges to Trade Union and NGO activism in the Tiruppur Garment Cluster, South India.' In *Hidden Hands in the Market: Ethnographies of Fair Trade, Ethical Consumption, and Corporate Social Responsibility*, edited by G. De Neve, P. Luetchford, J. Pratt, and D. C. Wood, 213–240. Bingley, UK: Emerald Group Publishing.

_____. 2009. 'Power, Inequality and Corporate Social Responsibility: The Politics of Ethical Compliance in the South Indian Garment Industry.' *Economic and Political Weekly* 44 (22): 63–72.

_____. 2014a. 'Fordism, Flexible Specialization and CSR: How Indian Garment Workers Critique Neoliberal Labour Regimes.' *Ethnography* 15 (2): 184–207.

_____. 2014b. 'Entrapped Entrepreneurship: Labour Contractors in the South Indian Garment Industry.' *Modern Asian Studies* 48 (5): 1302–33.

Delaney, A. 2004. 'Global Trade and Homework: Closing the Divide.' *Gender and Development* 12 (2): 22–28.

De Neve, G., and Prentice, R. 2017. *After Rana Plaza: Rethinking Garment Workers' Health and Safety*. Philadelphia: University of Pennsylvania Press (forthcoming).

DeNicola, A. O. 2003. 'Mediating Design, Manufacturing Tradition: Innovation in Bagru's Print Industry.' In *Institutions and Social Change*, edited by S. Singh, and V. Joshi. New Delhi: Rawat.

_____. 2004. Creating *Borders, Maintaining Boundaries: Traditional Work and Global Markets in Bagru's Handblock Textile Industry*. Unpublished PhD Thesis Submitted to Syracuse University, Syracuse.

_____. 2005. 'Working Through Tradition; Experiential Learning and Formal Training as Markers of Class and Caste in Indian Block Printing Industry.' *Anthropology of Work Review* 26 (2): 12–16.

Deshingkar, P. 2009. *Extending Labour Inspections to the Informal Sector and Agriculture*. Chronic Poverty Research Centre, Working Paper 154. London: ODI.

Deshingkar, P., and Farrington, J. 2009. *Circular Migration and Multilocational Livelihood Strategies in Rural India*, p. 16. New Delhi: Oxford University Press.

Deshpande, A. 2000. 'Recasting Economic Inequality.' *Review of Social Economy* 58 (3): 381–99.

_____. 2011. *The Grammar of Caste*. Oxford: Oxford University Press.

De Soto, H. 1989. *The Other Path: The Invisible Revolution in the Third World*, London: Tauris.

Development Commissioner for Handicraft 2013. *Rajiv Gandhi Shilpi Swasthya Bima Yojana*. GoI website. Accessed September 20, 2015. http://handicrafts.nic.in/welfare/rajivgandhi.htm.

Dey, I., and G. Grappi. 2015. 'Beyond Zoning: India's Corridors of Development and New Frontiers of Capital.' *The South Atlantic Quarterly* 114 (1): 153–70.

Doshi, S. 2012. 'The Politics of the Evicted: Redevelopment, Subjectivity, and Difference in Mumbai's Slum Frontier.' *Antipode* 45 (4): 844–65.

Dreze, J., and A. Sen. 2014. *An Uncertain Glory. India and Its Contradictions.* London: Penguin.

Elson, D. 1983. 'Nimble Fingers and Other Fables.' In *Of Common Cloth: Women in the Global Textile Industry*, edited by W. Enloe, and C. Chapkis. Amsterdam: Transnational Institute.

Elson, D., and R. Pearson. 1981. 'The Subordination of Women and the Internationalisation of Factory Production.' In *Of Marriage and the Market: Women's Subordination in International Perspective*, edited by K. Young, R. MacCullagh, and C. Wolkowitz. London: CSE Books.

Elson, D., C. Grown, and N. Cagatay. 2007. 'Mainstream, Heterodox and Feminist Trade Theory.' In *The Feminist Economics of Trade*, edited by D. Elson, C. Grown, and I. Van Staveren. London: Routledge.

Esbenshade, J. 2004. *Monitoring Sweatshops. Workers, Consumers and the Global Apparel Industry.* Philadelphia: Temple University Press.

ETI. 2006. *ETI homeworker guidelines: Recommendations for working with homeworkers*, ETI website. Accessed September 20, 2015. http://www.ethicaltrade.org/sites/default/files/resources/ETI%20Homeworker% 20guidelines, %20ENG.pdf.

_____. 2013. *Indian national homeworker group*, ETI website. Accessed September 20, 2015. http://www.ethicaltrade.org/in-action/programmes/the-indian-national-homeworker-group.

Federici, S. 2004. *Caliban and the Witch: Women, the Body and Primitive Accumulation.* Brooklyn, NY: Autonomedia.

_____. 2012. *Revolution at Point Zero: Housework, Reproduction, and Feminist Struggle.* Brooklyn, NY: PM Press.

Fieldhouse, D. K. 1994. *Merchant Capital and Economic Decolonization: The United Africa Company 1929–1989.* Oxford: Clarendon Press.

Fine, B. 2010. *Theories of Social Capital: Researchers Behaving Badly.* Pluto Press: London.

Foucault, M. 1989. *The Archaeology of Knowledge.* London: Routledge.

Frank, D. 2003. 'Where Are the Workers in Consumer-Worker Alliances? Class Dynamics and the History of Consumer-Labour Campaigns.' *Politics & Society* 31 (3): 363–79.

Fraser, N. 2014. 'Behind Marx's Hidden Abode: For an Expanded Conception of Capitalism.' *New Left Review* 86: 55–72.

Friedmann, H. 2005. 'From Colonialism to Green Capitalism: Social Movements and Emergence of Food Regimes.' In *New Directions in the Sociology of Global Development*, edited by F. H. Buttel, and P. McMichael, 229–267. Amsterdam: Elsevier.

Fröbel, F., J. Heinrichs, and O. Kreye. 1984. *The New International Division of Labour: Structural Unemployment in Industrialised Countries and Industrialisation in Developing Countries.* Cambridge: Cambridge University Press.

Fukunishi, T., and T. Yamagata. 2014. *The Garment Industry in Low-Income Countries - An Entry Point of Industrialisation.* IDE-JETRO Series. London: Palgrave Macmillan.

Garikipati, S. 2008. 'Agricultural Wage Work, Seasonal Migration and the Widening Gender Gap: Evidence from a Semi-Arid Region of Andhra Pradesh.' *The European Journal of Development Research* 20 (4): 629–48.

Gereffi, G. 1994. 'The Organisation of Buyer Driven Commodity Chains: How US Retailers Shape Overseas Production Networks.' In *Commodity Chains and Global Capitalism*, edited by G. Gereffi, and M. Korzeniewicz. Westport, Connecticut: Praeger Publishers.

Gereffi, G., and M. Korzeniewicz. 1994. *Commodity Chains and Global Capitalism.* Westport, Connecticut: Praeger Publishers.

Gereffi, G., J. Bair, and D. Spencer. 2002. *Free Trade and Uneven Development: The North American Apparel Industry after NAFTA.* Philadelphia: Temple University Press.

Ghosh, A. 2011. *River of Smoke.* London: John Murray.

Ghosh, J. 2009. *Never Done and Poorly Paid: Women's Work in Globalising India.* New Delhi: Women Unlimited.

Gibbon, P. 2001. 'Globalisation, Present-Day Capitalism, Commodity Chains.' In *Changing Global and Regional Conditions for Development in the Third World*, edited by J. Degnbol-Martinussen, and L. S. Lauridsen. Occasional Paper 21. Copenhagen: International Development Studies, Roskilde University.

Gibbon, P., and S. Ponte. 2005. *Trading Down: Africa, Value Chains, and the Global Economy.* Philadelphia: Temple University Press.

Gibbon, P., J. Bair, and S. Ponte. 2008. 'Governing Global Value Chains: An Introduction.' *Economy and Society* 37 (3): 315–38.

Gideon, J. 2007. 'Excluded from Health? Informal Workers' Access to Health Care in Chile.' *Bulletin of Latin American Research* 26 (2): 238–55.

Gilbert, C. 2008. 'Value Chain Analysis and Market Power in Commodity Processing with Application to the Cocoa and Coffee Sectors.' Rome: FAO, *Commodity Market Review*, pp. 5–34. Accessed September 20, 2015. ftp://ftp.fao.org/docrep/fao/010/a1487e/a1487e00.pdf.

Global Slavery Index. 2014. *The 2014 Global Slavery Index.* Australia: Hope for Children Organisation. Accessed September 20, 2015. https://d3mj66ag90b5fy.cloudfront.net/wp-content/uploads/2014/11/Global_Slavery_Index_2014_final_lowres.pdf.

Gooptu, N. 2013. *Enterprise Culture in Neoliberal India: Studies in Youth, Class, Work and Media.* London: Routledge.

Goto, K., and T. Endo. 2014. 'Upgrading, Relocating, Informalising? Local Strategies in the Era of Globalisation: The Thai Garment Industry.' *Journal of Contemporary Asia* 44 (1): 1–18.

Graeber, D. 2011. *Debt. The First 5,000 Years.* Brooklyn and London: Melville House.

Greenslade, R. 2011. 'Why the BBC Trust is Wrong to Have Found Against Panorama.' *The Guardian* (June 16). Accessed September 20, 2015. http://www.theguardian.com/media/greenslade/2011/jun/16/bbc-trust-investigative-journalism.

Guérin, I., B. D'Espallier, and G. Venkatasubramanian. 2013. 'Debt in Rural South India: Fragmentation, Social Regulation and Discrimination.' *The Journal of Development Studies*, 49 (9): 1155–71.

Gunther, M. 2013. 'Gap Spearheads New Alliance for Bangladeshi Worker Safety.' *The Guardian.* Accessed September 25, 2015. http://www.theguardian.com/sustainable-business/gap-alliance-bangladeshi-worker-safety.

Gupte, V. 2004. *Trade Union Movement in India a Brief History*, Mumbai: Mill Mazdoor Education Trust.

Hale, A., and J. Wills. 2005. *Threads of Labour: Garment Industry Supply Chains from the Workers' Perspective.* Oxford: Blackwell.

Hammer, N., R. Plugor, P. Nolan, and I. Clark. 2015. *New Industry on a Skewed Playing Field: Supply Chain Relations and Working Conditions in UK Garment Manufacturing* (Report). Centre for sustainable work and employment futures, University of

Leicester: Leicester. Accessed September 20, 2015. http://www2.le.ac.uk/offices/press/for-journalists/media-resources/Leicester%20Report%20-%20Final%20-to%20publish.pdf/.

Hanieh, A. 2011. *Capitalism and Class in the Gulf Arab States*. New York: Palgrave MacMillan.

Hardt, M., and A. Negri. 2004. *Multitude: War and Democracy in the Age of Empire*. New York: Penguin.

Hardy, J. 2013. 'New Divisions of Labour in the Global Economy.' *International Socialism: A quarterly Journal of Socialist Theory*, 137. Accessed September 2015. http://www.isj.org.uk/index.php4?id=868&issue=137.

Harriss, J. 1986. 'The Working Poor and the Labour Aristocracy in a South Indian City: A Descriptive and Analytical Account.' *Modern Asian Studies* 20 (2): 231–83.

Harriss-White, B. 1996. *A Political Economy of Agricultural Markets in South India: Masters of the Countryside*. New Delhi and London: Sage.

_____. 2003. *India Working-Essays on Society and Economics*. Cambridge: Cambridge University Press.

_____. 2008. *Rural Commercial Capital - Agricultural Markets in West Bengal*. Oxford: Oxford University Press.

_____. 2010. 'Globalization, The Financial Crisis and Petty Production in India's Socially Regulated Informal Economy.' *Global Labour Journal* 1 (1): 152–77.

_____. 2014. 'Labour and Petty Production.' *Development and Change* 45 (5): 981–1000.

Harriss-White, B., and N. Gooptu. 2001. 'Mapping India's World of Unorganized Labour.' *Socialist Register* 37: 89–118.

Hartmann, H. 1979. 'The Unhappy Marriage Between Marxism and Feminism: Towards a More Progressive Union.' *Capital and Class* 3 (2): 1–33.

Harvey, D. 2001. 'Globalization and the "Spatial Fix".' *Geographische Revue* 2: 23–30.

_____. 2004. 'The "New" Imperialism: Accumulation by Dispossession.' *Socialist Register* 40: 63–87.

Hashim, D. A. 2004. 'Cost and Productivity in India Textiles; Post MFA Implications.' ICRIER Working Paper 147. Accessed September 20, 2015. http://www.icrier.org/pdf/wp147.pdf.

Haynes, D. 2001. 'Artisan Cloth-Producers and the Emergence of Powerloom Manufacture in Western India, 1920–1950.' *The Past and Present Society* 172 (1): 170–98.

_____. 2012. *Small Town Capitalism in Western India: Artisans, Merchants and the Making of the Informal Economy, 1870–1960*. New York: Cambridge University Press.

Heyer, J. 2012. 'Labour Standards and Social Policy: A South Indian Case Study.' *Global Labour Journal* 3 (1): 91–117.

_____. 2013. 'Integration into a Global Production Network: Impacts on Labour in Tiruppur's Rural Hinterlands.' *Oxford Development Studies* 41 (3): 307–21.

Hensman, R. 2000. 'Organizing Against the Odds: Women in India's Informal Sector.' In *Socialist Register, Working Classes, Global Realities*, edited by L. Panitch, and C. Leys, 249–257. London: Merlin.

_____. 2010. *Workers, Unions and Global Capitalism: Lessons from India*. New York: Columbia University Press.

Hickey, S. and A. du Toit. 2007. *Adverse incorporation, social exclusion and chronic poverty*. Chronic Poverty Research Centre, Working Paper no. 81, University of Manchester.

Hobson, J. M. 2004. *The Eastern Origins of Western Civilisation*. Cambridge: Cambridge University Press.

Holmström, M. 1976. *South Indian Factory Workers: Their Life and Their World*. Cambridge: Cambridge University Press.

Hopkins, T., and I. Wallerstein. 1977. 'Patterns of Development of the Modern World System.' *Review* 1 (2): 11–45.

_____. 1986. 'Commodity Chains in the World Economy Prior to 1800.' *Review* 10 (1): 157–70.

Hoskins, T. 2014. *Stitched up: The Anti-Capitalist Book of Fashion*. London: Pluto.

Howard, A. 1997. 'Labor, History, and Sweatshops in the New Global Economy.' In *No Sweat: Fashion, Free Trade and the Rights of Garment Workers*, edited by A. Ross, 151–72. London: Verso.

Huws, U. 2001. 'The Making of a Cybertariat? Virtual Work in a Real World.' *Socialist Register* 37: 1–33.

_____. 2003. *The Making of a Cybertariat: Virtual Work in a Real World*, London: Merlin Press.

_____. 2014. *Labor in the Global Digital Economy: The Cybertariat Comes of Age*. New York: Monthly Review Press.

ILO and WTO. 2009. *Globalization and Informal Jobs in Developing Countries*. ILO and WTO: Geneva.

ILRF (International Labor Rights Forum). 2015. *Our Voices, Our Safety: Bangladeshi Garment Workers Speak Out*. Washington: ILRF. Accessed August 2, 2016. http://laborrights.org/sites/default/files/publications/Our%20Voices,%20Our%20Safety%20Online_1.pdf

Jacob, B. 2014. 'Fashion Revolution Day: Join Caryn Franklin and VV Brown and be a part of a label revolution.' Metro, UK. Accessed September 20, 2015. http://metro.co.uk/2014/04/16/fashion-revolution-day-join-caryn-franklin-and-vv-brown-and-be-a-part-of-a-label-revolution-4700188/.

Jeffery, R. 2014. 'The future of Human Rights in India.' *Discover Society*, Issue 12, Viewpoint. Accessed May 20, 2016. http://discoversociety.org/2014/09/02/viewpoint-the-future-of-human-rights-in-india/.

Jenkins, J. 2013. 'Organizing "Spaces of Hope": Union Formation by Indian Garment Workers.' *British Journal of Industrial Relations* 51 (3): 623–43.

Jenkins, Rob. 2004. 'Labour Policy and the Second Generation of Economic Reforms in India.' *India Review* 3 (4): 333–63.

Jenkins, Rhys. 2005. 'Globalization, Corporate Social Responsibility and Poverty.' *International Affairs* 81 (3): 525–40.

Jenkins, R., Pearson, R. and Seyfang, G. 2002. *Corporate Responsibility and Labor Rights-Codes of Conduct in the Global Economy*. London: Earthscan Publications.

John, M. E. 2013. 'The Problem of Women's Labour: Some Autobiographical Perspectives.' *Indian Journal of Gender Studies* 20 (2): 177–212.

Jonas, A.E.G. 1996. 'Local Labour Control Regimes: Uneven Development and the Social Regulation of Production.' *Regional Studies* 30 (4): 323–338.

Joshi, V., and H. Joshi. 1976. *Surplus Labour and The City: A Study of Bombay*. Delhi: Oxford University Press.

Jureidini, R. 2014. *Arab Gulf States: Recruitment of Asian Workers. Gulf Labour Markets and Migration* (GLMM). Working paper 3, European University Institute (EUI) and Gulf Research Center (GRC). Accessed September 23, 2015. http://cadmus.eui.eu/ bitstream/handle/1814/32149/GLMM%20ExpNote_03-2014.pdf?sequence=1.

Kabeer, N. 2000. *The Power to Choose: Bangladeshi Women and Labour Market Decisions in London and Dhaka*. London: Verso.

_____. 2004. 'Globalisation, Labour Standards and Women's Rights: Dilemmas of Collective (in)Action in an Interdependent World.' *Feminist Economics* 10 (1): 3–35.

Kabeer, N., and S. Mahmud. 2004. 'Rags, Riches and Women Workers: Export-Oriented Garment Manufacturing in Bangladesh.' In *Chains of Fortune: Linking Women Producers and Workers Within Global Markets*, edited by M. Carr, 133–162. London: Commonwealth Secretariat.

Kalhan, A. 2008. 'Permanently Temporary Workers in Global Readymade Garment Hub in Bangalore.' *Indian Journal of Labour Economics* 51 (1): 115–28.

Kalhan, A., and M. Franz. 2009. 'Regulation of Retail: Comparative Experience.' *Economic and Political Weekly* 44 (32): 56–64.

Kalpagam, U. 1981. 'Labour in Small Industry: Case of Export Garments Industry in Madras.' *Economic and Political Weekly* 16 (48): 1957–63 & 1965–68.

_____. 1994. 'Labour in Small Industry: The Case of the Garment Export Industry in Madras city.' In *Labor and Gender: Survival in Urban India*, edited by U. Kalpagam. New Delhi: Sage.

Kamau, P. 2013. *Chinese Ascendancy in the Global Clothing Industry - Implications for Sub-Saharan Africa*. SSRC Working paper, presented at the conference 'Making Sense of the China-Africa Relationship: Theoretical Approaches and the Politics of Knowledge', November 18–19, 2013, Yale University. Accessed September 20. http://china-africa. ssrc.org/wp-content/uploads/2014/10/Kamau-Final.pdf.

Kandiyoti, D. 1988. 'Bargaining with Patriarchy.' *Gender and Society* 2 (3): 274–90.

Kannan, K. P. 2009. 'Dualism, Informality and Social Inequality, An Informal Economy Perspective of the Challenge of Inclusive Development in India.' *Indian Journal of Labour Economics*, 52 (1): 1–32.

Katz, C. 2004. *Growing Up Global: Economic Restructuring and Children's Everyday Lives*. Minneapolis, MN: University of Minnesota Press.

Kaur, A. 2014. 'Plantation Systems, Labour Regimes and the State in Malaysia, 1900–2012.' *Journal of Agrarian Change* 14 (2): 190–213.

Khatun, Y. 2014. 'The Fashion Revolution.' *The Huffington Post*. Accessed September 20, 2015. http://www.huffingtonpost.co.uk/yasmin-khatun/the-fashion-revolution_b_5200488.html.

Kiely, R. 2008. 'Poverty Through 'insufficient exploitation and/or globalization? Globalized production and new dualist fallacies.' *Globalizations* 5 (3): 419–32.

Kishore, V. 2014. *Ricardo's Gauntlet- Economic Fiction and the Flawed Case for Free Trade*. London and New York: Anthem Press.

Klein, N. 2000. *No Logo: No Space, No Choice, No Jobs: Taking Aim at the Brand Bullies*. London: Flamingo.

Knowles, C. 2015. *Flip-Flop. A Journey through Globalisation Backroads*. London: Pluto.

Kodoth, P., and V. J. Varghese. 2011. *Emigration of Women Domestic Workers from Kerala: Gender, State Policy and the Politics of Movement*. CDS working paper 445. Trivandrum: CDS.

Kohli, A. 1999. 'Where Do High Growth Political Economies Come From? The Japanese Lineage of Korea's Developmental State.' In *The Developmental State*, edited by M. Woo-Cummings. Ithaca: Cornell University Press.

Krishnamoorthy, S. 2004. *Structure of the Garment Industry and Labor Rights in India - The Post MFA Context*. New Delhi: Centre for Education and Communication.

Krishnaraj, M. 1987. '*New Opportunities and Old Terms, the Case of the Garment Industry in India*.' Mumbai: Research Centre for Women's Studies, SNDT Women's University.

Kumar, A. 2014. 'Interwoven Threads: Building a Labour Countermovement in Bangalore's Export-Oriented Garment Industry.' *CITY* 18 (6): 789–807.

Kumar, A., and J. Mahoney. 2014. 'Stitching Together: How Workers are Hemming Down Transnational Capital in the Hyper-Global Apparel Industry.' *Working USA. The Journal of Labour and Society* 17 (2): 187–210.

Kundu, A., and N. Sarangi. 2007. 'Dynamics of Labour Market Under Globalisation: Changing Characteristics of Informal Employment in India.' *The Indian Journal of Labour Economics* 50 (2): 201–216.

Kusakabe, K., and R. Pearson. 2010. 'Transborder Migration, Social Reproduction and Economic Development: A Case Study of Burmese Women Workers in Thailand.' *International Migration* 48 (6): 13–43.

Lal, T. 2004. *Diagnostic Study, Report & Action Plan for the Ready Made Garment Cluster*. New Delhi: GoI, SISI Okhla, Cluster Development Executive Section.

Lan, T. 2014. 'Industrial District and the Multiplication of Labour: The Chinese Apparel Industry in Prato, Italy.' *Antipode* 47 (1): 158–78.

Lawrence, F. 2015. 'Costco and CP Foods face lawsuit over alleged slavery in prawn supply chain,' in *The Guardian*, 19 August. Accessed January 15, 2016. http://www.theguardian.com/global-development/2015/aug/19/costco-cp-foods-lawsuit-alleged-slavery-prawn-supply-chain.

LeBaron, G., and A. J. Ayers. 2013. 'The Rise of a 'New Slavery'? Understanding African Unfree Labour Through Neoliberalism.' *Third World Quarterly* 34 (5): 873–92.

Lee, J., and G. Gereffi. 2013. 'Global Value Chains, Rising Power Firms and Economic and Social Upgrading.' *Critical Perspectives on International Business* 11 (3/4): 319–339.

Leonard, K. 2003. 'South Asian Workers in the Gulf: Jockeying for Places.' In *Globalization Under Construction: Governmentality, Law, and Identity*, edited by R. W. Perry, and B. Maurer, pp. 134–153. Minneapolis, MN: University of Minnesota Press.

Lerche, J. 2007. 'A Global Alliance Against Forced Labour? Unfree Labour, Neo-liberal Globalisation and the International Labour Organisation.' *Journal of Agrarian Change* 7 (4): 425–52.

_____. 2010. 'From "Rural Labour" to "Classes of Labour": Class Fragmentation, Caste and Class Struggle at the Bottom of the Indian Labour Hierarchy.' In *The Comparative Political Economy of Development: Africa and South Asia*, edited by B. Harriss-White, and J. Heyer, 67–87. London: Routledge.

_____. 2012. 'Labour Regulations and Labour Standards in India: Decent Work?' *Global Labour Journal* 3 (1): 16–39.

Lessinger, J. 2000. 'Work and Love: the Limits of Autonomy for Female Garment Workers in India.' *Anthropology of Work Review* 23 (1–2): 13–18.

Lichtenstein, N. 2009. *The Retail Revolution: How Wal-Mart Created a Brave New World of Business*. New York: Metropolitan Books.

Lim, L. 1990. 'Women's Work in Export Factories: The Politics of a Cause.' In *Persistent Inequalities: Women and World Development*, edited by I. Tinker, 101–122. New York: Oxford University Press.

Lyimo, M. 2010. *Sexual Harassment: An Insight into the Indian Garment Industry*. Report, Bangalore: Cividep. Accessed April 4, 2016. http://cividep.org/backdoor/wp-content/uploads/2013/01/Sexual-Harassment-Report-MahooLyimo-_Oct-2010.pdf

Lund-Thomsen, P., K. Nadvi, A. Chan, N. Khara, and X. Hong. 2012. 'Labour in Global Value Chains: Work Conditions in Football Manufacturing in China, India and Pakistan.' *Development and Change* 43 (6): 1211–37.

Lund-Thomsen, P., and N. M. Coe. 2015. 'Corporate Social Responsibility and Labour Agency: The Case of Nike in Pakistan.' *Journal of Economic Geography* 15 (2): 275–96.

Maini, G. 2004. *The Giant Awakens: Punjab, Industry and Growth*. New Delhi: India Research Press.

Makino, M. 2014. 'Pakistan: Challenges for Women's Labour Force Participation.' In *The Garment Industry in Low-Income Countries - An Entry Point of Industrialisation*, edited by T. Fukunishi, and T. Yamagata, 132–176. Palgrave McMillan: London. IDE-JETRO series.

Manzo, K. 2005. 'Modern Slavery, Global Capitalism & Deproletarianisation in West Africa.' *Review of African Political Economy* 32 (106): 521–34.

Marcus, G. E. 1995. 'Ethnography in/of the World System: The Emergence of Multi-Sited Ethnography.' *Annual Review of Anthropology* 24: 95–117.

Marshall, A. 1961. *Principles of Economics*. London and New York: Macmillan for the Royal Economic Society (originally published in 1922).

Marx, K. 1990. *Capital: A Critique of Political Economy. Volume I*. London: Penguin (Reprint of the classic Pelican Books version, 1976, introduced by Ernest Mandel. Original year of publication 1867).

Mason, P. 2015. 'How to Turn a Liberal Hipster into a Capitalist Tyrant in One Evening.' *The Guardian* (24 May). Accessed September 13, 2015. http://www.theguardian.com/commentisfree/2015/may/24/turn-a-liberal-hipster-into-global-capitalist-world-factory.

Mathew, J. 2016. *Margins of the Market: Trafficking and Capitalism across the Arabian Sea*. Oakland, California: University of California Press

Mazumdar, I., and N. Neetha. 2011. 'Gender Dimensions: Employment Trends in India, 1993–94/2009–10.' *Economic and Political Weekly* 46 (43): 118–26.

McCormick, D. 1999. 'African Enterprise Clusters and Industrialisation: Theory and Reality.' *World Development* 27 (9): 1531–51.

McCormick, D., and P. Kamau. 2013. *Adjusting to Chinese Ascendancy in the Global Clothing Industry: African Clothing Exports in the Post-MFA Era*. ACFRN Working Paper 12/1. Accessed September 20, 2015. www.acfrn.uonbi.ac.ke.

McDougall, D. 2008. 'The Hidden Face of Primark Fashion.' *The Guardian* (June 22). Accessed September 20, 2015. http://www.theguardian.com/world/2008/jun/22/india.humanrights.

McGrath, S. 2013. 'Fuelling Global Production Networks with *Slave Labour?* Migrant Sugar Cane Workers in the Brazilian Ethanol GPN.' *Geoforum* 44: 32–43.

McMichael, P. 2009. 'A Food Regime Genealogy.' *The Journal of Peasant Studies* 36 (1): 139–170.

_____. 2012. 'The Land Grab and Corporate Food Regime Restructuring.' *The Journal of Peasant Studies* 39 (3–4): 681–701.

Meagher, K. 1995. 'Crisis, Informalisation and the Urban Informal Sector in Sub-Saharan Africa.' *Development and Change* 26: 259–83.

_____. 2006. 'Social Capital, Social Liabilities, and Political Capital: Social Networks and Informal Manufacturing in Nigeria.' *African Affairs*, 105/421: 553–582.

_____. 2010. *Identity Economics: Social Networks and the Informal Economy in Nigeria.* Suffolk, UK: James Currey.

_____. 2011. 'Informal Economies and Urban Governance in Nigeria: Popular Empowerment or Political Exclusion?' *African Studies Review* 54 (2): 47–72.

Merk, J. 2014. 'The Rise of Tier 1 Firms in the Global Garment Industry: Challenges for Labour Rights Advocates.' *Oxford Development Studies* 42 (2): 277–95.

Meskins Wood, E. 2002. *The Origin of Capitalism. A Longer View.* London: Verso.

Mezzadra, S. and Nielsen, B. 2013. *Border as Method, or, the Multiplication of Labor.* Durham: Duke University Press.

Mezzadri, A. 2005a. 'Calamita' Innaturali.' *Peacereporter* (June 1). Accessed September 20, 2015. http://it.peacereporter.net/articolo/2724/Calamit%E0+innaturali.

_____. 2005b. 'Il prezzo di vecchie e nuove trasformazioni' ('The price of old and new transformations'). *Peacereporter (May 10).* Accessed September 2015. http://it.peacereporter.net/articolo/2422/Il+prezzo+di+vecchie+e+nuove+trasformazioni.

_____. 2007. 'The Limitation of Corporate Social Responsibility in the Indian Garment Sector: A Case Study from the Delhi Industrial Area at the End of the Multi Fibre Agreement.' In *At the Crossroads: South Asian Research, Policy and Development in a Globalised World,* edited by SDPI, 16–35. Islamabad: SDPI/Sama.

_____. 2008. 'The Rise of Neoliberal Globalisation and the 'New Old' Social Regulation of Labour: The Case of Delhi Garment Sector.' *Indian Journal of Labour Economics* 51 (4): 603–18.

_____. 2009a. 'Neoliberalism, Industrial Restructuring and Labour: Lessons from the Delhi Garment Industry.' In *Economic Transitions to Neoliberalism in Middle Income Countries: Policy Dilemmas, Economic Crises, Forms of Resistance,* edited by A. Saad Filho, and G. L. Yalman. London: Routledge.

_____. 2009b. *The Architecture of Production and Labour Control in the Indian Garment Industry: Informalisation and Upgrading in the Global Economy.* Unpublished PhD thesis. London: SOAS.

_____. 2010. 'Globalisation, Informalisation and the State in the Indian Garment Industry.' *International Review of Sociology* 20 (3): 491–511.

_____. 2012. 'Reflections on Globalisation and Labour Standards in the Indian Garment Industry: Codes of Conduct Versus "Codes of Practice" Imposed by the Firm.' *Global Labour Journal* 3 (1): 40–62.

_____. 2014a. 'Indian Garment Clusters and CSR Norms: Incompatible Agendas at the Bottom of the Garment Commodity Chain.' *Oxford Development Studies* 42 (2): 217–37.

_____. 2014b. 'Backshoring, Local Sweatshop Regimes and CSR in India.' *Competition and Change* 18 (4): 327–44.

_____. 2014c. 'Cambodian Sweatshop Protests Reveal the Blood on Our Clothes.' *The Conversation UK* (January 8). Accessed September 20, 2015. http://theconversation.com/cambodian-sweatshop-protests-reveal-the-blood-on-our-clothes-21811.

_____. 2015a. 'Labour Regimes in the Garment Sector in India: Global, National, & Local Conditions of Competition & Capital Dynamics.' In *Labour Regimes in the Indian Garment Sector: Capital-Labour Relations, Social Reproduction and Labour Standards in the National Capital Region (NCR)*, edited by A. Mezzadri, and R. Srivastava. Final ESRC Report for the project 'Labour Conditions and the Working Poor in China and India.'

_____. 2015b. 'Labour Regimes in the Garment Sector in India: Home-Based Labour, Peripheral Labour.' In *Labour Regimes in the Indian Garment Sector: Capital-Labour Relations, Social Reproduction and Labour Standards in the National Capital Region (NCR)*, edited by A. Mezzadri, and R. Srivastava. London: SOAS. Final ESRC Report for the Project 'Labour Conditions and the Working Poor in China and India.'

_____. 2015c. 'Free to Stitch, or Starve: Capitalism and Unfreedom in the Global Garment Industry.' *Open Democracy: Beyond Trafficking and Slavery* (February 25). Accessed May 22, 2015. https://www.opendemocracy.net/beyondslavery/alessandra-mezzadri/free-to-stitch-or-starve-capitalism-and-unfreedom-in-global-garmen.

_____. 2015d. *Garment sweatshop regimes: The Informalisation of Social Responsibility over Health and Safety Provisions'*. CDPR SOAS Working paper 30.

_____. 2016. 'The informalization of capital and interlocking in labour contracting networks.' *Progress in Development Studies* 16 (2): 124–169.

Mezzadri, A., and Srivastava, R. 2015. *Labour Regimes in the Indian Garment Sector: Capital-Labour Relations, Social Reproduction and Labour Standards in the National Capital Region (NCR)*. London: SOAS. Final ESRC Report for the Project 'Labour Conditions and the Working Poor in China and India.'

Mies, M. 1982. *The Lace Makers of Narsapur: Indian Housewives Produce for the World Market*. London: Zed.

_____. 1986. *Patriarchy and Accumulation on a World Scale: Women in the International Division of Labour*. London: Zed.

Milberg, W. 2008. 'Shifting Sources and Uses of Profits: Sustaining US Financialisation within Global Value Chains.' *Economy and Society* 37 (3): 420–51.

Miles, R. 1987. *Capitalism and Unfree Labour: Anomaly or Necessity?* London and New York: Tavistock.

Miller, D. 2010. *Stuff*. London: Polity.

Mitchell, C., S. A. Marston, and C. Katz. 2003. 'Introduction: Life's Work: An Introduction, Review, and Critique.' *Antipode* 35 (3): 415–42.

Mitchell, K. 2004. *Crossing the Neoliberal Line: Pacific Rim Migration and the Metropolis*. Philadelphia, PA: Temple University Press.

Mitter, S., G. Fernandez, and S. Varghese. 2004. 'On the Threshold of Informalisation: Women Call Centre Workers in India.' In *Chains of Fortune: Linking Women Producers & Workers with Global Markets,* edited by M. Carr, 165–183. London: Commonwealth Secretariat.

Molyneux, M. 1979. 'Beyond the Domestic Labour Debate.' *New Left Review* (I/116): 3–27.

Monaco, L. 2015. *Bringing Operaismo to Gurgaon: A Study of Labour Composition and Resistance Practices in the Indian Auto Industry*. Unpublished PhD thesis. London: SOAS, Department of Development Studies.

Moser, C. O. N. 1978. 'Informal Sector or Petty Commodity Production: Dualism or Dependence in Urban Development?' *World Development* 6 (9/10): 1041–64.

Mosse, D. 2010. 'A Relational Approach to Durable Poverty, Inequality and Power.' *The Journal of Development Studies* 46 (7): 1156–78.

Mukhopadhyay, S. 1997. 'Locating Women within Informal Sector Hierarchies.' *Indian Journal of Labour Economics* 40 (3): 483–92.

Muzi, L. 2014. 'Thousands of African Child Migrants Feared in Thrall to Italian Traffickers.' *The Guardian* (17 October). Accessed September 20, 2015. http://www.theguardian.com/profile/luca-muzi.

Nadvi, K. 2008. 'Global Standards, Global Governance and the Organization of Global Value Chains.' *Journal of Economic Geography* 8: 323–43.

Narasimhan, T. E., and A. Sethi. 2014. 'Women on Night Shift: A Lesson from Tamil Nadu.' *Business Standard* (August 12). Accessed September 20. http://www.business-standard.com/article/current-affairs/women-on-night-shift-a-lesson-from-tamil-nadu-114081200027_1.html.

NCEUS. 2007. *Report on Conditions of Work and Promotion of Livelihoods in the Unorganised Sector*. New Delhi: Government of India. Accessed September 20, 2015. http://nceus.gov.in/Condition_of_workers_sep_2007.pdf last access February 20, 2014.

NCR Planning Board. 2015. *NCR Constituent Areas*. Accessed September 20, 2015. http://ncrpb.nic.in/ncrconstituent.php.

Neetha, N. 2002. 'Flexible Production, Feminisation and Disorganisation: Evidence from Tiruppur Knitwear Industry.' *Economic and Political Weekly* 37 (21): 2045–52.

Neveling, P. 2017. 'Capital over Labor: Health and Safety in Export Processing Zones Garment Production since 1947.' In *After Rana Plaza: Rethinking Garment Workers' Health and Safety*, edited by G. De Neve, and R. Prentice. Philadelphia: University of Pennsylvania Press (forthcoming).

Newman, S. 2009. 'Financialization and Changes in the Social Relations Along Commodity Chains: The Case of Coffee.' *Review of Radical Political Economics* 41 (4): 539–59.

Noordegraaf, L. 1997. 'The New Draperies in the Northern Netherlands, 1500–1800.' In *The New Draperies in the Low Countries and England, 1300–1800*, edited by N. B. Harte. Oxford: Oxford University Press, pp. 173–195.

Novak, P. 2015. 'Refugees Status as a Productive Tension.' *Transnational Legal Theory*, 6 (2): 287–311.

NTUI. 2014. *GATWU Wins Historic Increase in Minimum Wages for Garment Workers in Bangalore*. Accessed September 20, 2015. http://ntui.org.in/ntui-news/item/gatwu-wins-historic-increase-in-minimum-wages-for-garment-workers-in-bangal/.

O'Keefe, K., and S. Narin. 2013. 'H&M Clothes Made in Collapsed Cambodian Factory.' *The Wall Street Journal* (May 21). Accessed September 20, 2015. http://www.wsj.com/articles/SB10001424127887324787004578497091806922254.

O'Laughlin, B. 2008. Governing Capital? Corporate Social Responsibility and the Limits of Regulation. *Development and Change* 39 (6): 945–57.

_____. 2010. *Questions of Health and Inequality in Mozambique*. Cadernos IESE (Instituto de Estudos Sociais e Economicos, Maputo) 4. Accessed September 20, 2015. http://www.iese.ac.mz/lib/publication/cad_iese/CadernosIESE_04_Bridget.pdf.

_____. 2013. 'Land, Labour and the Production of Affliction in Rural Southern Africa.' *Journal of Agrarian Change* 13: 175–96.

_____. 2015. 'Trapped in the Prison of the Proximate: Structural HIV/AIDS Prevention in Southern Africa.' *Review of African Political Economy* 42 (145): 342–61.

Ong A. 1988. 'The Production of Possession: Spirits and the Multinational Corporation in Malaysia.' *American Ethnologist* (Medical Anthropology) 15 (1): 28–42.

Oya, C. 2010. *Rural Inequality, Wage Employment and Labour Market Formation in Africa: Historical and Micro-Level Evidence*. Working Paper 96. Geneva: ILO.

Palma, G. 2011. 'Homogeneous Middles vs. Heterogeneous Tails, and the End of the "Inverted-U": It's All About the Share of the Rich.' *Development and Change* 42 (1): 87–153.

Palpacuer, F. 2008. 'Bringing the Social Context Back in: Governance and Wealth Distribution in Global Commodity Chains.' *Economy and Society* 37 (3): 393–419.

_____. 2017. 'Voluntary Versus Binding Forms of Regulation in Global Production Networks: Exploring the "Paradoxes of Partnership" in the European Antisweatshop Movement.' In *After Rana Plaza: Rethinking Garment Workers' Health and Safety*, edited by G. De Neve, and R. Prentice, Philadelphia: University of Pennsylvania Press (forthcoming).

Palriwala, R., and N. Neetha. 2011. 'Stratified Familialism: The Care Regime in India Through the Lens of Child Care.' *Development and Change* 12 (4): 1–30.

Pande, A. 2010. 'Commercial Surrogacy in India: Manufacturing a Perfect Mother-Worker.' *Signs* 35 (4): 969–92.

Parakuni, G., L. Ceresna, A. Raju, P. Ray, and C. Leffler. 2015. *Mind the Gap: How the Global Brands are not Doing Enough to Ensure a Dignified Life for Workers in the Garment & Electronics Industry in India*. Report by Framtiden I Vare Hender (FIVH) and Cividep. Oslo: (FIVH). Accessed September 20, 2015. http://www.indianet.nl/pdf/MindTheGap.pdf.

Parry, J. 2013. 'Company and Contract Labour in a Central Indian Steel Plant.' *Economy and Society* 42 (3): 348–74.

Patel, R. 2010. *Working the Night Shift: Women in India's Call Center Industry*. Stanford: Stanford University Press.

Pattenden, J. 2016a. *Labour, State and Society in Rural India, A Class-Relational Approach*. Manchester University Press: Manchester.

Pattison, P. 2013. 'Revealed: Qatar's World Cup "Slaves".' *The Guardian* (25 September). Accessed September 15, 2015. http://www.theguardian.com/world/2013/sep/25/revealed-qatars-world-cup-slaves.

Pearson, R., and K. Kusakabe. 2012. *Thailand's Hidden Workforce: Burmese Migrant Women Factory Workers*, London: Zed.

Perrons, D. 2004. *Globalisation and Social Change: People and Places in a Divided World*. London: Routledge.

Phillips, A., and Taylor, B. 1980. 'Sex and Skill: Notes towards a Feminist Economics.' *Feminist Review* 6: 79–88.

Phillips, N. 2011. Informality, Global Production Networks and the Dynamics of 'Adverse Incorporation.' *Global Networks* 11: 380–97.

Phillips, N., R. Bhaskaran, D. Nathan, and C. Upendranadh. 2013. 'The Social Foundations of Global Production Networks: Towards a Global Political Economy of Child Labour.' *Third World Quarterly*. 35 (3): 428–46.

Picherit, D. 2009. *The Multiple Times of Debt- Bondage and Its Practices in Southern India: Temporary Protection and Over-Indebtedness.* Rural Microfinance and Employment (RuMe) Working Paper 2009–11.

Piketty, T. 2014. *Capital in the 21ˢᵗ Century.* Belknapp Press and Harvard University Press.

Plankey-Videla, N. 2012. *We Are in This Dance Together: Gender, Power, and Globalization at a Mexican Garment Firm.* New Brunswick, NJ: Rutgers University Press.

Powell, B. 2014. *Out of Poverty: Sweatshops in the Global Economy.* New York: Cambridge University Press.

Portes, A., and K. Hoffman. 2003. 'Latin American Classes' Structures: Their Composition and Change during the Neoliberal Era.' *Latin America Research Review* 38 (1): 41–82.

Prentice, R. 2014. 'A Year After Rana Plaza, Still Unearthing its Causes.' *OpenDemocracy.* Accessed September 20, 2015. https://www.opendemocracy.net/opensecurity/rebecca-prentice/year-after-rana- plaza-still-unearthing-its-causes.

_____. 2015. *Thiefing A Chance: Factory Work, Illicit Labor, and Neoliberal Subjectivities in Trinidad.* Boulder: University Press of Colorado.

Preston, P. W. 1996. *Development Theory: An Introduction.* Oxford: Blackwell Publishers.

Prugl, E. 1996. 'Home-Based Producers in Development Discourse.' In *Homeworkers in Global Perspective: Invisible no More,* edited by E. Boris, and E. Prugl. New York and London: Routledge.

Pun, N. 2005a. '*Made in China: Women Workers in a Global Workplace.*' London and Durham: Duke University Press.

_____. 2005b. 'Global Production, Company Codes of Conduct and Labour Conditions in China: A Case Study of Two Factories.' *The China Journal* 54: 101–13.

_____. 2007. 'The Dormitory Labor Regime: Sites of Control and Resistance for Women Migrant Workers in South China.' *Feminist Economics* 13 (3–4): 239–58.

Pun, N., and C. Smith. 2007. 'Putting Transnational Labour Process in its Place: The Dormitory Labour Regime in Post-Socialist China.' *Work, Employment and Society* 21 (1): 27–45.

Pun, N., A. Y. Liu, and H. L. Lu. 2015. *Labor Conditions and the Working Poor in China and India.* Final Report presented in 2014 (March 30-April 1) at the Final Workshop for the ESRC-DfID Project 'Labour Conditions and the Working Poor in China and India,' London: SOAS.

Quirk, J. 2015. 'Reparations are too confronting: let's talk about "modern-day slavery" instead.' *Open Democracy, Beyond Trafficking and Slavery* (7 May). Accessed January 20, 2016. https://www.opendemocracy.net/beyondslavery/joel-quirk/reparations-are-too-confronting-let's-talk-about-'modernday-slavery'-instead.

Rairikar, B. R. 1999. *Social Security for Homebased Women Workers-Mumbai City and Suburbs.* Mumbai: Ambekar Institute of Labour Studies in Association with Friedrich Ebert Stiftung.

Raju, S. 2013. 'The Material and the Symbolic: Intersectionalities of Home-Based Work in India.' *Economic and Political Weekly* 48 (1): 60–8.

Rakowski, C. A. 1994. 'Convergence and Divergence in the Informal Sector Debate: a Focus on Latin America, 1984–92.' *World Development* 22 (4): 501–16.

Ramamurthy, P. 2004. 'Why is Buying a Madras Cotton Shirt a Political Act? A Feminist Commodity Chain Analysis.' *Feminist Studies* 30 (3): 734–69.

Ramaswamy, K. V., and G. Gereffi. 2001. 'India's Apparel Exports: The Challenge of Global Markets.' *Developing Economies* 28 (2): 186–210.

Rammohan, K. T., and R. Sundaresan 2003. 'Socially Embedding the Commodity Chain: An Exercise in Relation to Coir Yarn Spinning in Southern India.' *World Development*, 31 (5): 903–23.

Rani, U., and J. Unni. 2004. 'Unorganised and Organised Manufacturing in India, Potential for Employment Generating Growth.' *Economic and Political Weekly* 39 (41): 4569–80.

Richey, L. A., and S. Ponte. 2011. *Brand Aid: Shopping Well to Save the World*. Minneapolis: University of Minnesota Press.

Riello, G., and P. Parthasarathi. 2010. *The Spinning World: A Global History of Cotton Textile, 1200–1850*. Oxford: Oxford University Press.

Riello, G., and T. Roy. 2010. *How India Has Clothed the World: The World of South Asian Textiles, 1500–1850*. Leiden: Brill.

Rigg, J. 2006. 'Land, Farming, Livelihoods, and Poverty: Rethinking the Links in the Rural South.' *World Development* 34 (1): 180–202.

Rizzo, M. 2011 '"Life is War"! Informal Transport Workers and Neoliberalism in Tanzania, 1998–2009.' *Development and Change* 42 (5): 179–206.

Rosen, E. 2002. *Making Sweatshops: The Globalization of the US Apparel Industry*. Berkeley, CA: University of California Press.

Roy, T. 1999. *Traditional Industry in the Economy of Colonial India*. Cambridge: Cambridge University Press.

_____. 2008. 'Sardars, Jobbers, Kanganies: The Labour Contractor and Indian Economic History.' *Modern Asian Studies* 42: 971–98.

_____. 2013. *India in the World Economy: From Antiquity to the Present*. Cambridge: Cambridge University Press.

_____. 2014. 'Trading Firms in Colonial India.' *Business History Review* 88: 9–42.

RoyChowdhury, S. 2005. 'Labor Activism and Women in the Unorganized Sector, Garment Export Industry in Bangalore.' *Economic and Political Weekly*, 40 (22–23): 2250–55.

_____. 2015. 'Bringing Class Back In: Informality in Bangalore.' *Socialist Register* 51 (Transforming Classes) 51: 73–92.

Rudrappa, S. 2015. 'India's Reproductive Assembly Line.' In *Reproduction and Society: Interdisciplinary Readings*, edited by C. Joffe, and J. Reich, 110–115. New York: Routledge.

Ruthven, C. 2015. 'Bangalore or bust: can India's clothing factories offer freedom to rural recruits?' *The Guardian* (Video, 14 September). Accessed September 20, 2015. http://www.theguardian.com/news/video/2015/sep/14/bangalore-india-clothing-factories-freedom-rural-recruits-video.

Ruwanpura, K. N. 2011. 'Women Workers in the Apparel Sector: A Three-Decade (r) evolution of Feminist Contributions?' *Progress in Development Studies* 11 (3): 197–209.

_____. 2013. 'Scripted Performances? Local Readings of "Global" Health and Safety Standards: The apparel Sector in Sri Lanka.' *Global Labour Journal* 4 (2): 88–108.

Ruwanpura, K. N., and Wrigley, N. 2011. 'The Cost of Compliance? Views of Sri Lankan Apparel Manufacturers in Times of Global Crisis.' *Journal of Economic Geography* 11: 1031–49.

Saad-Filho, A. 2013. 'The "Rise of the South": Global Convergence at Last?' *New Political Economy* 19 (4): 578–600.

Saad-Filho, A., and D. Johnston. 2005. *Neoliberalism: A Critical Reader.* London: Pluto Press.

Saad-Filho, A., and J. Weeks. 2013. 'Curses, Diseases and Other Resource Confusions.' *Third World Quarterly* 34 (1): 1–21.

SACOM. 2011. *iSlave Behind the iPhone Foxconn Workers in Central China.* Hong Kong: SACOM. Accessed September 20, 2015. http://sacom.hk/wp-content/uploads/2011/09/20110924-islave-behind-the-iphone.pdf.

Salzinger, L. 2003. *Genders in Production.* Berkley: University of California Press.

Sanyal, K. 2007. *Rethinking Capitalist Development: Primitive Accumulation, Governmentality and Post-Colonial Capitalism.* New Delhi: Routledge.

Saptari, R. 2012. 'Production Systems and Forms of Labour Control in the Javanese Cigarette Industry; 1920s–1930s.' In *Working on Labour: Essays in Honour of Jan Lucassen*, edited by M. Van der Linden and L. Lucassen 99–124. Leiden: Brill.

Sarkar, A. 2011. 'Unsolved Mysteries.' The Telegraph Calcutta (July 14). Accessed September 20, 2015. http://www.telegraphindia.com/1110714/jsp/opinion/story_14234363.jsp.

Sarkar, T. 2005. 'Handicrafts and "Cluster Development Approach": The Hand Block Printed Textiles Cluster of Jaipur.' In *Industrial Clusters: Cases and Perspectives*, edited by K. Das, 172–198. Aldershot: Ashgate.

Sassen, S. 2000. 'Counter-Geographies of Globalization and the Feminization of Survival.' *Journal of International Affairs* 53 (2): 504–24.

Schumacher, R. 2013. 'Deconstructing the Theory of Comparative Advantage'. *World Economic Review* 2: 83–105.

Seabrook, J. 2015. *The Song of the Shirt: The High Price of Cheap Garments, from Blackburn to Bangladesh.* London: Hurst.

Seguino, S. 2000 'Accounting for Gender in Asian Economic Growth.' *Feminist Economics* 6 (3): 27–58.

Selwyn, B. 2012a. 'Beyond Firm-Centrism: Re-Integrating Labour and Capitalism into Global Commodity Chain Analysis.' *Journal of Economic Geography* 12: 205–26.

_____. 2012b. *Workers, State and Development in Brazil: Powers of Labour, Chains of Value.* Manchester: Manchester University Press.

_____. 2013. 'Social Upgrading and Labour in Global Production Networks: A Critique and an Alternative Conception.' *Competition and Change* 17 (1): 75–90.

Selwyn, B., and S. Miyamura. 2014. 'Class Struggle or Embedded Markets? Marx, Polanyi and the Meanings and Possibilities of Social Transformation.' *New Political Economy* 19 (5): 639–61.

Sen, A. 1999. *Development as Freedom.* New York: Oxford University Press.

Sender, J. 2016. 'Backward Capitalism in Rural South Africa: Prospects for Accelerating Accumulation in the Eastern Cape.' *Journal of Agrarian Change*. 16(1): 3–31.

Sethi, A. 2012. *A Free Man: A True Story of Life and Death in Delhi*. London: Jonathan Cape.

Shaikh, A. 2005. 'The Economic Mythology of Neoliberalism.' In *Neoliberalism, A Critical Reader*, edited by A. Saad-Filho and D. Johnston, 41–49. London: Pluto.

Shah, A., and Harriss-White, B. 2011. 'Resurrecting Scholarship on Agrarian Transformations.' *Economic and Political Weekly*, September 24, 2011, XLVI(39): 13–18.

Sharma, H. C. 1989. 'Handloom Weavers of the Punjab Under British Rule: A Study of Socio-Economic Change.' In *The Punjab Past and Present*. Patiala: Punjabi University 23 (42).

Sharma, M. 2005. 'Globalisation with a Female Face: Issues from South Asia.' In *Exploring Gender Relations: Colonial and Post Colonial India*, edited by S. Kak, and B. Pati, 463–490. New Delhi: Nehru Memorial Museum and Library.

Sharma, S. 2013. 'Social Responsibility in India - The Emerging Discourse & Concerns.' *The Indian Journal of Industrial Relations* 48 (4): 582–96.

Shukla, A., and Bansal, P. 2003. *Diagnostic Study, SME Hosiery Cluster, Ludhiana Punjab*. Ludhiana: UNIDO Cluster Development Programme.

Shyam Sunder, K. R. 2005. 'State in Industrial Relations System in India: from Corporatist to Neoliberal?' *Indian Journal of Labour Economics* 48 (4): 917–37.

_____. 2011. 'Employment Relations in India in the Post-reform Period: Positives, Challenges and Opportunities.' *Indian Journal of Labour Economics* 54 (1): 89–111.

Siegmann, K. 2005. 'The Agreement on Textiles and Clothing: Potential Effects on Gendered Employment in Pakistan.' *International Labour Review* 14 (4): 401–21.

_____. 2009. *The Trade and Gender Interface: A Perspective from Pakistan*. Islamabad: Sustainable Development Policy Institute.

Silver, S. 2003. 'Introduction.' *Forces of Labour. Workers' Movements and Globalisation Since 1970*. Cambridge: Cambridge University Press, 1–40.

Silver, B. J., and G. Arrighi. 2001. 'Workers North and South.' *Socialist Register*, 64 (4): 53–76.

Singh, A. 2010. 'Human Resource: A Cause of Concern for Ludhiana Hosiery Industry.' *Asia Pacific Business Review* 6: 157–164.

Singh, N., R. Kaur, and M. Kaur Sapra. 2004. *Continents Wide Layers Deep: The Ready Made Garment Industry in the Times of Restructuring*. New Delhi: National Council of Applied Economic Research.

Singh, N., and M. Kaur Sapra. 2007. 'Liberalisation in Trade and Finance: India's Garment Sector.' In *Trade Liberalisation and India's Informal Economy*, edited by B. Harriss-White, and A. Sinha, 42–127. New Delhi: Oxford University Press.

Singh, R. 2011. *The Fabric of Our Lives: The Story of Fabindia*. New Delhi: Penguin.

Sinha, S. 2013. 'Workers and Working Classes in Contemporary India: A Note on Analytic Frames and Political Formations.' In *Beyond Marx: Confronting Labour-History and the Concept of Labour with the Global Labour-Relations of the Twenty-First Century*, edited by M. Van der Linden, and K. H. Roth, 145–172. Leiden: Brill.

Sisters for Change and Munnade. 2016. *Eliminating Violence Against Women at Work: Making Sexual Harassment Laws Real for Karnataka's Women Garment Workers*. Accessed on

August 2, 2016. http://sistersforchange.org.uk/wp-content/uploads/2016/06/SFC_ WomenatWork_FullReport_25June2016.pdf

Smith, C., and Pun, N. 2006. 'The Dormitory Labour Regime in China as a Site for Control and Resistance.' *The International Journal of Human Resource Management* 17 (8): 1456–70.

Smith, A., Rannie, A., Dunford, M., Hardy, J., Hudson, R., and Sadler, D. 2002. Networks of Value, Commodities and Regions: Reworking Divisions of Labour in Macro-Regional Economies. *Progress in Human Geography* 26 (1): 41–63.

SOMO and ICN. 2014. *Flawed Fabric: The Abuse of Girls and Women Workers in the South Indian Textile Industry.* Netherlands: SOMO and ICN. Accessed September 20. http:// www.somo.nl/publications-en/Publication_4110.

Spinanger, D., and S. Verma. 2003. *The Coming Death of the ATC and China's WTO Accession: Will Push Come to Shove for Indian T&C Exports?* Mimeo. Kiel: Kiel Institute for World Economics.

Srinivasulu, K. 1996. '1985 Textile Policy and Handloom Industry: Policy, Promises and Performance.' *Economic and Political Weekly* 31 (49): 3198–3206.

Srivastava, R. 1989. 'Interlinked Modes of Exploitation in Indian Agriculture During Transition: A Case Study.' *Journal of Peasant Studies* 16 (4): 493–522.

_____. 2005. *Bonded Labour in India: Its Incidence and Pattern.* ILO Working paper 43. Geneva: ILO.

_____. 2012. 'Changing Employment Conditions of the Indian Workforce and Implications for Decent Work.' *Global Labour Journal* 3 (1): 63–90.

_____. 2015. 'Capital-Labour Relationships in Formal Sector Garment Manufacturing in the Delhi National Capital Region of India.' In *Labour Regimes in the Indian Garment Sector: Capital-Labour Relations, Social Reproduction and Labour Standards in the National Capital Region (NCR)*, edited by A. Mezzadri, and R. Srivastava. Final ESRC Report for the project 'Labour Conditions and The Working Poor in China and India.' London: SOAS.

Standing, G. 1989. 'Global Feminization through Flexible Labor.' *World Development* 17 (7): 1077–95.

_____. 1999. 'Global Feminization through Flexible Labor: A Theme Revisited.' *World Development* 27 (3): 583–602.

_____. 2007a. 'Offshoring and Labor Recommodification in the Global Transformation.' In *Global Capitalism Unbound: Winners and Losers from Offshore Outsourcing*, edited by E. Paus, 41–60. New York: Palgrave MacMillan.

_____. 2007b. *Work After Globalisation: Building Occupational Citizenship.* Cheltenham: Edward Elgar.

_____. 2010. *The Precariat: The New Dangerous Class.* London: Bloomsbury Academic.

_____. 2014. 'Understanding the Precariat Through Labour and Work.' *Development and Change* 45 (5): 963–80.

Starosta, G. 2010a. 'Global Commodity Chains and the Marxian Law of Value.' *Antipode* 42 (2): 433–65.

_____. 2010b. 'The Outsourcing of Manufacturing and the Rise of Giant Global Contractors: A Marxian Approach to Some Recent Transformations of Global Value Chains.' *New Political Economy* 15 (4): 543–63.

Stein, L. 1962. *The Triangle Fire*. Ithaca: ILR Press (Centennial Edition, 2011).

Taussig, M. 1980. *The Devil and Commodity Fetishism in South America*. Chapel Hill: University of North Carolina Press.

Taylor, M. 2007. 'Rethinking the Global Production of Uneven Development.' *Globalizations* 4 (4): 529–42.

_____. 2011. 'Race You to the Bottom . . . and Back Again? The Uneven Development of Labour Codes of Conduct.' *New Political Economy* 16 (4): 445–62.

Tewari, M. 1996. *When the Marginal Becomes Mainstream: Lessons from Half Century of Dynamic Small Firm Growth in Ludhiana, India*. Unpublished PhD Thesis submitted to MIT, Cambridge, Massachusetts.

_____. 1999. 'Successful Adjustment in Indian Industry: The Case of Ludhiana's Woollen Knitwear Cluster.' *World Development* 27 (3): 1651–71.

_____. 2008. 'Varieties of Global Integration: Navigating Institutional Legacies and Global Networks in India's Garment Industry.' *Competition & Change* 12 (1): 49–67.

The Economic Times 2005. *SC clears auction of 7 NTC mills* (May 11). Accessed September 20, 2015. http://articles.economictimes.indiatimes.com/2005-05-11/news/27489581_1_ntc-mills-other-mills-jupiter-mills.

The Guardian 2011. 'BBC to Apologise on Air to Primark for Panorama Documentary' (June 16). Accessed September 20, 2015. http://www.theguardian.com/media/2011/jun/16/bbc-to-apologise-on-air-primark.

The Telegraph 2011. 'BBC Forced to Apologise for "Faked" Panorama Documentary Accusing Primark of Child Labour.' *The Telegraph, UK* (June 17). Accessed September 20, 2015. http://www.telegraph.co.uk/culture/tvandradio/8580751/BBC-forced-to-apologise-for-faked-Panorama-documentary-accusing-Primark-of-child-labour.html.

The Times of India. 2005. 'Jupiter Mills' Sale Draws Four Top Bids.' In *The Times of India* (24 March 2015).

Thoburn, J. 2009. *The Impact of World Recession on the Textile and Garment Industries in Asia*. Working Paper 17/2009. Vienna: UNIDO.

Tronti, M. 1966. *Operai e Capitale*. Roma: Einaudi. Collana 'Biblioteca dell'Operaismo', terza edizione (2006).

Tsing, A. 2009. 'Supply Chains and the Human Condition.' *Rethinking Marxism: A Journal of Economics, Culture & Society* 21 (2): 148–176.

Uchikawa, S. 1998. *Indian Textile Industry: State Policy, Liberalization and Growth*, New Delhi: Manohar.

_____. 2012. 'The Development of Apparel Industrial Cluster in India: A Comparison between Ludhiana and Tiruppur.' In *The Linkage between Agriculture and Industry in India* edited by S. Uchikawa, 1–15. Tokyo: IDE. Accessed September 20, 2015. http://www.ide.go.jp/Japanese/Publish/Download/Report/2011/pdf/103_ch1.pdf.

_____. 2014. *Industrial Clusters, Migrant Workers, and Labour Markets in India*. IDE-Jetro series. London: Palgrave McMillan.

UNIDO. 1997. *Diagnostic Study of Textile Hand Printing Cluster of Jaipur*. Internal report. Jaipur: UNIDO Cluster Development Programme.

_____. 2004a. *Ludhiana, Knitwear and Hosiery Cluster.* Internal report. Ludhiana: UNIDO Cluster Development Programme.

_____. 2004b. *Jaipur Hand-Block Printed Textile Cluster.* Internal report. Jaipur: UNIDO Cluster Development Programme.

United States Department of Labour 2015. *The Triangle Shirtwaist Factory Fire of 1911.* Accessed September 24, 2015. http://www.dol.gov/shirtwaist/.

Unni, J., and U. Rani. 2008. *Flexibility of Labour in Globalising India, The Challenge of Skills and Technology.* New Delhi: Tulika Books.

Unni, J., and S. Scaria. 2009. 'Governance Structure and Labour Market Outcomes in Garment Embellishment Chains.' *Indian Journal of Labour Economics* 52 (4): 631–50.

Van Schendel, W. 2012. 'Green Plats into Blue Cakes: Working for Wages in Colonial Bengal's Indigo Industry.' In *Working on Labour: Essays in Honour of Jan Lucassen,* edited by M. Van der Linden, and L. Lucassen, 47–74. Leiden: Brill.

Vérité. 2010. *Indian Workers in Domestic Textile Production and Middle East-Based Manufacturing, Infrastructure and Construction.* Accessed September 20, 2015. http://digitalcommons.ilr.cornell.edu/cgi/viewcontent.cgi?article=2176&context=globaldocs.

Vijayabaskar, M. 2001. 'Industrial Formation under Conditions of Flexible Accumulation: the Case of a Global Knitwear Node in South India.' Unpublished PhD Thesis submitted to Jawaharlal Nehru University, New Delhi and Centre for Development Studies (CDS), Thiruvananthapuram.

_____. 2005. 'Flexible Accumulation and Labour Markets: Case of the Tiruppur Knitwear Cluster.' In *Indian Industrial Clusters,* edited by K. Das. Aldershot: Ashgate.

Vijayabaskar, M., and Kalaiyarasan, A. 2014. 'Caste as Social Capital: The Tiruppur Story.' *Economic and Political Weekly* 49 (10): 34–38.

Vogel, L. 1983. *Marxism and the Oppression of Women: Toward a Unitary Theory.* London: Pluto.

Wade, R. 1990. *Governing the Market: Economic Theory and the Role of the Government in East Asian Industrialization.* Princeton: Princeton University Press.

Wallace, J. 2014. 'Workers of the World, Faint!' *New York Times* (January 17). Accessed January 25, 2015. http://www.nytimes.com/2014/01/18/opinion/workers-of-the-world-faint.html.

Wallerstein, I. 2009. 'Production Networks and Commodity Chains in the Capitalist World-Economy.' In *Frontiers of Commodity Chain Research,* edited by J. Bair, 83–89. Stanford: Stanford University Press.

War on Want. 2011. *Stitched-up. Women Workers in the Bangladeshi Garment Sector.* London: War on Want. Accessed September 20, 2015. http://old.waronwant.org/attachments/Stitched%20Up.pdf.

Warren, B. 1973. 'Imperialism and Capitalist Industrialisation.' *New Left Review* 81: 3–44.

Watts, M. J. 1994. 'Life Under Contract: Contract Farming, Agrarian Restructuring, and Flexible Accumulation.' In *Living Under Contract: Contract Farming and Agrarian Transformation in Sub-Saharan Africa,* edited by P. D. Little, and M. J. Watts, 21–77. Madison: University of Wisconsin Press.

Webster, E. 2010. 'From Critical Sociology to Combat Sport?' A Response to Michael Burawoy's 'From Polanyi to Pollyanna: The False Optimism of Global Labour Studies.' *Global Labour Journal* 1 (3): 384–87.

Webster, E., R. Lambert, and A. Bezuidenhout 2008. *Grounding Globalisation: Labour in the Age of Insecurity*. London: Blackwell.

Weeks, J. 2014. *The Economics of the 1%*. London and New York: Anthem Press.

Wilkinson-Weber, C. M. 1999. *Embroidering Lives: Women's Work and Skill in the Lucknow Embroidery Industry*. New York: State University of New York Press.

Wilson, F. 2011. 'Historical Roots of Inequality in South Africa.' *Economic History of Developing Regions* 26 (1): 1–15.

Wood, A. 1994. *North-South Trade, Employment and Inequality: Changing Fortunes in a Skill-Driven World*. Oxford: Clarendon Press.

_____. 1995. 'How Trade Hurt Unskilled Workers.' *Journal of Economic Perspectives* 9 (3): 57–80.

Wood, A., and Ridao-Cano, C. 1997. *Skill, Trade and International Inequality*. IDS Working paper 47. Accessed September 20, 2015. https://www.ids.ac.uk/ids/bookshop/wp/WP47.pdf.

World Bank. 1993. *The East Asia Miracle: Economic Growth and Public Policy*. World Bank Policy Research Report. Oxford: Oxford University Press.

Wright, M. 2006. *Disposable Women and Other Myths of Global Capitalism*. New York: Routledge.

Yadav, A. 2015. 'Workers Riot at Two Work-Sites, in Himachal Pradesh and Haryana.' *Scroll.in* (September 18). Accessed September 20, 2015. http://scroll.in/article/735850/workers-riot-at-two-factories-in-himachal-pradesh-and-haryana.

_____. 2016. 'Bengaluru Protests Represent a New Wave of Militant Worker Expression, say Union Leaders.' *Scroll.in* (April 22). Accessed August 2, 2016. http://scroll.in/article/806968/bengaluru-protests-represent-a-new-wave-of-militant-worker-expression-say-union-leaders

Index

Lightning Source UK Ltd.
Milton Keynes UK
UKHW022156280720
367334UK00004B/49